A JOURNAL OF A VOYAGE TO THE SOUTH SEAS

SYDNEY PARKINSON

A JOURNAL
OF A VOYAGE TO
THE SOUTH SEAS

by

Sydney Parkinson

CALIBAN BOOKS

© Caliban Books 1984

This edition first published 1984
by Caliban Books
25 Nassington Road,
Hampstead, London, N.W.3

ISBN 0 904573 51 6

Library of Congress Cataloguing in Publication Data

Parkinson, Sydney, 1745?–1771.
 Journal of a voyage to the South Seas in HMS Endeavour.

 Reprint. Originally published: London: Printed for
C. Dilly, 1784.
 1. Cook, James, 1728–1779. 2. Parkinson, Sydney,
1745?–1771. 3. Endeavour (Ship). 4. Voyages around
the world. 5. Oceania—Discovery and exploration.
I. Title.

G420.C65P32 1984   910′.45   83-62658
ISBN 0-904573-51-6

Printed and bound in Great Britain by
A. Wheaton & Co. Ltd., Exeter.

A
JOURNAL
OF A
VOYAGE to the SOUTH SEAS,

In his MAJESTY's Ship

The ENDEAVOUR:

FAITHFULLY TRANSCRIBED

From the Papers of the late SYDNEY PARKINSON,

Draughtſman to SIR JOSEPH BANKS, BART. in his Expedition with
DR. SOLANDER round the World;

AND EMBELLISHED

With Twenty-nine VIEWS and DESIGNS, engraved by CAPITAL ARTISTS.

TO WHICH IS NOW ADDED,

REMARKS on the PREFACE,

By the late JOHN FOTHERGILL, M.D. F.R.S. &c.

LONDON:

Printed for CHARLES DILLY, in the POULTRY; and JAMES PHILLIPS,
in GEORGE-YARD, LOMBARD-STREET.
M DCC LXXXIV.

ADVERTISEMENT.

THE following *Journal* of the circumnavigation undertaken in 1768, and completed in 1771, has met with publick approbation. Sydney Parkinson, the author, was draughtsman to Sir Joseph Banks, Bart. and the engravings, taken from his drawings, have been esteemed a valuable addition to the *Journal*, as, perhaps, no plates hitherto published have conveyed a more faithful representation of the originals from whence the drawings were painted. This young artist was a person of unblemished character, and strict veracity; and his *Journal* may, therefore, be considered as consonant to truth in every relation.

Both before and since the period of the voyage here described, the Journals of other circumnavigators have been published; which, together, form such an ample history of a part of the southern hemisphere, hitherto but little known, that I deemed an abridgment of them would prove a useful appendage to Sydney Parkinson's original work : I employed, therefore, a writer of literary reputation to execute this summary, which is now offered to the publick. To every paragraph are annexed marginal references to the original Journals; which, while they form an accurate epitome of the several voyages, enable the reader to refer to them with the greatest facility and exactness.

The

ADVERTISEMENT.

The *Preface* to Sydney Parkinson's *Journal* was drawn up after his death, at the requeſt of his brother, Stanfield Parkinson, the original editor, by the late Dr. Kenrick, who was totally unacquainted with Dr. Fothergill, as he informed me at the time he was employed in writing, and whoſe ſole apology was the pecuniary emolument of his labour. I have preſerved this *Preface*, as well as added Dr. Fothergill's *Remarks* upon it, in juſtification of his conduct.

As controverſial performances, I did not think them of ſufficient importance to inſert them in my edition of Dr. Fothergill's works; and more eſpecially as the unmerited ſuſpicions which gave riſe to the *Preface*, no longer ſubſiſted. The brother of Sydney Parkinſon is dead: in his laſt illneſs Dr. Fothergill was conſulted, and kindly attended him; and after his deceaſe the family diſpoſed of the copy-right of the Journal to Dr. Fothergill, thereby evincing a thorough dependence upon him, and the moſt unequivocal acknowledgment of his rectitude.

Since the Doctor's deceaſe, the whole has been conveyed into my poſſeſſion; and, beſides the additions already enumerated, which may be had ſeparately, I have prefixed a geographical chart of the tracts of the late circumnavigators, in order to render the work as complete as poſſible for thoſe who may not have purchaſed the original, or who wiſh to poſſeſs an elegant collection of South American views and portraits.

JOHN COAKLEY LETTSOM.

London,
June 1, 1784.

✠✠✠

CONTENTS.

PART I.

COmprehending the occurrences that happened from the ſhip's departure from England to its arrival in the South-Seas; particularly

PART II.

Comprehending the occurrences met with from leaving Yoolee-Etea to the time of the ſhip's departure from the coaſt of New-Zealand.

Singular

P A R T   III.

Comprehending the incidents that happened from the time of the ſhip's leaving New-Zealand, to its arrival at and departure from Batavia for Europe.

P A R T   IV.

P R E F A C E.

PREFACE.

By the EDITOR

UNqualified to addrefs the public, as a writer, I fhould have contented myfelf with giving the following journal to the world, without the formality of *preface*, had not the circumftances, which have delayed, and the arts that have been practifed to fupprefs, its publication, made fome explanation on this head particularly neceffary.

The unmerited afperfions which have been caft on me, for afferting a right to pay this tribute to the memory of a deceafed brother, and to poffefs a bequeathed, analienated, pittance of his little fortune, earned at the hazard, and purchafed, as I may fay, at the expence, of his life, render it indeed incumbent on me to defend a reputation, as injurioufly attacked as fuch dear-bought property has been unjuftifiably invaded.

It is yet with regret I find myfelf reduced to this neceffity; as the perfons, of whom I complain, are men, from whofe fuperior talents and fituation in life better things might be expected; however they have, in this inftance, been mifemployed in ftriving to baffle a plain, unlettered, man; who, though he thinks it is his duty to be refigned under the difpenfations of providence, thinks it alfo equally his duty to feek every lawful redrefs from the oppreffive acts of vain and rapacious men.

Sydney Parkinfon, from whofe papers and drawings the journal, now prefented to the public, has been faithfully tranfcribed and delineated, was the younger fon

of

of the late Joel Parkinſon, brewer, of Edinburgh, one of the people commonly called Quakers, and, as I am told, well known and eſteemed by men of all ranks in that city. His ſucceſs in life, however, was by no means equal to that probity of mind and purity of manners, for which he was eminently diſtinguiſhed; a generoſity of diſpoſition inducing him to be improvidently remiſs in proſecuting the recovery of his juſt debts: a circumſtance, which, aggravated by other ſiniſter accidents, rendered his family, on his deceaſe, dependent on their own talents and induſtry for their future ſupport. His ſon Sydney was put to the buſineſs of a woollen-draper; but, taking a particular delight in drawing flowers, fruits, and other objects of natural hiſtory, he became ſoon ſo great a proficient in that ſtile of painting, as to attract the notice of the moſt celebrated botaniſts and connoiſſeurs in that ſtudy. In conſequence of this, he was, ſome time after his arrival in London, recommended to Joſeph Banks, Eſq. whoſe very numerous collection of elegant and highly-finiſhed drawings of that kind, executed by Sydney Parkinſon, is a ſufficient teſtimony both of his talents and application.

His recommendation being ſo effectually confirmed by theſe proofs of ingenuity and induſtry, Joſeph Banks made him the propoſal of going in the capacity of botanical draughtſman, on the then intended voyage to the South-ſeas. An inſatiable curioſity for ſuch reſearches prevailed over every conſideration of danger, that reaſonably ſuggeſted itſelf, as the neceſſary attendant of ſo long, ſo perilous, and, to my poor brother, ſo fatal a voyage! He accordingly accepted Joſeph Banks's offer; though by no means an alluring one, if either views of profit, or perhaps even prudence, had influenced his determination. His appointment, for executing ſuch drawings of ſingular botanical ſubjects and curious objects of natural hiſtory as might occaſionally be met with on the voyage, was ſettled at eighty pounds *per annum*. In this capacity, and under this moderate encouragement, Sydney Parkinſon undertook to accompany Joſeph Banks to the South-Seas; making his will before his departure, in which he bequeathed the ſalary, which might be due to him at the time of his deceaſe, to his ſiſter Britannia, and appointed me his reſiduary legatee.

The

The occurrences and events that attended the expedition are minutely related in the following sheets : the contents of which, though destitute of the embellishments of stile and diction, may serve to shew with what assiduity the curious journalist pursued his observations, and what accuracy he aimed at, not only in the particular walk of his profession of natural history, but also in describing the persons, languages, customs, and manners of the natives of the several islands and continents they visited.

And here let me be indulged in the spontaneous effusions of a heart still affected with the loss of a loving and a beloved brother, while I declare how I have heard many of the surviving companions of this amiable young man dwell with pleasure on the relation of his singular simplicity of conduct, his sincere regard for truth, his ardent thirst after knowledge, his indefatigable industry to obtain it, and his generous disposition in freely communicating, with the most friendly participation, to others, that information which perhaps none but himself could have obtained. That this is more than probable will appear, on comparing the different manner in which Sydney and his associates passed their time, in the most interesting situations. While many others, for want of a more innocent curiosity or amusement, were indulging themselves in those sensual gratifications, which are so easily obtained among the female part of uncivilized nations, we find him gratifying no other passion than that of a laudable curiosity ; which enabled him inoffensively to employ his time, and escape those snares into which the vicious appetites of some others betrayed them. It doth equal honour to his ingenuousness and ingenuity, to find him protected by his own innocence, securely exercising his pleasing art amidst a savage, ignorant, and hostile, people ; engaging their attention by the powers of his pencil, disarming them of their native ferocity, and rendering them even serviceable to the great end of the voyage, in chearfully furnishing him with the choicest productions of the soil and climate, which neither force nor stratagem might otherwise have procured.

By such honest arts and mild demeanor he soon acquired the confidence of the inhabitants of most places, at which the voyagers went on shore ; obtaining thus,

as

as I am well informed, with remarkable facility, the knowledge of many words in various languages, hitherto little, if at all, known in Europe.

These paved the way also to his success in acquiring a choice and rare collection of curiosities, consisting of garments, domestic utensils, rural implements, instruments of war, uncommon shells, and other natural curiosities, of considerable value: of so much value, indeed, as even to seduce men of reputed sense, fortune, and character, to attempt, by means unworthy of themselves, to deprive me of what, after the loss sustained in the death of so deserving a brother, one would think none ought to envy me the gain.

It has happened otherwise; and I am now to enter on the disagreeable task of submitting to the public, before whom I have been traduced, a relation of the manner in which the greater part of his effects hath been hitherto detained from me, and the use of those I got denied me, through my implicit confidence in false friends, and the specious arts of covetous and designing strangers.

On the arrival of Joseph Banks in London, about the middle of July, 1771, he informed me, by letter, of the death of Sydney Parkinson, my brother; acquainting me, at the same time, of his having taken possession of his effects, as the only person that could do it *; of which he was ready to give a proper account to his executors. I waited, of course, immediately on Joseph Banks; who appeared to sympathize with me on account of my brother, with whose services he seemed highly satisfied, and declared he suffered a considerable loss by his death; telling me, after a short conversation on the subject, that he was then much confused with a multiplicity of concerns, but that, as soon as his hurry of business was over, he would give me an account of my brother's effects.

Being soon after informed, that Joseph Banks had told James Lee, of Hammersmith, that my brother had bequeathed to him, James Lee, a journal of the

---

* I am, however, since informed, that it is usual, in such cases, for the captain of the ship to take possession of the effects of the deceased; causing at the same time a regular inventory to be taken of them before two competent witnesses.

voyage, and some other papers, which were unfortunately lost; I took occasion to ask Joseph Banks about this circumstance, who confirmed it; telling me that he had made a search among the ship's company for the said journal, but could not find it. At this time he also told me that he expected to get his goods up from the ship in a few days, and that, when they arrived, I should receive the things bequeathed me by my brother; among which he observed there were some curiosities he should be glad to purchase. I replied that when I should receive and be inclined to part with them, I would give him the preference.

Several weeks having elapsed without hearing any thing of my legacy, I waited on Joseph Banks, and, as I thought in the civilest terms, desired him to account with me on this head. He was, or affected to be, extremely angry with me, however; saying his own affairs were not yet settled, and, till they were, he could not settle mine. I answered, that I did not insist on a final adjustment immediately, but thought it necessary to make some enquiry about the matter, lest there might be some perishable commodities among my brother's effects, which would suffer by being kept so long in the package, and therefore required to be inspected. On this he flew, in a rage, to a bureau, that stood in a room adjoining, and began to uncord it with great violence, and in much apparent confusion. On my remonstrating that what he was doing was at present needless, he desisted, and, calling his servant, gave him a written inventory; telling him at the same time to deliver me the things therein mentioned; contained in a bureau, a large Chinese chest, a trunk with two locks, a Dutch box, and some other smaller chests, jars, and boxes.

They were accordingly delivered me the next day, unlocked and without keys, although the inventory implied that all the locks had keys to them excepting that of a tea-chest. On examining into the contents of the several packages also, I found the things did not agree with the inventory †. I missed also some things,

b which

---

† Particularly some linen was found not inventoried, and two New-Zealand arrows were missing. The large chest, instead of being full of curiosities, as mentioned in the inventory, was not a third part full, and most of the things that were in it were damaged or perished. The upper part of the bureau, said to contain curiosities and sundries, contained nothing but a stuffed bird, a few manuscripts

and

which I knew my brother had taken with him, and which were not mentioned at all in the inventory; fuch as a filver watch, two table-fpoons, and a pair of gold fleeve-buttons; all which, however, it is poffible my brother might have loft or difpofed of on the voyage. But, as I thought it not very probable, I was induced to en-quire, of fome of the officers belonging to the Endeavour, into the manner in which my brother's effects were taken care of; and, in particular, after the journal, faid to be loft, and more of his papers and drawings, which I expected to have found.

The refult of this enquiry afforded no reafons to confirm me in the good opinion I had hitherto entertained of Jofeph Banks; in whofe integrity and generofity I had before placed the utmoft confidence. By one perfon, who was particularly inti-mate with my brother, I was informed that he died poffeffed of feveral curious drawings of the natives of New-Zealand and other fubjects, which he had taken at his leifure hours, in prefence of the informant, for his own amufement and par-ticular ufe; having given feveral of them away as prefents to the officers on-board, and that to the knowledge of Jofeph Banks, who never pretended to have the right, he hath fince been pleafed to fet up, to all and every the labours, in feafon and out of feafon, of his indefatigable draughtfman. * From another of the fhip's company I learned, that, immediately after Sydney Parkinfon's deceafe, on the 26th of January, 1771, Jofeph Banks, attended by Dr. Solander, went into his cabbin; when the captain's clerk accidentally paffing by, they called him, and defired him to take an inventory of the deceafed's effects: which he did, by writing down what was dictated. † On being fhewn the abovementioned inventory, he faid it was the clerk's hand-writing; but, on being afked if he thought it contained the whole of Sydney Parkinfon's effects, he replied " No, nothing like it." He was then fhewn the cu-riofities

and fketches of no great moment, and a parcel of written mufic; which latter could hardly belong to my brother, who knew nothing of a fcience, of which his religious profeffion prohibited him the ftudy. Perhaps the fundries were his journal and drawings faid to be loft; the place of which, thefe mufical manufcripts (undoubtedly belonging to Jofeph Banks, who is a connoiffeur in the art,) afterwards fupplied.

* It is here to be obferved, that Sydney Parkinfon was engaged to Jofeph Banks as a botanical draughtf-man only; fo that he was under no obligation to delineate other fubjects for Jofeph Banks, who took out another draughtfman, one Alexander Buchan, with him for that purpofe; who likewife fell a fa-crifice to the viciffitudes of climate and fatigues of the voyage.

† This circumftance was afterwards confirmed to me by the clerk himfelf.

riofities received of Jofeph Banks; on viewing which he declared, that the deceafed, to his knowledge, poffeffed many things not to be found among them, particularly a quantity of feeds of curious plants, many birds and animals preferved in fpirits, many lances, bludgeons, and other weapons ufed in war, likewife houfehold uten-fils and other inftruments, purchafed of the natives of the newly-difcoverd iflands in the South-Seas; together with the third of a leager ‡ of the beft arrack, bought at Batavia. In refpect to the loft journal, he faid that Sydney Parkinfon had been extremely affiduous in collecting accounts of the languages, cuftoms, and manners, of the people, wherever the fhip touched at, and had drawn up a very fair journal, which was looked upon, by the fhip's company, to be the beft that was kept; par-ticularly as to the account it contained of the new-difcovered iflands, and of the people refiding at, or trading to, Batavia. He added, that Sydney Parkinfon had made, at his leifure hours, a great many drawings of the people at Otaheite and the neighbouring iflands, as alfo of the New-Zealanders, particularly of fome who were curioufly marked in the face; and that he frequently fat up all night, drawing for himfelf or writing his journal; and as for the account of its being loft, he looked upon it as a farce, as he was fure Jofeph Banks took particular care of every thing belonging to Sydney Parkinfon, and had all his effects under his own eye. ‖

The reader will obferve, that, though I look on thefe informants to be perfons of veracity, and doubt not they would make good their information, if called on in a court of judicature, I do by no means charge Jofeph Banks, on hear-fay evidence, with the embezzlement or detention of effects I never faw; he has enough to an-fwer for, as a man of credit and probity, in hitherto detaining from me the things I was afterwards prevailed on to entruft him with, on his promife to return them. The information I received, however, could not fail of alarming my fufpicion; which I communicated to fome friends, who advifed me to file a bill in chancery to compel Jofeph Banks to come to a juft account. But, having a man of character and fortune to deal with, I was loth to take violent meafures, in hopes he might be in-duced by fair means to do me juftice.

At the end of about five weeks, I received a meffage from him, appointing me to come the next afternoon to fettle with him. I waited on him accordingly, at the

b 2   time

‡ About fifty five gallons.
‖ The above account was corroborated by another of the fhip's company, who fmiled at the relation of the Journal's being loft, and at the enquiry that was pretended to be made concerning it.

time appointed; when I found him attended by his attorney. He received me very coldly, and complained that I had ufed him ill in making enquiries, among the people belonging to the fhip, concerning my brother's effects; he afked me if I had taken out letters of adminiftration, which he told me it was neceffary I fhould do previous to our finally fettling accounts.

At this meeting, therefore, little paffed, except the adjuftment of the value of fome few of my brother's effects, that Jofeph Banks chofe to keep, or had fold. To this fucceeded, indeed, a fhort, but fomewhat warm, altercation, about the above-mentioned journal and drawings; to which Jofeph Banks claimed a right, in qua-lity of my brother's employer. As I could not be brought to acknowledge this title in him to any thing but the drawings in natural hiftory, which only my brother was employed to execute; he admitted there were in his hands a few manufcripts, which were bequeathed to James Lee beforementioned; fetching a fmall bundle of pa-pers out of a bureau and throwing them down on the table.

Being a good deal flurried with the difpute, and finding nothing could be then determined on, I took no farther notice of them, at that time, than juft to obferve that the manufcripts were my brother's hand-writing.

I obferved however to Jofeph Banks, that Dr. Solander had informed me, that, when my brother was taken ill, he called him afide, and told him he was appre-henfive he fhould die; in which cafe he faid he hoped he had done every thing to Jofeph Banks's fatisfaction, and doubted not but Jofeph Banks would do the juft thing by him; at the fame time defiring that James Lee might have the *perufal* of his manufcripts. Jofeph Banks denied his knowledge of any fuch circumftance; on which his attorney prefent afked if he had any written voucher that the papers were bequeathed to James Lee, and was anfwered in the negative; Jofeph Banks then faying that if Dr. Solander fhould fay that James Lee was to have the perufal only of thofe writings, he would give up the point. At this inftant the doctor came into the room, when I put the queftion to him, and he confirmed, without hefi-tation, what I had afferted. When Dr. Solander left the room, neverthelefs, Jofeph Banks fnatched up the papers, and locked them up in his bureau; telling me to go and adminifter to my brother's will, and he would acquaint me when it

would

would be convenient to him for me to wait on him to make an end of the affair. And thus our interview concluded.

In a day or two after, I took out letters of adminiſtration, as next of kin ; † and having waited a conſiderable time, to no purpoſe, in expectation of hearing from Joſeph Banks, I applied to Dr. John Fothergill, a common friend of my late bro-ther and Joſeph Banks, to inform him how I had been treated ; telling him, at the ſame time, I intended to file a bill in chancery againſt his friend Banks. The doctor diſſuaded me from it, as it would be very expenſive, and promiſed to think of ſome method of bringing about an accommodation. Soon after, he engaged to mediate between us, and, in appearance, much to the ſatisfaction of Joſeph Banks ; between whom ſeveral interviews, of courſe, took place on the occaſion.

During the negotiation, I was informed by Dr. Fothergill, that Joſeph Banks de-ſired to have the inſpection of the ſhells and other curioſities, which had been de-livered to me by his order, as beforementioned ; which, by the doctor's perſua-ſion, I was prevailed on to conſent to, as alſo to agree to preſent Joſeph Banks with ſpecimens of ſuch as he might not have in his own collection ; which he ſaid could be but few, as Sydney Parkinſon always gave him the choice of what he procured and collected.

It was not, I own, without ſome reluctance that I conſented to ſend theſe things to Joſeph Banks's houſe ; but, on Dr. Fothergill's engaging that I ſhould have the whole or the greateſt part of them back, I yielded to his remonſtrances, and ſent a cheſt-of-drawers, a large trunk, and a wainſcot coach-ſeat-box, containing,.

Thirty pieces of the cloth made and worn at Otaheite and the neighbouring iſlands.

Fifteen ditto of matting and New-Zealand garments.

A great number of fiſh-hooks, and various utenſils and inſtruments uſed by the people on the ſouthern iſlands. Theſe were contained in the wainſcot box, which was full of them.

A very

---

‡ Elizabeth Parkinſon, the mother of Sydney, having relinquiſhed her right of adminiſtering.

A very large parcel of curious shells, corals, and other marine productions, many of them beautiful and rare. Besides many other particulars.

Of these curiosities, the shells alone Dr. Fothergill had valued at two hundred pounds: yet neither the shells, nor any thing else, hath Joseph Banks to this day returned me. The reasons he gives for the detention are, that I have used him ill; that he hath given a valuable consideration for them; and, in short, that he will keep them. Of this pretended valuable consideration I am now to speak. On the readiness I shewed to oblige Joseph Banks with such of the shells as he might not have in his collection, Dr. Fothergill informed me, that Joseph Banks, in great good humour and apparent generosity, told him, he had much reason to be satisfied with the services of Sydney Parkinson, and the chearfulness with which he executed other drawings than those of his own department; supplying, in fact, the loss of Joseph Banks's other draughtsman, who died in the beginning of the voyage. On this account, Joseph Banks was pleased to say, it had been his constant intention to make Sydney Parkinson a very handsome present, had he lived to return to England. His intention was now to take place, therefore, towards his brother and sister; to whom he would make the like present, in consideration of such extra-service, or, as Joseph Banks himself expressed it, a *douceur* to the family for the loss they sustained in the death of so valuable a relation. There being due to the deceased upwards of a hundred and fifty pounds salary, the sole property of my sister Britannia, and Joseph Banks chusing to keep some of the effects bequeathed to me, as beforementioned, it was agreed, between Dr. Fothergill and Joseph Banks, that the latter should make up the sum five hundred pounds, to be paid into the hands of me and my sister.

Matters being thus settled, a meeting of all parties was agreed on; which took place on the 31st of January, 1772, when I waited on Joseph Banks with my sister Britannia, meeting there Dr. Fothergill according to appointment.* After a short introduction,

---

* It may not be improper to observe here, that I proposed to Dr. Fothergill the taking my attorney with me on the occasion: but this the doctor opposed; saying, " No, by no means, Joseph Banks " will be offended."

introduction, Jofeph Banks, inftead of enquiring about my letters of adminiftration, as I expected, produced, for us to fign, a receipt, written on ftamped paper, and
couched in the ftrongeft terms of a general releafe, in which he himfelf was ftiled
executor, or adminiftrator, to the laft will of my brother; and, as I underftood it,
importing a renunciation of my right of adminiftration in favour of Jofeph Banks.
This furprizing me, I immediately took out of my pocket the letters of adminiftration, which I had myfelf procured by Jofeph Banks's advice and direction ;
upon which he feemed highly difpleafed, flew into a great paffion, and faid the
whole affair was then overturned : but, on the interpofition of Dr. Fothergill, and
my reprefenting to him that what I had done was by his own order, he having
before told me it was neceffary, and that till I had adminiftered he could not fettle
with me, he became fomewhat pacified, and agreed to pay the five hundred pounds,
on receiving a common receipt, deferring the execution of a general releafe to another opportunity, This receipt was dictated, to the beft of my remembrance, by
Dr. Fothergill, and was figned by me and my fifter Britannia ; I leaving with Jofeph Banks my letters of adminiftration, for the purpofe of having a more proper
and formal releafe drawn up.   Before the figning of the above receipt, however,
I defired Jofeph Banks to deliver me that bundle of my brother's manufcripts,
which he had before fhewn me : On which Dr. Fothergill interfered ; and, faying
they fhould be returned him, and no improper ufe made of them, Jofeph Banks delivered them.

While Jofeph Banks was gone to fetch the papers, I intimated to Dr. Fothergill, that, the fhells and other curiofities not having been returned me according to
promife, it was proper to take notice of it now, and that, unlefs they were returned, I would not fign the receipt.   But to this intimation Dr. Fothergill haftily
replied, " No, no ; thou feeft he is now in a paffion, and it will be improper to
" fpeak of them ;" adding, that he placed fo much confidence in Jofeph Banks's
integrity, that he would anfwer for the return of at leaft the greateft part of them.
And thus our meeting ended.

On the examination of the papers, thus delivered to me by Jofeph Banks, I
found them to be the memorandums and materials, from which, I conceived, my
brother

brother had written his loft journal: which being defirous of preferving for my own fatisfaction, as well as the entertainment of my friends, I caufed them to be faithfully tranfcribed; returning the originals back to Jofeph Banks, as well to comply with Dr. Fothergill's promife to him, as to induce him to return me the fhells and curiofities he ftill detained.

It was in vain I expected Jofeph Banks would keep his word with me. On the 26th of March, 1772, he fent me back, indeed, my drawers and boxes quite empty, without the civility even of a meffage by the bearers. I complained, of courfe, to Dr. Fothergill, who afterwards faid he could obtain no fatisfaction for me. After feveral fruitlefs attempts to obtain it myfelf, therefore, I wrote to Jofeph Banks, acquainting him, that, if he did not immediately return the curiofities, I would inform the world of the whole tranfaction between us, and endeavour to indemnify myfelf by publifhing alfo my brother's journal.* To this letter I received the following anfwer.

Mr. PARKINSON.

I fhall in the prefent, as well as at all times, refer the difpute between us to Dr. Fothergill's deter-mination: not that I feel confcious of having done any thing amifs, but that I feel loth to endure your fcurrilous letters, fuch as I fhall fhew him upon this occafion.

With this you receive the adminiftration.

Notwithftanding this declaration of his willingnefs to refer our difpute to the decifion of Dr. Fothergill, Jofeph Banks took no ftep whatever toward an accommodation; nor did he ever fhew Dr. Fothergill, as the latter informed me, any of thofe pretended fcurrilous letters he mentions.

On

* Not that at this time I was furnifhed with fufficient materials to render it worthy of being laid before the public; having received no drawings or defigns of any confequence whatever from Jofeph Banks. On application, however, to feveral of the fhip's company, and by a fortunate accident, I recovered foon after other manufcripts of my brother's, together with thofe drawings which embellifh the following fheets: not one of which did I receive from Jofeph Banks.

On hearing of Jofeph Banks's intended voyage to Iceland, I thought it neceffary, therefore, to purfue the advice of my friends, by endeavouring to come at my brother's journal and drawings, which I had now fo much reafon to think were concealed from me, and to derive what emolument I could from their publication. To this end I caufed the following advertifement to be inferted in the news-papers.

HIS MAJESTY'S SHIP ENDEAVOUR.

Whereas a Journal was kept on-board the faid fhip, during her late voyage round the world, by Sydney Parkinfon deceafed, late draughtfman to Jofeph Banks, Efq. which, from the great variety of particulars it contained relative to the difcoveries made during the faid voyage, was allowed by the fhip's company to be the beft and moft correct that was taken; and whereas the faid Sydney Parkinfon had, at his leifure hours, made drawings of many of the natives of the new-difcovered iflands, and had alfo taken views of feveral places in the faid iflands, which he intended as prefents to his friends; which faid Journal and Drawings are pretended to have been loft. And whereas there is great reafon to think that they have been fecreted by fome perfon or perfons for his or their own emolument. This is to give Notice, that if any one can give Information where the faid Journal and Drawings are fo fecreted, fo that the Heir at Law to the faid Sydney Parkinfon may come by his lawful property, by applying to Stanfield Parkinfon in little Pulteney Street, they fhall receive One Hundred Guineas Reward.

N. B. It is fuppofed that they are not many Miles from New Burlington Street.†

In confequence of this advertifement, and perfonal application to feveral of the officers and others on-board the fhip Endeavour, I procured, by purchafe, loan, and gift, not indeed the fair copy of my brother's journal, but fo many of his manufcripts and drawings, as to enable me to prefent the following work, in its prefent form, to the public.

As I made no fecret of my defign, and was known to have employed the proper artifts to execute it, I was now folicited and entreated by Jofeph Banks's friends to defift : Dr. Fothergill, in particular, offered me, at different times, feveral fums of money, to drop my intended publication, notwithftanding he knew Jofeph Banks ftill detained my curiofities, contrary to agreement, and refufed to come to

c   any

---

† By this intimation, it is plain I meant to infinuate, that I thought the Journal was in the hands of Jofeph Banks : but I fhould never have thought of publifhing fuch an advertifement, had I ever meant to have fold him my brother's papers, as Dr. Fothergill afterwards affirmed I had done.

any accommodation. Nay, James Lee, of whom I have before spoken, proceeded, indiscreetly, to attempt to intimidate me from my design, by pretending himself to have a right to my brother's manuscripts. His letter to me on that occasion may serve to shew the manner in which I was beset, and what methods were taken to induce me, if possible, to relinquish my right.

To STANFIELD PARKINSON.

SIR,

I have heard of your unaccountable behaviour to my good friend doctor Fothergill relative to your intending to publish your brother's papers, after he had passed his word for your making no improper use of them, contrary to the intention of the lender, for they *was* only lent as a *peice* of indulgence, which the doctor *beged* for you, the use you intend to make of this indulgence in my opinion carrys with it the colour of an action so fraught with ingratitude and matchless impudence that should you proceed in it, you will bring a lasting stain on your name and family, and may be followed by the ruin of both.

I little thought that a brother of my late worthy friend Sidney Parkinson, could have even thought of such a peice of treachery, it makes me shudder at your vicious turn of mind , while I *lemante* ever having had any knowledge of a man of such wretched principles. I advise you to desist, and take shame on you before it is *to* late, and that you will for the sake of your family save your reputation which once lost is seldom to be recovered.

One thing more I must tell you which perhaps you think I did not know, which is that in your brother's will, that he left with his sister before he went abroad, he left some legacys to my daughter Ann. amongest other things some paintings that *was* in your hands. I have likeways heard there was something left to me in the will Mr. Banks brought home. You have taken no notice of these things to me, I imputed your *scilence* to your avarice and did not think it worth my while to disturb you about it. but since I have heard of your determination, I must tell you if you proceed further in your publication I am determined to call you to an account. the papers you are about to publish, *is* by right mine, I have Mr. Banks's word for it that your brother left them to me. and I will *disput* your title to them, as I have witness's of your brother leaving em to me as my property. Consider the contents of this letter and act like a man of honour, or consider the consequence of doing wrong.

Vineyard 26th Nov. 1772.   I am, &c.

JAMES LEE.

To this strange epistle I returned the following answer.

JAMES LEE,   11th Mo. 1772.

I received a letter from thee last Friday, the contents of which, as coming from the friend of my dear brother, greatly amazed me, as thou chargest me therein with crimes of the blackest dye ; but as
they

they are only charges without foundation, the greater part being, according to thy own confeſſion, founded on hearſay evidence, I can eaſily clear myſelf from them, and ſhall therefore anſwer them in the order in which they appear in thy letter.

Thou ſayeſt I intend to publiſh my brother's papers, notwithſtanding Dr. Fothergill gave his word that I ſhould make no improper uſe of them, contrary to the intention of the lender —— From which I infer that thou art of opinion that by publiſhing my brother's papers I ſhall make an improper uſe of them. —— I cannot ſee any impropriety at all in publiſhing what is my own property, not only in my own opinion but that of all my friends. And that my brother's papers were ſuch I ſhall make appear when I come to anſwer another part of thy letter: And being my property, Dr. Fothergill had no authority for ſaying I ſhould not make uſe of them. He might as well have ſaid I ſhould not ſell another piece of furniture out of my ſhop. That I did not, being preſent, contradict what the doctor ſaid, was I confeſs, a fault, but owing to the hurry and confuſion I was in at that time through the altercation between J. Banks and myſelf.

I always had, and ſtill have the greateſt regard for Dr. Fothergill, having in many inſtances experienced his friendſhip. I ſhould be ſorry thy charge of ingratitude in me towards him ſhould be true — I have ſtated the caſe between him and me, reſpecting my intended publication, to many of my friends, and they were all clearly of opinion that the doctor remained entirely excuſed from any thing he had ſaid reſpecting the papers, and the blame, if any, wholly devolved on me.

In regard to what thou haſt advanced, that the papers were lent as a piece of indulgence which the doctor begged for me, I muſt beg leave to contradict thee, and to tell thee that thou wert miſinformed : the doctor, at the time I was with him at Joſeph Banks's houſe, never ſpoke about the papers till I had demanded them as my property, and which I had done ſeveral times before. Joſeph Banks produced them before the doctor ſpake about them, and in all probability they would have given me without any condition, as Joſeph Banks never requeſted any.

I had been for a long time paſt ſurprized at not hearing from, or ſeeing, thee, eſpecially as I had wrote to thee of my intentions reſpecting my brother's Journal ; but the great ſecret, or reaſon thereof is at laſt come out. It ſeems then that thou haſt heard that I have kept ſome legacies bequeath'd to thy daughter Ann, which were left in my brother's will that he depoſited in my ſiſter's hands before he went abroad ; amongſt other things, ſome paintings that were in my hands : And, that by a will Joſeph Banks brought over there was ſomething left to thee, which I have taken no notice of to thee. This is a heavy charge, but from which (as I have already ſaid) I can eaſily exculpate myſelf.

In the will left with my ſiſter, a copy of which Dr. Fothergill has, and to which I have adminiſtred, is the following clauſe.

" 3dly, I deſire that my paintings on vellum, &c. may be given to thoſe for whom they are
" marked on the back, and whatever utenſils that are uſeful in painting or drawing to Mr. Lee's
" daughter, my ſcholar."

I have, accordingly, as bound by ſolemn affirmation at Doctors Commons, ſent thy daughter all my brother's drawing and painting utenſils, that I received from Joſeph Banks or had by me, and have diſpoſed of the paintings as directed by my brother in his own hand writing on the back of them ; if any of them had been marked for thy daughter ſhe wou'd of courſe have had them with the utenſils.

Among

Among the papers I received from J. Banks there was a copy of the will he left with my fifter: If Jofeph Banks brought over any other will of my brother's, it is more than I know of. I fuppofe if he had, it would have been produced before now, as it muft of courfe have fet afide that he left at home, and to which J. Banks knew I adminiftered.

I therefore indeed *did not think thou* KNEWEST *all* that thou haft charged me with on this head.

Thou fayeft that the papers I am about to publifh are thine, and that thou haft Jofeph Banks's word for it. If by the papers thou meaneft the Manufcript of my brother's Journal, I muft tell thee I have it not, it being in Jofeph Banks's poffeffion, to whom I fent it, in order to oblige Dr. Fothergill. What I have are indeed taken from my brother's papers, but contain far more than what that manufcript does; the other part thereof I have been furnifhed with by fome friends of my late brother.

But allowing that what I am going to publifh was no more than what that manufcript contained, thou wouldft find it a difficult matter to perfwade me out of my Right of publication, and muft bring with thee into a court of Equity fomething more ftrong for Evidence than what thou haft mentioned; as I have Dr. Solander as a witnefs to the contrary, who faid in the prefence of Jofeph Banks's lawyer, whom I can produce as an Evidence, and in my hearing, that my brother defired that thou waft to have only the *perufal* of them. Jofeph Banks's lawyer afked him, at that very time, if he had it in writing, that my brother's papers were bequeathed to thee; who anfwered in the Negative; on which the lawyer pronounced them to be my property. And Jofeph Banks was fo well fatisfied at what Dr. Solander then uttered, that he faid he gave it up.

I think thou wilt find I have fufficiently cleared myfelf from thy charges exhibited againft me, which I have done: not that I am any ways fearful of thy threats, for I fhall be at all times ready to anfwer thy fuits, but that I am defirous of living peaceably with all men.

As for the words, *matchlefs impudence, treachery, wretched principles, avarice,* and fuch like, which thou haft applied to me, I regard them as wrote in heat of paffion; and *advife thee* (to make ufe of thy own phrafe) *to take fhame on thee* for having written them, as alfo for having unjuftly charged me with crimes I never committed.

I always have, and I truft I always fhall, act as a man of honour, and I well know the confequence of doing wrong. I hope, after reading this, thou wilt alfo act as becomes fuch towards

STANFIELD PARKINSON.

Perfifting ftill in the preparations for publifhing my book, and turning a deaf ear to Dr. Fothergill's remonftrances, as not being of fo friendly a nature as I thought becoming him, I forfeited his good-will, and he became all at once as much my declared enemy as he had been before my pretended friend. He traduced my reputation before others, complained of my ingratitude to him, and my injuftice to Jofeph Banks; appearing to join with Dr. John Hawkefworth, the compiler of the fouth-fea voyages now publifhed, in reprefenting my book as an un-

fair

fair and furreptitious publication.* To this purpofe indeed Dr. Hawkefworth caufed an advertifement to be inferted in the public news-papers ; in anfwer to which I thought it incumbent on me to infert one, in my own defence ; afferting my right to my brother's papers, and my refolution to publifh them.

To delay this defign, and, if poffible, fupprefs my book, which was almoft ready to appear, Dr. Hawkefworth, whofe compilation was not fo forward, filed a bill in chancery againft me, fetting forth that I had invaded his property, by printing manufcripts and engraving defigns, which I fold to Jofeph Banks, and which Jofeph Banks had *afterwards* fold to him : even Dr. Fothergill fupporting this mifreprefentation, by affirming that I had made fuch fale to Mr. Banks, of which he was a witnefs. On this application an injunction was granted by the court of chancery, to ftop the printing and publifhing of my work. Nay, Dr. Hawkefworth, not contented with praying for the fuppreffion of my book, modeftly defired alfo to have delivered up to him the printed copies of it, which I had, at the expence of feveral hundred pounds, prepared to offer the public.

Put

---

* As a proof how far Dr. Fothergill did interest himfelf on this occafion, I beg leave to give an extract of a letter from a relation at Newcaftle on the fubject.

Dear Coufin,   Newcaftle, 29th Jan. 1773.

—— This will inform thee thy favours came duely to hand, and that I was not a little furprized at Mr. Lee's letter and his change of fentiments refpecting Mr. Banks, as his friendfhip for my late coufin feemed fo great, and by thine I find I am the only perfon who have caufe of complaint and whofe friendfhip yet remains unftaggered. —— But now to what I know of Dr. F's letter to J. K. —— The latter called upon me one day and afked me if I knew of any Journal that was printing here, publifhed by my coufin. I told him no ; but there was one printing at London, which I expected would be finifhed by the middle of this month ; he then read the Dr's letter, wherein after faying how ill thou had treated both him and Mr. Banks, he fays from the regard he had to his promife, he offered thee £. 50 to ftop the publication, which thou refufedft, as he fuppofed only through a mercenary view, to extort more money from him ; which however he did not offer.‖ This was the meaning and the words pretty much the fame, as well as I can remember, in fhort he faid fo much that notwithftanding all I could offer in thy vindication and infifting that the Journal was certainly the property of the family, as well as every curiofity Coufin had collected in the Voyage, yet the Dr. had ftated his cafe in fuch terms, that James King looks on thee as highly culpable. Had my coufin at firft infifted by the proper method of the Law for his brother's laft will and Effects, as I advifed, he would not only have had a great deal more of the Effects, but have faved both Expence and preferved the friendfhip of the Dr. and Mr. Lee. However if the Book be ready, I hope a Number may be fold fo as to defray the Expence and afford thee fomething over ; but am of opinion if they are not out foon, it will be a very great difadvantage. —— Thy truly affectionate Coufin,

J. GOMELDON.

‖ This is not true. The doctor did offer firft fifty and afterwards one hundred and fifty pounds.

Put thus to the trouble and expence of defending a fuit in chancery, and the publication of my book being delayed when juft ready to appear, I had yet no remedy but that of putting in a full anfwer to the bill, and praying a diffolution of the injunction. This I at length obtained; the reafons for continuing the injunction not appearing fatisfactory to the court; and indeed the pretended transfer of the property in my brother's manufcripts, from me to Jofeph Banks, and from Jofeph Banks to Dr. Hawkefworth, being attended with a circumftance, that, on the very face of it, might reafonably fuggeft fome collufion. This was, that the alledged date of the affignment of fuch property, from Banks to Hawkefworth, was prior to that of the receipt for the five hundred pounds before-mentioned, given by Stanfield and Britannia Parkinfon to Banks, on which the pretended right of the latter to fuch manufcript was founded. Can it be fuppofed, that a man of Dr. Hawkefworth's difcretion and abilities would enter into an engagement of this nature, and make a purchafe of fuch moment, without enquiring into the title of the vender?

Be this as it may, fuch is the fact. Indeed the whole purpofe of the bill appears to be litigious, and calculated to anfwer no other end than to delay my publication, till he fhould get the ftart of me and publifh his own: and this end, to my great damage and lofs, it hath anfwered. In the mean while, and pending the fuit between us, it is faid that this prudential author fold the property of his own book, for no lefs a fum than fix thoufand pounds: a fum that probably would not have been given for it, had not an injunction been obtained againft the publication of mine; which contains an authentic journal of the laft and principal voyage, viz. that of his majefty's fhip The Endeavour.

Having thus given a fimple unvarnifhed narrative of the caufes of the delay of this publication, I fubmit its encouragement to the judgement, and candour of the public. I cannot help concluding, however, with a fhort reflection or two on the conduct of my principal oppreffors.

That of Jofeph Banks, in particular, argues a high degree of infolence or avarice, poffeffed, as he was, of fo large a collection of curiofities, as well as of my

brother's

brother's drawings and defigns, was it not covetous in him to defire alfo the little
ftore bequeathed to me? Might not I cite, on this occafion, the parable of the
prophet, and fay to this gentleman, as Nathan did unto David, *thou art the man?*
Would it not be with propriety alfo that I fhould look on his friend, Dr. Fothergill,
as a kind of Ahithophel, by whofe pernicious counfel I gave the ftaff out of my
own hands, and by whofe officious meddling, to fay no worfe of it, I have been involved in an expenfive and troublefome law-fuit? a proceeding the more reprehen-
fible in him, as it is inconfiftent with the peaceful rules of that religious fociety to
which we mutually belong. As to Dr. Hawkefworth, I fhall only fay of him,
that, for a man of reputed piety, he hath behaved on this occafion with fufficient
eagernefs after worldly profit; and hath fhewn, that, whatever be his theory of
moral fentiments, he is practically qualified for the higheft poft, in which the exer-
cife of felfifh talents may be difplayed, and a defire of inordinate gain be grati-
fied.*

In refpect to the comparative merits of his book and mine, it is not for me to
fay any thing. If I have juftified myfelf in the eye of the impartial world for perfifting in this publication, I fhall leave the works of my brother to fpeak his talents; ‡
thinking I have paid a proper refpect to his memory, though it fhould be faid of his
journal, that its only ornament is truth, and its beft recommendation, characteriftic
of himfelf, its genuine fimplicity.

Little-Pultney-ftreet, Golden-fquare,
June 5, 1773.

Stanfield Parkinfon.

* It is faid this gentleman hath been lately made an Eaft-India director.

‡ Of thofe works are all, or moft, of the drawings, publifhed in Dr. Hawkefworth's narrative of
the voyage of the fhip Endeavour; although, while the name of the engraver is pompoufly difplayed,
that of the draughtfman, or original defigner, is meanly and invidioufly fuppreffed.

A JOURNAL

EXPLANATORY REMARKS

ON THE

PREFACE

TO

SYDNEY PARKINSON'S JOURNAL

OF A

VOYAGE TO THE SOUTH-SEAS.

BY JOHN FOTHERGILL, M.D. FR. S.

TO an ingenuous mind, however innocent, it is a humiliating circumstance to be accufed : even a confcioufnefs of integrity, both in act and intention, cannot always efface the remembrance of unmerited, unjuft imputations.

I feel myfelf no otherways affected by the accufations I am going to refute ; and if I have borne them longer than my friends thought I fhould have done, I neither was indifferent, nor incapable of refuting them.

I muft here acquaint the reader, that the preface to Sydney Parkinfon's Journal was not written by the perfon who figns it. That he fupplied the materials, I have no doubt ; he was indeed " unqualified to addrefs the publick"— " an unlettered man"—and was he capable of anfwering for himfelf I might fay more. He had the fortune however to find out a perfon, whofe talents and difpofition were exactly fuitable to fuch a work, and who has, indeed, " varnifhed " his materials" admirably. I know the nominal author was incapable of writing a line of it—nay, thofe letters put down as his own have been corrected ; otherwife, a much larger field of Italicks might have appeared than are fo invidioufly pointed out in a letter, which does the writer's heart great credit with every friend to truth and humanity. It is of confequence to the parties accufed, that the reader fhould know this circumftance, and that whilft he is

perufing

perufing the preface to this journal, he is to confider it as the production of a venal pen, and of a writer who has had very little regard to either truth or character.

Another circumftance the reader ought likewife to be acquainted with—The unfortunate Stanfield Parkinfon, who figns this preface, is now infane, in confinement, and muft probably remain fo for life.* I write, therefore, as if I was treating of a perfon dead, and utterly incapable of anfwering for himfelf— no fmall difadvantage to an accufed perfon, when the accufer is not prefent to fupport his charges—under fuch a fituation, the fuppofition that he poffibly could have done it, ftands againft the accufed.

A fhort hiftorical detail of this whole tranfaction, will perhaps be the moft fatisfactory means of enabling the reader to judge for himfelf, whether the parties charged in this preface are guilty, and deferve the cenfures therein paffed upon them ; or ought not only to be acquitted, as having acted with honour, but applauded for generofity.

I knew Parkinfon's father when I ftudied at Edinburgh ; I believe he deferved the character beftowed upon him in the preface, and I retain a juft efteem for his memory.

When I removed from the city, about the year 1767, to my prefent abode in Harpur-Street, I became a member of that part of our religious fociety which is in Weftminfter, and to which likewife I found Stanfield Parkinfon belonged.

The regard I had for the father, led me to inquire into the fituation of the fon, who I found was an Upholfterer by trade ; Sydney Parkinfon, whofe journal follows, was then in town, and had engaged to accompany Jofeph Banks, Efq; as his draughtfman, in his intended voyage to the South Seas. Being intro-duced to me in this character, I gave him fome fmall proofs that I confidered

* Since this was written, he died infane in Luke's hofpital,

him

him not only as a young man of much ingenuity, but of an unblemifhed character, and one, who, for his friends fake, I could wifh to countenance.

After he embarked in the Endeavour, I took friendly notice of Stanfield Parkinfon, for his father's and brother's fake; I occafionally employed him in fome little affairs in the way of his bufinefs, lent him money on a preffing emergency, and fhewed him every proper mark of regard.

Some time after the return of the Endeavour, he called to inform me, that he thought himfelf ill ufed by Jofeph Banks; that he could neither obtain his brother's effects, nor a fettlement of the account, and added many other accufations.

I informed him my engagements were fuch, that it was not in my power to fpare time to inquire into fuch matters; that the gentleman he complained of would, I doubted not, render him the ftricteft juftice, and more than this, be generous, if he would have patience and allow proper time for adjufting his affairs. I faid this on a prefumption, which I found afterwards fufficiently juftified, that a gentleman of J. Banks's character could never fubmit to do any thing mean and unbecoming that rank in which he ftood with the publick, on account of an undertaking which is yet unequalled.

Stanfield Parkinfon repeatedly called upon me, to folicit my affiftance in terminating this affair. Even his advocate acknowledges that I diffuaded him from all harfh meafures; and this acknowledgment ought to have fuperfeded the infinuation of "officious meddling." But to throw a great deal of dirt, in hopes that fome will ftick, feems to be the eftablifhed maxim of this writer. In confequence of thefe reiterated applications, I wrote to J. Banks, to whom I was then perfonally a ftranger, and acquainted him, "That at Stanfield "Parkinfon's requeft, I had taken the liberty to interfere in a bufinefs that "did not concern me, and to which I thought myfelf very unequal, but "fhould be much pleafed if I could bring them together in fuch a way as to "terminate the mifunderftanding between them in an amicable manner."

In

In anfwer to this, I received the following letter, which, to my great fatis-faction, I lately found amongft my papers, and which, I think, will afford the moft convincing proof of our intentions. Another letter or two paffed between us on the fubject, which, thinking the matter only temporary, were deftroyed. The letter follows :

" DEAR SIR,

" I 'F E E L myfelf very much obliged to you, for having interefted yourfelf
" in fettling the difputes between me and the Executors of Sydney Parkin-
" fon, deceafed; efpecially, as I always feared that without the good offices of
" fome difinterefted perfon, equally to be trufted by both parties, they would
" inevitably end in a law-fuit of the moft pettyfogging nature, which would
" at once defeat any intention I had of ferving them, and lead them into an
" ufelefs expence.

" On leaving England, I agreed to give eighty pounds a year to S. Parkin-
" fon, befides his living of all kinds, as my draughtfman, to make drawings
" for me : of this agreement, £. 151. 8s. 1d. is now due to his executors,
" befides fome fmall fum for fuch cloths, &c. of his, as I could difpofe of,
" or make ufe of in the fhip, which I chofe rather to do, than bring them
" home liable to be damaged, as thofe which came home were in fome
" degree.

" Curiofities of all kinds I gave up to them, and fuch of his papers as I
" had, excepting only fome loofe fheets of a journal, which feemed to be only
" foul copies of a fair journal that I never found, and which is now the chief
" object of their enquiry; thefe foul papers, as all the journal I had, was to
" be given to Mr. Lee, for his reading, by S. Parkinfon's own defire, expreffed
" to Dr. Solander juft before he died : the curiofities I offered to purchafe at
" the time I delivered them, at fuch price as the executors fhould put upon
" them, but was refufed.

" Now

" Now as S. Parkinſon certainly behaved to me, during the whole of his
" long voyage, uncommonly well, and with unbounded induſtry made for me
" a much larger number of drawings than I ever expected, I always did and
" ſtill do intend to ſhew to his relations the ſame gratitude for his good ſervices
" as I ſhould have done to himſelf; the execution of this my intention was only
" delayed by the fear of being involved in a vexatious law-ſuit after all.

" Now you, ſir, in converſation with Dr. Solander, have been ſo good as to
" ſuggeſt a mode of pleaſing all parties, which I confeſs I very much approve
" of; the only thing that now remains is, that, as a friend to both, you
" think of a certain ſum to be paid by me to them, as an acknowledgement of
" S. Parkinſon's good ſervices, taking or not the curioſities, &c. juſt as may
" ſeem to you moſt proper : in this, if you are good enough to undertake it,
" I beg leave to hint, that I do not at all mean to be ſparing in my acknowledg-
" ment ; but to err rather on the other ſide, that any one who may hear the
" tranſaction may rather ſay that I have been generous than otherwiſe.

" Your obliged, and very

" Affectionate humble ſervant,

" J O S E P H   B A N K S."

Being thus left ſolely to compromiſe the difference between the parties, I
endeavoured to view them both in the moſt impartial and diſpaſſionate light.
Whether my opinion was the moſt prudent, is now ſubmitted to others to
determine ; that it appeared to me the moſt equitable and impartial, I can
ſafely aſſert.

I did

I did not find there was any ftipulated time referved for the fole ufe of Sydney Parkinfon during this expedition. His falary was fixed, his fupport engaged for—and of right, his time was the property of J. Banks, who paid this falary, and gave this fupport.

It followed then that the whole of S. Parkinfon's labour as a draughtfman, or in whatever manner he might be employed towards promoting the object of this voyage was the property of his employer. This I confidered as including notes, minutes, draughts, and other articles that required time to execute; which time was his mafter's.

But as it appeared, that he had ufed extraordinary diligence; had given the moft ample fatisfaction to J. Banks, both in refpect to application and ability; that he was now no more, and could claim from him no farther acknowledgment, I judged that more than barely his wages was due, and embracing the liberty allowed me to propofe what was generous, I thought if the fum of £151, which was due to the executors of this young man, was made up £500, it would be a moft ample acknowledgment of his fervices; and prompt any other perfon who might attend in a fecond voyage, (which was then in agitation) in the fame ftation, to exert himfelf with vigour, when he had before him fuch an inftance of generous attention to extraordinary fervices. I endeavoured to make it my own cafe, both one fide and the other. J. Banks very readily fell in with the propofal, and fettled at the fame time a penfion upon a black woman, the wife of a faithful black fervant who went out with him, and perifhed by the cold of Terra del Fuego.

With regard to the collection made by Sydney Parkinfon, it feemed to approach very near being the property of J. Banks; yet part of it might be purchafed—might be given him for particular fervices—might be collected at times when it would be unreafonable to expect he fhould be labouring at all. In thefe things I allowed him to be interefted, yet with this referve, that if he had collected any curiofities, which were not in the general collection, it would

be

be right for J. B. to have every thing of that kind, as the collection could not have been made without his expence and affistance.

I propofed, therefore, in refpect to thefe things, that J. B. fhould have the privilege of looking them all over—of felecting from them whatever might be agreeable to him, and returning the reft to Stanfield Parkinfon.

When Sydney went out, I requefted him, if he met with any rare marine productions, which did not interfere with the general bufinefs, that he would be kind enough to referve a few fpecimens for me—this he promifed, and had he lived would, I doubt not, have gratefully performed.

Stanfield allowed me to look over this part of his collection ; requefting me at the fame time to lay afide a few of fuch as I thought rare for his coufin at Newcaftle. This I performed ; took care in felecting for myfelf thofe I thought proper, that the reft of the collection fhould be as valuable as poffible, by leaving duplicates, and in good condition.

At my requeft, and in purfuance of the opinion, that it was neceffary that every curious article not in the general collection, if any fuch there fhould be, ought to make a part of it, both the fhells I had felected for myfelf and S. P.'s relation, as well as thofe from whence they were taken, were all fent back to J. Banks, who after fome time returned to me all thofe I had picked out, and thofe only. In this part of my negociation I was unfortunate. I had not made myfelf fufficiently underftood. I meant that after J. B. had taken out of Sydney Parkinfon's collection, whatever he might think fit to add to his own collection, not only thofe which I had felected, but the reft likewife fhould have been returned. Papers, manufcripts, drawings, and whatever related to the object of this voyage, the promotion of knowledge, were unexceptionably to be given up to J. Banks, who thought himfelf likewife entitled to the reft of the curiofities, as well as the manufcripts, papers, &c. in confideration of the ample fatisfaction he had made, having prefented the family with £349 more than was due to Parkinfon ; forty-nine of which he judged to be more than an

equivalent

equivalent for the whole of his collection ; as indeed it proved to be from the prices they fold at in fubfequent auctions.

After the fhells were returned to me, I defired Parkinfon to fay what would content him for thofe I had felected. He told me that a dealer, who had feen the whole collection which his brother had made, in his abfence, faid they were worth two hundred pounds. I never fixed any value upon them. I never faw the whole, nor examined any part of his collection but the fhells and corals. It is therefore an abfolute untruth that I fixed any price upon this collection.

There is nothing more difagreeable than to fix a value upon another's property; efpecially where that valuation has no certain ftandard. Things of this nature are to be rated according to opinion only. Determined therefore to follow the example I had propofed, I paid liberally for thofe I felected— above twice the real value, as the fame kinds have fince been fold for at publick auctions. I told him at the time, he muft not expect to difpofe of the reft on the like terms.

Incapable of feeling the generofity of my conduct, he immediately con-cluded, that what remained in the hands of J. Banks, were of much greater value than he had fufpected; and from that moment, became importunate to have every thing returned : and this, perhaps, was a principal motive to his future ungenerous and ungrateful conduct. The reader of Parkinfon's preface, when he has confidered thefe circumftances, will perhaps acquit me of the charge of having acted the part of a " pretended friend." If he does, what name muft the man deferve, who had bafenefs enough to forge the injurious epithet ?

The fum of £500, which I had propofed to be paid by J. Banks, to the executors of Sydney Parkinfon, as a full compenfation for his extra-ordinary diligence, inftead of £151, was accepted by both parties. I was prefent at the payment, a witnefs to the receipt, and hoped the difpute was amicably and honourably terminated.

Stanfield

Stanfield Parkinson then requested he might have the perusal of his deceased brother's papers. J. Banks complied with this request, though not without hesitation ; the event too plainly proved, he had stronger reasons for his reluctance than I was aware of : he knew the man much better than I did. Thinking that it must afford Stanfield much satisfaction to peruse these last remains of his brother's industry, I requested it as a favour, engaging, as I thought I might do it safely, that no improper use should be made of them ; I meant by printing, or communicating them to the publick in any mode whatsoever. My request was complied with, and he was put in possession of all the papers in J. Banks's custody.

That J. Banks was dissatisfied with the manner, at least, in which Parkinson made the request, was evident, and not without sufficient reason. After such an instance of generosity, as he had just exhibited to Parkinson's family, to have the shadow of a claim urged with heat, was not a little irritating.

By Parkinson's own confession in the preface, as soon as he had got the papers into his hands, it appears, that he immediately set to work to get them transcribed, engravings to be made from some drawings of his brother's, and to put the whole as fast as he could into a form for publication.

Some weeks after the business was, as I thought, happily terminated, I was informed, that Parkinson was preparing his brother's papers for the press. I sent for him immediately, to enquire into the truth of this report, and learned from him, to my astonishment, that the papers were transcribing for this purpose.

I asked, if he had forgot that I pledged myself to J. Banks, that no improper use should be made of them, in his hearing ; and that he made not the least objection to my engaging on his behalf in this manner : and told him that it was a piece of the blackest treachery such a transaction could admit of, and he was treating me with no less ingratitude than injustice, silently to acquiesce with

my

my engaging for him, perhaps at the very moment he was refolving to avail himfelf of my good nature and humanity towards him, to do an irreparable injury to J. Banks and myfelf.

I entreated him, if he had any regard for his own intereft and reputation, that he would immediately defift from a project, which would be ruinous in all probability to himfelf, and leave me expofed to reproaches, on my part wholly undeferved. The reader will much more eafily conceive than I can exprefs, what I felt on this occafion.

I urged him to lay afide an intention, which, if carried into execution, might involve us both in an imputation of notorious treachery.—Entreated him to recollect in what manner I had behaved to his brother, and himfelf, ever fince I had known them; the acts of kindnefs I had repeatedly done to himfelf, and his family.—That it would be forfeiting, not only my future friendfhip, but the regard of every one who fhould be made acquainted with this fignal act of ingratitude.—That his conduct would be a reproach to the whole fociety we belonged to, and that J. Banks, if he was not generous enough to think me incapable of it, might accufe me as a party in his guilt. He then promifed to defift, upon my engaging to pay the expences he had incurred, for tranfcribing and engraving. I ordered him to bring me the amount of his expences, he did fo, juft as I was preparing to fet out for Chefhire—I offered him a draft for the money; but he chofe to ftay for it till my return from the country. At which time, when I fent for him to finifh the affair, I was informed the work was advancing, and that the expences were at leaft £300.

In vain I reprefented to him this double aggravation of his criminal conduct. All that I could urge was received with an obftinate refolution to perfevere.

He faid that J. Banks had ufed him ill, by retaining all the articles fent to him, fome of which ought to have been returned to him, and were of as much

value

value as the fum he had received; and that he was therefore determined to do himfelf juftice, by publifhing his brother's papers, and informing the publick of his reafons.

This complaint I told him ought firft to have been made to me, as I ftood guarantee to J. Banks, that no fuch ufe fhould be made of his papers as was then intended; if J. Banks had withheld any thing that was juftly due to him, I was obliged to fee juftice done him, and fhould do it, either by application to J. Banks, or out of my own pocket. But all was in vain. Can the reader think, as S. Parkinfon has infinuated, that becaufe I declared this conduct ungrateful, therefore my friendfhip till now was " meer pretence ?"

Finding all my endeavours to put a ftop to this unexpected treacherous behaviour ineffectual, I prevailed upon a reputable fenfible perfon, of our perfuafion, and a member of the fame meeting, to meet Parkinfon at my houfe, to endeavour, if poffible, to put an end to this moft difagreeable bufinefs; we met accordingly. What paffed amongft us on this occafion, will probably appear moft fatisfactorily to the reader, from the mediator's own account of it, which I copied from his memorandum.

" Subftance of what paffed at Dr. Fothergill's houfe, November the 22d,
" between Stanfield Parkinfon and Dr. Fothergill, in the prefence of John
" Hatch, who, a few days after, put it down in writing, to affift his memory,
" if he fhould be called upon as an evidence in the cafe.

" J. Fothergill requefted J. Hatch would meet Stanfield Parkinfon, at
" J. F.'s houfe, which he did Nov. 22, 1772.

" J. F. then informed J. Hatch, with the occafion of this appointment.
" The following is the purport of what paffed between J. F. S. Parkinfon,
" and John Hatch, on this occafion.

" That

" That S. P. had a difpute with Jofeph Banks, which was likely to be
" attended with a law-fuit ; but in order to ferve S. P. and prevent fo much
" trouble and expence, J. F. at the defire of S. P. had taken upon him to
" endeavour to fettle the matter between them, which J. F. had effected in
" the following manner :

" That Jofeph Banks inftead of paying S. Parkinfon the fum of one hundred
" and forty pounds, or thereabouts, which was due to his deceafed brother
" Sydney Parkinfon, fhould pay Stanfield Parkinfon the fum of five hundred
" pounds : for which S. P. fhould let J. Banks felect fuch fhells, &c. from
" his late brother's collection, as to make J. Banks's complete ; and that S. P.
" fhould make no ufe of his late brother Sydney Parkinfon's papers or
" drawings : to which agreement Stanfield Parkinfon being prefent made no
" objection.

" But J. F. complained, that contrary to this agreement he found S. P.
" was preparing to publifh his brother's obfervations, which S. P. acknow-
" ledged was true, and faid he had expended upwards of fixty pounds on that
" account.

" J. F. remonftrated with him on the injuftice of fuch a procedure, and
" faid for the fake of their own credit, and to avoid difputes, he (J. F.)
" defired S. P. would fend him an account of what had been expended in
" preparing for the publication, and he (J. F.) would pay it him.

" Accordingly the bill was fent, amounting to upwards of fixty pounds ;
" this happened to be about the time when J. F. was going into the country
" for fome weeks, who foon after his return fent for S. P. in order to pay the
" aforefaid bill.

" But to his great furprife, S. P. told J. F. the work was ftill going on,
" and that the fum of £300 was now expended thereon.   J. F. again
" remonftrated

" remonftrated with S. P. on the great injuftice done him as a mediator
" between them, but to no purpofe, S. P. ftill perfifting in publifhing.

" A little while after S. P. was withdrawn, J. F. defired J. Hatch would let
" S. P. know that J. F. would pay this farther expence, provided he would
" drop the publication : to which J. H. replied, that S. Parkinfon told J. H.
" that the work was ·carrying on fo faft that he could not drop it ; on which
" account J. H. did not carry this propofal to S. P."

Having thus made ufe of every method in my power, but ineffectually, to
prevent the publication of a work obtained from its rightful owner in this
treacherous manner, nothing remained for me to do, but to affure my much
injured friend J. Banks, that I felt the moft poignant diftrefs on this occafion :
and that whilft I had been folely intent upon ferving both parties, I had been
made the inftrument of injuring him fo materially.

Though I knew Parkinfon himfelf was incapable of publifhing the papers
which he had thus furreptitioufly obtained ; yet it was not to be doubted, but
he might readily find fome needy writer, who would fupply his defects, and
perhaps rejoice at an opportunity of defaming thofe who were moft juftly
entitled to commendation.

When the work appeared, this apprehenfion was fully juftified ; it was
ufhered to the publick by a preface profeffing much fpecious candour, but
containing a feries of falfehood, mifreprefentation, and abufe. To thefe is
oppofed the explanation here exhibited, and it is now before the publick, and
will probably be before pofterity, who will have no partial regards to the
accufer or defendants : both have the right of appeal to that tribunal, to
explain the motives of their conduct, and muft fubmit to the equity of their
decifion.

That applications were made by a legal procefs to ftop the appearance
of this work by the publifher and bookfellers concerned in the edition
of

of Capt. Cook's Voyages, is true, and for very obvious reasons; the sale of it would lessen their benefits, in proportion to its value and its sale. The hope of gain had been Parkinson's chief object—he knew that a much more honourable place * might and would have been reserved for doing justice to his brother's merit, than in a preface filled with invective and unjust insinuations against his brother's warmest friends. Could poor Sydney have foreseen that he was furnishing avarice and malevolence with the means of traducing such men, he would have swerved from the instructions of his cordial and intelligent friend,† who desired him to " minute every thing he saw, and " trust nothing to his memory.'"

It may not be improper here to mention a fact, which, though of no great consequence in itself, is of moment to those who are under the disagreeable necessity of justifying their conduct before the publick.

Parkinson's plea for printing his brother's papers, was, " That Jos. Banks " never returned him any of the clothes, utensils, &c. which were sent to " Jos. Banks for his inspection."

It was stipulated expressly, that every thing of this nature should be put into the hands of Jos. Banks. But it is evident, that Parkinson had reserved many drawings; whence, otherwise, came the plates which appear in this work?

And there are now in my possession, some clothes and instruments which were collected by Sydney Parkinson, which I purchased of Stanfield Parkinson's executors after his decease, and which were never sent to J. Banks, though *all* were promised. Hence it is very evident, this supposed detention, which might readily have been adjusted, was not the sole cause of the unrighteous act —but the hope of acquiring a large sum of money by the sale of this journal.

However artfully the tale was told, yet the publick could not readily adopt the partial and invidious narrative; they could not believe the account was true; it bore too evident marks of partiality, rancour, and injustice. And

* The Natural History of this Voyage.   † James Lee.

sensible

fenfible people could not but fufpect the like temper might poffibly pervade the work; and that the fame difregard to truth, the fame varnifh, might be employed to work up a recital of events and circumftances, more fuited to the compiler's ideas, than the reality of a journal.

But there feems not much reafon to apprehend the latter was the cafe. The revifer feems to have followed his original pretty clofely. What errors it contains were chiefly made by the author, and it was not likely the editor could correct them.

Perhaps it may be afked, whence it happened that two perfons, whofe characters have been thus fharply attacked, could quietly remain fo long under fuch imputations? I fhall anfwer for myfelf, and in doing that, fhall perhaps fuggeft fome reafons why J. Banks was as filent myfelf.

The confcioufnefs of my innocence, and the difintereftednefs of my views in this tranfaction, with a hope that the general tenour of my life, would prevent my fuffering greatly in the opinion of thofe who knew any thing concerning me, alleviated much the fenfe of the injuries done to me; and a perfuafion, that fenfible and impartial people, to whom J. Banks and myfelf were unknown, would difcover in the narrative itfelf, fo many inftances of paffion and partiality, as would lead them to fufpect the charges to be the product of difappointment and malevolence.

Men who wifh to pafs without blame through life, naturally endeavour to have none imputed to them; not even undefervedly. It is fcarcely poffible for perfons of any feeling, not to wifh to leave behind them an unfullied reputation; and this not only for their own fakes, but for the fake of their friends, and their connections. Not forgetting, likewife, that they owe example to the publick.

Two reafons prevented me from attempting the juftification I now fubmit to the reader's confideration before this time. The firft, Parkinfon and

myfelf

myfelf were members of a community which enjoins it as an indifpenfible obligation, not to appeal to the publick, in matters of difpute or difagreement, till the means prefcribed by that community have been tried to reconcile the difference.

Agreeable to this fundamental maxim, Parkinfon ought firft to have applied for juftice, had I injured him, in the ufual forms of our procedure. Inftead of this, he at once, contrary to all advice, traduced me before the publick, and violated the rules of his profeffion. Had I followed in a reply, I fhould have been as guilty as himfelf; guilty of breaking through a regulation, that has been thought to do credit to our inftitution. I bore it therefore patiently, till a feafon might arrive when probably he might be, by the interpofition of the fociety, made fenfible of the breach of order, might be induced to reflect on the injuftice he had done me, and, from conviction, do juftice to a much injured character to the utmoft of his power. To endeavour to make people fenfible of their miftakes by forbearance, by reafon, and the motives drawn from religious confiderations, is the method we employ on thefe occafions.

Soon after the publication of this journal, the fociety finding one of their members expofed to publick cenfure, by another of the fame profeffion, could not avoid taking notice of it in due form, and they treated with Parkinfon, to make him fenfible of the breach he had made in the rules of their difcipline. After much labour, he was made to comprehend it fo far as to own it, and was forry for it. A written acknowledgment to be entered in the minutes of the fociety, is always expected on thefe occafions; whilft this was framing, fuch evident marks of infanity appeared, as to render it of no confequence to proceed with him any further.

The refult of thefe proceedings, with thofe who are guilty of breaches of order, is to accept of their acknowledgment, if it appears to be competent and fincere; and this acknowledgment reinftates the offender in his former ftate of memberfhip. If he proves refractory, he is declared not to belong to the fociety, in which cafe he is open to the common modes of profecution.

Till,

Till, therefore, Parkinson had either reinstated himself in the society, by acknowledging and making proper satisfaction for the breach of a rule, which is not only known to the society itself, but to many intelligent people of other communities; or till he was disowned for refusing this satisfaction— no proper mode of proceeding to do myself justice presented itself. If, he remained a member, my application must be to the society. If he refused submission to them, he would be no longer considered as a member, and I should then be left at liberty to seek redress as circumstances might require. It would be tedious and not interesting, to produce undeniable evidence in support of this narrative. So much as is here offered, will, I hope, be received with indulgence, when it is considered I am rescuing myself from charges that must otherwise remain unrefuted, perhaps, as long as letters are esteemed either in this or other nations; for the engravings in this work, as well as the importance of the voyage, will always give the book a place in the libraries of the inquisitive.

It is not improbable, but that a hope of gaining considerably by the sale of this book, might be a very strong inducement to Parkinson to trample in this manner on the laws of friendship, gratitude, and justice. Some of the Endeavour's crew, who soon came about him, after their arrival in England, for their own private ends, buoyed him up with hopes of vast advantage from his brother's labours. This rendered him deaf to all advice; induced him to break the promise he had made me to stop the publication; involved him in many difficulties in respect to his circumstances; and, it is much to be feared, contributed to his ruin. He owned to some of his acquaintance before his faculties were quite disordered, " That he had used me wickedly."

It became necessary soon after his confinement, to look into his affairs, when it appeared, that not much more was left than would barely satisfy his creditors. His wife died a little before he became quite insane, and his children are maintained by the society, of which he was a member.

Amongst

Amongſt his effects were found ſome remains of his brother's collection of clothes and utenſils, though but few, and about four hundred copies of this journal : thoſe who had the management of his concerns, made me an offer of theſe copies, which I bought at their own price, together with the plates belonging to this work.

There had always appeared to me a great difficulty in reſpect to a juſtification of myſelf from his charges : to do this in a common news-paper, or in a pamphlet, though it might ſerve the preſent purpoſe, yet the calumny would be handed down to poſterity ; and if an exculpation gained the notice of a few cotemporaries, it ſtood but little chance of ſurviving when perſonal regard was at an end.

I chearfully accepted the offer made me of purchaſing the remaining copies, as the poſſeſſion of them would afford me an opportunity of tranſmitting to future time, ſuch an account of this tranſaction as might enable thoſe who peruſed the charge, to judge of it fairly for themſelves.

When the reader reflects on the ſeveral circumſtances here related, and conſiders this poor man as neceſſitous, diſappointed in his views, and under the commencement of inſanity, it will not be difficult to account for his extraordinary behaviour to perſons who had acted in all things towards him with diſintereſtedneſs and generoſity.

J O H N   F O T H E R G I L L.

POSTSCRIPT.

S O O N after the publication of Parkinson's Journal, a gentleman to whom I was very well known, and who is now abfent on duty, in a remote part of the world, was fo much affected with the injurious treatment I had met with, as to be at the pains of drawing up the following remarks on the preface, with a view to get them inferted in the Monthly Review. With this intention he put them into my hands, where they have lain ever fince. As, on perufing them, I find they have touched upon fome circumftances which are not directly noticed in the preceding narrative, it feemed not improper to add them to thefe remarks.

To the Publifher of the Monthly Review.

Among the many ufes to the publick of a literary review, it cannot be the leaft, nor out of character, to convey a candid defence againft an unjuft attack. In virtue of this plea it is that I claim your infertion of this addrefs to you.

A kind of folemn appeal to the publick having been lodged in Mr. Parkinfon's preface to his publication of certain remains of his brother's journal and draughts, on his voyage to the South-Seas, in the Endeavour, againft the ill treatment pretended to have been received by him, relative to fuch his edition ; in which appeal he has efpecially involved Dr. Fothergill ; it is from a particular regard of this gentleman's character, that the following

remarks

remarks are derived : yet does the love of truth fo far in me out-weigh all partiality, that the points of the greateft importance to the decifion, are principally taken from Mr. Parkinfon's own account of the matter, without falfifying any fact, or ftraining any inference.

Upon the face then of the premifes it appears, that Dr. Fothergill, without the fhadow of any intereft fo much as infinuated, but prefumptively with the beft of intentions, and agreeably to his well known ufual humanity, interfered for the fervice and fatisfaction of Mr. Parkinfon, to whofe " religious fociety," to ufe Mr. Parkinfon's own words, the doctor alfo belonged : it was under this friendly mediation that Mr. Banks, whofe debt to the deceafed for his· falary is not pretended to have been more than about one hundred and fifty pounds, confented to add the fum of three hundred and fifty pounds, which furely was a noble addition, and might very well be allowed to include in it, at once, the gratuity intended as a *douceur* to the family, for the lofs they fuftained in the death of fo valuable a relation, and a confideration as well for any diftinction that could be fet up between the drawings of the hired botani- cal draughtfman, and thofe of the draughtfman in general, as for all the vaft treafure of cockle fhells, plants, ftuffed birds, favage garments, utenfils, and implements of war, faid to have been left, of infinite curiofity, no doubt ; but hardly of fo much value as to tempt Mr. Banks to cheat Mr. Parkinfon's heirs of them.

That Mr. Banks, however, imagined that this additional fum of three hundred and fifty pounds gave him a right to a fair and full clearance (and perhaps the reader may imagine fo too) ftands prefumably proved by his having prepared a general releafe, to be figned by Mr. Parkinfon and fifter on their receipt of the fum, thus even generoufly made up five hundred pounds ; and that it was not figned by them appears, by Mr. Parkinfon's own account, to have been purely owing to fome delay made neceffary by a point of form. (See preface, p. xv.)

That

That Dr. Fothergill might, at that time, promife his good offices for Mr. Banks's letting him have fome of thofe curiofities back that Mr. Parkinfon there fays he wifhed to have back, is not at all improbable, if it be true that he expreffed at that time fuch a wifh ; but that he fhould make the receiving them back a condition of his figning the receipt of the £500, is not, perhaps, quite fo credible. Whoever, alfo, will think it worth his while to perufe Mr. Parkinfon's own account, his own confeffion of prefence at Dr. Fothergill's engaging for the return of the brother's manufcript, and not contradicting fuch engagement, will hardly not fee and feel that he was bound by it in honour and in juftice.

To how poor a prevarication and fubterfuge has he recourfe in his pitiful chicanery about the expreffion of making an improper ufe of his brother's papers ! Can he think to impofe on any one, that by that " improper ufe" he did not underftand himfelf precluded from publifhing any thing of his brother's, relative to that voyage, which Mr. Banks might wifh not to be publifhed ?

By all accounts then, not even excluding Mr. Parkinfon's own ftate of the cafe, it appears, that after a final end had (by Mr. Banks's juftice pufhed to the length of great generofity) been put to any further claim on this part of Mr. Parkinfon, for any debts or effects of his brother's, he expreffed a very natural curiofity to have the perufal of his journal and manufcripts, very lawfully and honourably in Mr. Banks's poffeffion. Upon which Mr. Banks, with a miftruft which Mr. Parkinfon has fince abundantly juftified, expreffing an unwillingnefs to truft them out of his hands, Dr. Fothergill, in that true fpirit of humanity which conftantly characterifes him, obferved, that it would be rather hard to deny a brother fuch a natural gratification, and interceded for Mr. Banks's letting Mr. Parkinfon have them, faying, " They fhould be " returned, and no improper ufe made of them." (See preface, p. xv.)

Now

Now what that improper ufe meant, I prefume, there is no reader who will not inftantly conftrue and allow that Mr. Parkinfon was at leaft in honour bound by it, relatively to Dr. Fothergill, who had thus humanely and kindly undertaken for him.

What the fentiments of an intimate friend of his brother's were, who, in a letter to this Parkinfon, accufes him of a treachery and avarice that make him fhudder for his treatment of fo worthy a perfon as Dr. Fothergill, the reader may fee in page xviii of that preface, and judge whether Parkinfon's anfwer to it does not add to the criminality of the ingratitude and breach of truft contained in the tranfaction, the meannefs of fhuffling and equivocation in an endeavour to juftify it.   Mean while the fituation of Dr. Fothergill is fingularly cruel; his humanity, his tendernefs for a brother's fuppofed fraternal feelings, a defire of procuring him a fatisfaction he judged but natural, having made him undertake for one whom he could not conceive poffible to be guilty of fo mean, fo difhonourable a procedure, have expofed him to the reproaches of Mr. Banks, if one fo much of a gentleman as Mr. Banks could be capable of not doing juftice to the intention, however hurt by the confequences: while, on the other hand, Mr. Parkinfon has in his preface aimed at prefenting him to the publick in the light of one who is an accomplice of Mr. Banks's in his oppreffive procedure, and partial to his injuftice, at the fame that it will clearly appear, that nothing could be more generous than Mr. Bank's dealing with Mr. Parkinfon; nor more humane and friendly, than Dr. Fothergill's interpofition in his favour.   And fuch his return from him! Upon which let the reader himfelf decide, whether this cafe is not one of thofe that may fairly be added to the catalogue, already terribly too long, of inftances of the danger of doing good.   And the reader will alfo pleafe to obferve, that in the premifes there have been no confequences drawn but what palpably arife from facts of Mr. Parkinfon's own furnifhing.

F I N I S.

EASTERN HEMISPHERE.

North Pole

South Pole

Engraved by Samuel John Neele, No. 352 Strand.

WESTERN HEMISPHERE.

North Pole

South Pole

Engraved by Samuel John Neele Nº 352 Strand.

A

JOURNAL

OF A

VOYAGE to the SOUTH SEAS,

In his Majefty's Ship The ENDEAVOUR.

ON the 22d of July, 1768, I went on board the fhip, ENDEAVOUR, then lying in the Galleons Reach, in the river Thames: on the 3d of Auguft arrived in the Downs; and then failed for Plymouth Sound, where we anchored on the 14th, and took on board fome more feamen, with a few marines. Mr. Banks, Dr. Solander, Mr. Green, with their attendants, alfo joined us at this port; and our number was then increafed to ninety fix. Having taken in fome more ftores and guns, and made a few neceffary alterations in the fhip, on the 26th of Auguft we failed from Plymouth, with the wind at N. N. W. but it did not continue long in that quarter, but changed to S. W. where it held till the 2d of September, foon after which, we difcovered Cape Ortugal. From this time, till the 4th of October, we had variable winds, and then we faw Cape Finiftere at about ten leagues diftance.

We continued our courfe, and met with no material occurrence till the 12th; then we difcovered Puerto Santo, about nine leagues off; foon after we faw the ifland of Madeira; and, on the 13th, in the morning, anchored in Fonchiale Bay.

This

This country is very mountainous, yet it is cultivated to the very tops of the mountains; and, being covered with vines, citrons, oranges, and many other fine fruit-trees, it appears like one wide, extended, beautiful, garden. During our ftay on this ifland we refided at Fonchiale, which is the capital. Mr. Banks and Dr. Solander lodged at the houfe of the Britifh conful, W. Cheap, efq. and made feveral excurfions into the country.

A great part of the beft provifions ufed on this ifland are imported from England and other parts of Europe, efpecially fuch as are eaten at dinner; from whence alfo they import moft of their utenfils and wearing-apparel; fo that many of the neceffaries of life bear a very high price amongft them.

While the fhip lay in this harbour, we had the misfortune of lofing Mr. Ware, the chief-mate, who was a very honeft worthy man, and one of our beft feamen. His death was occafioned by an unlucky accident which happened to him while he ftood in the boat to fee one of the anchors flipped. The buoy-rope happening to entangle one of his legs, he was drawn overboard and drowned before we could lend him any affiftance.

Having taken in a fupply of water, wines, and other neceffaries, on the 19th of September we proceeded on our voyage, with the wind at E. S. E. and on the 22d faw the iflands of Salvages, at about two leagues and a half diftance. They lie between Madeira and the Canaries, are fmall and uninhabited.

On the 23d we fell in with the trade-winds at N. E. and on the fame day dif-covered the peak of Teneriffe.

On the 24th we failed between that peak and the grand Canary iflands. In our paffage we faw fome land birds, and caught two of them, which were very much like our water wag-tail.

On the 29th, we had a view of the ifland of Bona Vifta, at about four leagues diftance.

Nothing

Nothing material occurred from the 29th to the 7th of October; then we had variable winds, with fome fhowers of rain; and the dampnefs of the air greatly affected all our iron utenfils. We caught two fea fwallows, and feveral curious marine animals, of the molufca tribe, fuch as fea-worms, ftar-fifh, and fea urchins.

On the 21ft, we reached the S. E. trade wind, and continued our courfe without any remarkable occurrence till the 8th of November; then we difcovered land at about eight leagues diftance, and fpoke with the crew of a Portugueze fifhing veffel, of whom Mr. Banks bought a great quantity of fifh, among which were dolphins and breams, which afforded much fpeculation to our naturalifts. After having left the veffel, we ftood in for the land, which proved to be the Brazils; and coafted along the fhore till the 13th, and then failed into the harbour of Rio de Janeiro, which lies in latitude 22° 56′ fouth, and longitude 42° 45′ weft; but before we arrived in the harbour, the captain had fent Mr. Hicks, the firft lieutenant, and the chief mate, in the pinnace, to the viceroy, to obtain a pilot; however, as the wind was fair, the captain ventured to continue failing on, and was affifted by fignals from the forts.

The viceroy detained the lieutenant and the mate, and fent back the pinnace with three of his own officers in it (of which one was a colonel) but no pilot. The colonel told us, that our officers would only be detained till the fhip fhould be examined, according to cuftom: we therefore ftood forward into the harbour, and anchored near the north end of Ilhos dos Scobros, or Snakes Ifland; but the colonel would not permit any of us to go afhore.

Our lieutenant had been inftructed to evade anfwering any queftions the Portugueze might afk him refpecting our deftination; or at leaft to anfwer them with referve: the captain thought fuch queftions would be impertinent, as our veffel was a fhip of war; and the lieutenant obferved thefe directions.

The viceroy held a council, the refult of which was, to prohibit any perfon coming on fhore from our fhip; but they condefcended to order all neceffary

fupplies

supplies to be fent to us. We were difpleafed on receiving this intelligence, as we had expected to have met with agreeable entertainment on fhore. Mr. Banks and Dr. Solander appeared much chagrined at their difappointment: but, notwith-ftanding all the viceroy's precautions, we determined to gratify our curiofity, in fome meafure, and having obtained a fufficient knowledge of the river and harbour, by the furveys that we had made of the country, we frequently, unknown to the centinel, ftole out of the cabin window at midnight, letting ourfelves down into a boat by a rope; and, driving away with the tide till we were out of hearing, we then rowed to fome unfrequented part of the fhore, where we landed, and made excurfions up into the country, though not fo far as we could have wifhed to have done. The morning after we went afhore, my eyes were feafted with the pleafing profpects that opened to my view on every hand. I foon difcovered a hedge in which were many very curious plants in bloom, and all of them quite new to me. There were fo many, that I even loaded myfelf with them. We found alfo many curious plants in the fallading that was fent to us; and defired the people that brought it to procure us, if poffible, all the different forts that grew upon the ifland.

We had plenty of fifh from the markets every day, of which they are furnifhed with a great variety.

We often picked off fome curious molufca from the furface of the fea; and alfo land infects of feveral kinds alive, which floated round the fhip upon the water.

The country, adjacent to the city of Rio de Janeiro, is mountainous, full of wood, and but a very little part of it appears to be cultivated. The foil near the river is a kind of loam, mixt with fand; but farther up in the country we found a fine black mould. All the tropical fruits, fuch as melons, oranges, mangoes, lemons, limes, cocoa nuts and plantains, are to be met with here in great plenty. The air, it feems, is but feldom extremely hot, as they have a breeze of wind from the fea every morning; and generally a land wind at night *.

* S. Parkinfon had not been idle from the time he left England, having, as appeared by a letter from him to his brother, finifhed 100 drawings on various fubjects, and taken fketches of many more; which he intended to have finifhed if he had lived to return.

On

On the 7th of December, 1768, our neceſſary proviſions, and other ſupplies, having been taken on board, we left the harbour of Rio de Janeiro, coaſting along the Brazils, and met with nothing worthy of note till the 22d of the ſame month, except, that in coming out of the harbour, Mr. Flowers, an experienced ſeaman, fell from the main ſhrouds into the ſea, and was drowned before we could reach him.

On the 22d, we ſaw a great many birds of the procellaria genus, in latitude 39° 37′ S. and longitude 49° 16′ W. and we alſo met with ſhoals of porpoiſes of a very ſingular ſpecies.

On the 23d of December, we obſerved an eclipſe of the moon; and about ſeven in the morning a bright cloud in the weſt, from which a ſtream of fire proceeded : it bore away to the weſtward, and about two minutes after we heard two loud explofions like that of a cannon; and then the cloud ſoon diſappeared.

On the 24th, we caught a logger-head tortoiſe, which weighed one hundred and fifty pounds; and ſhot ſeveral birds, one of which was an albatros, that meaſured, from the tip of one wing to the other, nine feet one inch; and from the beak to the tail two feet one inch and a half. Some time after, we met with ſome birds of the ſame kind that meaſured fourteen feet from the tips of the wings.

The thermometer, in the middle of the day, was from 66 to 69; and in the evening 62, when the air was not ſo dry.

On the 29th, we ſaw ſeveral parcels of rock weed; and, from this time to the 30th, the weather was very unſettled; the wind ſometimes blowing very hard; at others only a moderate gale; and then quite calm.

For ſeveral evenings, ſwarms of butterflies, moths, and other inſects, flew about the rigging, which we apprehended had been blown to us from the ſhore. Thouſands of them ſettled upon the veſſel; Mr. Banks ordered the men to gather them

up;

up ; and, after felecting fuch as he thought proper, the reft were thrown overboard ; and he gave the men fome bottles of rum for their trouble.

On the 31ft, we had much thunder, lightening, and rain, and faw feveral whales: we faw alfo fome birds about the fize of a pigeon, with white breafts and grey beaks.

On the 4th of January, 1769, we faw a cloud which we took for Pepy's Ifland, and made toward it till we were convinced of our miftake. The air at this time was cold and dry, and we had frequent fqualls of wind.

On the 6th, we faw feveral penguins, with many other fea birds ; and, on the 7th, had an exceeding hard gale of wind from S. W. in latitude 51° 25′ S. and longitude 62° 44′ W. We fuppofed ourfelves not far from Falkland's Iflands, but, not knowing their longitude, we could not fo readily find them.

From feveral circumftances which occurred on the 8th, it was concluded that we had failed between Falkland's Iflands and the main land; and were in hopes of touching at the former place, from which we defigned to have forwarded fome letters to Europe.

On the 11th, we difcovered Terra del Fuego; but, having contrary winds, and being apprehenfive of danger from the foulnefs of the ground, which we difcovered by founding, we kept out at fea.

On the 16th, the wind changing in our favour, we approached the land; and at length anchored in Port Maurice's Bay, fituated in latitude 54° 44′ S. and longitude 66° 15′ W. Some of our principal people went afhore, and found feveral pieces of brown European broad cloth, in a hut that had been deferted by the natives. Mr. Banks and Dr. Solander collected a great number of plants, fhot feveral birds, and returned to the fhip much pleafed with their adventure.

On the 17th we left Port Maurice's Bay ; and, at about one o'clock in the afternoon, anchored in the bay of Good Succefs.

We

Plate. I.

1. Man, Woman & Child, Natives of Terra del Fuego, in the Dress of that Country.

We had not been long arrived before fome Indians appeared on the beach at the head of the bay; the captain, Mr. Banks, and Dr. Solander, went on fhore, and foon after returned on board with three of them, whom we cloathed in jackets; gave them fome bread and beef, part of which they ate, and carried the remainder with them afhore: We gave them alfo fome rum and brandy; but, after tafting it, they refufed to drink any more, intimating, by figns, that it burnt their throats. This circumftance may ferve to corroborate the opinion of thofe, who think that water is the moft natural, and beft drink for mankind, as well as for other animals.

One of the Indians made feveral long orations to the reft; but they were utterly unintelligible to every one of us. Another of them feeing the leathern cover of a globe lie in the cabin, found means to fteal it, and fecrete it under his garment, which was made of a fkin of fome animal, and carried it afhore, undifcovered; where he had no fooner arrived, than he fhewed his prize to the very perfon it belonged to, and feemed to exult upon the occafion, placing it upon his head, and was highly delighted with it.

The natives make a very uncouth and favage appearance, [fee pl. I.] having broad flat faces, fmall black eyes, low foreheads, and nofes much like thofe of negroes, with wide noftrils, high cheeks, large mouths, and fmall teeth. Their hair, which is black and ftreight, hangs over their foreheads and ears, which moft of them had fmeared with brown and red paint; but, like the reft of the original inhabitants of America, they have no beard. None of them feemed above five feet ten inches high; but their bodies are thick and robuft, though their limbs are fmall. They wear a bunch of yarn made of guanica's * wool upon their heads, which, as well as their hair, hangs down over their foreheads. They alfo wear the fkins of guanicas and of feals, wrapped round their fhoulders, fometimes leaving the right arm uncovered. Both men and women wear necklaces, [fee pl. XXVI. fig. 14] and other ornaments made of a fmall pearly perriwincle, very ingenioufly plaited in rows with a kind of grafs. We faw alfo an ornament made of fhells,

* An animal fomething like a fheep but of the fize of a mule, and has a thick fleece.

which

which was ten yards long.   The fhells that compofed it were of feveral fizes ; the
largeft, about the fize of a damafcene ftone, were placed at one end, from whence
they gradually leffened to the other end of the ftring, where the fhells were not
bigger than a pepper corn.   The larger ornaments are worn about their waifts.
Many of both fexes were painted with white, red, and brown, colours, in different
parts of their bodies ; and had alfo various dotted lines pricked on their faces. The
women wear a flap of fkin tied round their loins ; and have alfo a fmall ftring round
each ancle : they carry their children on their backs, and are generally employed
in domeftic drudgery.

These poor Indians live in a village [fee pl. II.] on the fouth fide of the bay,
behind a hill ; the number of their huts is about thirteen, and they contain near
fifty people, who feem to be all the inhabitants of this dreary part of the ifland,
where it is very cold, even in the midft of fummer.

Their huts are made of the branches of trees, covered with guanica and feal
fkins ; and, at beft, are but wretched habitations for human beings to dwell in.

Their food is the flefh of feals and fhell-fifh, particularly mufcles, of which we
have feen fome very large.

They ufe bows and arrows with great dexterity.   The former are made of a
fpecies of wood fomewhat like our beech ; and the latter of a light yellow wood
feathered at one end, and acuated at the other with pieces of clear white chryftal,
chipped very ingenioufly to a point.   [See pl. XXVI. fig. 26.]

There are dogs upon this ifland two feet high, with fharp ears.

Having feen feveral rings and buttons upon the natives, we concluded that they
muft have had fome communication with the Indians in the Streights of Magellan ;
but they appeared to be unacquainted with Europeans.

The Bay of Good Succefs is about three miles in extent, from eaft to weft ; two
miles in breadth   is defended from eaft w   by Staten-land.   Near the fhore it is
                                                                                                    very

Plate II.

A. Buchan del.   J. Newton Sculp.

View of a Village in the Bay of Good Success, in the Island of Terra del Fuego.

very foul, and full of rocks; abounding with great quantities of fea weed. The
foundings are regular from fourteen, to four fathoms; and, at the bottom of the bay,
there is a fine fandy beach.

During our ftay on this ifland, the naturalifts collected a great many plants, and
other curiofities, moft of which are non-defcript : but an unfortunate accident happened in one of their excurfions; Mr. Banks, Dr. Solander, Mr. Buchan, with
feveral attendants, two of whom were negroes, went far up into the country, and
at length afcended the hills, which they found covered with fnow, and the air
upon them fo intenfely cold, that they ftaid but a fhort time. On their return,
they miffed their way, and wandered about for a confiderable time, not knowing
whither they went; but at length they found their former track. While the naturalifts were fearching for plants upon the hill, two negroes and a failor, who were
left to guard the liquor and provifion, having made too free with the brandy-bottle,
were rendered incapable of keeping pace with the reft of the company, who made
all poffible fpeed, hoping to have reached the fhip before the day clofed in upon
them, dreading the confequence of being expofed in a ftrange land, and an inhof-
pitable clime ; but time, that waits for no man, brought on the night, which put
an end to their hopes, and excited the moft alarming apprehenfions : Being out
of breath, fatigued, and difpirited, and almoft benumbed with cold, particularly
Dr. Solander, infomuch that he was unable to walk, and was carried near two
hours on their fhoulders ; and it was thought he would not have furvived the perils
of the enfuing night. In this haplefs fituation, they held a confultation on what
was beft to be attempted for their prefervation, till the light of the morning fhould
return ; and determined, if poffible, to kindle a fire, which they happily effected,
gathering together fome wood, and, by the help of their fowling pieces, and
fome paper, fetting it on fire. The cold was fo intenfe, that they found it would
not be fafe to lie down, left they fhould fall afleep, and be frozen to death ; where-
fore they walked round it all night. The three men who were left behind, being
tired, fat down in the woods, and fell afleep, but one of them providentially foon
awoke, ftarted up, and, being apprehenfive of the imminent danger they were in,
attempted to roufe his companions, but they were too far funk into the fleep of
death to be recovered. In this forlorn fituation the man could not expect to fur-
vive them long, and therefore he fled for his life, hallooing as he went along, in
hopes

hopes that fome of the company would hear him, which, after wandering fome time in a pathlefs wildernefs, they happily did, and anfwered him as loud as their enfeebled voices would admit: Overjoyed at the event, he refumed frefh courage, and, making toward the part from which the found proceeded, at length came up with them. Touched with fympathy for his companions, he told the company of the condition in which he left them; and they were difpofed to have yielded them affiftance, but, it being almoft dark, there was not any probability of finding them, and the attempt would have been attended with the rifque of their own lives; they therefore declined it. However, the next morning, after break of day, they difpatched the man in queft of his companions, whom he at length found frozen to death; but the dog that had been with them all the night had furvived them : he found him fitting clofe by his mafter's corpfe, and feemed reluctant to leave it; but at length the dog forfook it, and went back to the company ; they all fet out immediately towards the fhip, which they reached about 11 o'clock in the forenoon, to our great joy, as we had defpaired of their return.

Having furnifhed ourfelves with wood and water, and let down our guns and lumber below deck, to be better prepared for the high gales which we expected in going round Cape Horn; on the 21ft of January, 1769, we weighed anchor, and left the Bay of Good Succefs, and proceeded on our voyage through the Straits of Le Maire, which are formed by Cape Antonio on Staten-land, and Cape Vincent on Terra del Fuego to the north; and on the fouth by Cape Bartholomew on Statenland, and a high promontory on Terra del Fuego, paffing between them, and are about nine leagues long, and feven broad.

The land on both fides, particularly Staten-land, affords a moft difmal profpect, being made up chiefly of barren rocks and tremendous precipices, covered with fnow, and uninhabited, forming one of thofe natural views which human nature can fcarce behold without fhuddering. — How amazingly diverfified are the works of the Deity within the narrow limits of this globe we inhabit, which, compared with the vaft aggregate of fyftems that compofe the univerfe, appears but a dark fpeck in the creation! A curiofity, perhaps, equal to Solomon's, though accompanied with lefs wifdom than was poffeffed by the Royal Philofopher, induced fome of

us

us to quit our native land, to inveſtigate the heavenly bodies minutely in diſtant regions, as well as to trace the ſignatures of the Supreme Power and Intelligence throughout ſeveral ſpecies of animals, and different genera of plants in the vegetable ſyſtem, " from the cedar that is in Lebanon, even unto the hyſſop that ſpringeth out of the wall :" and the more we inveſtigate, the more we ought to admire the power, wiſdom, and goodneſs, of the Great Superintendant of the univerſe; which attributes are amply diſplayed throughout all his works ; the ſmalleſt object, ſeen through the microſcope, declares its origin to be divine, as well as thoſe larger ones which the unaſſiſted eye is capable of contemplating : but to proceed.

On the 25th, we ſaw Cape Horn, at about five leagues diſtance, which, contrary to our expectations, we doubled with as little danger as the North Foreland on the Kentiſh coaſt; the heavens were fair, the wind temperate, the weather pleaſant, and, being within one mile of the ſhore, we had a more diſtinct view of this coaſt, than perhaps any former voyagers have had on this ocean.

The point of the Cape is very low ; and at the S. E. extremity there are ſeveral iſlands, called, by the French, Iſles d'Hermitage ; and near it are ſeveral ragged rocks. The Cape is in latitude 55° 48′ S. and longitude 67° 40′ W. We ſounded in fifty-five fathom, and found round ſtones, and broken ſhells.

On the 30th, we reached to latitude 60° 2′ S. and longitude 73° 5′ W. variation 24° 54′ E. This was our higheſt ſouthern latitude ; and from thence we altered our courſe, ſteering W. N. W. with but little variation, having pleaſant weather, and ſhort nights, until the 16th of February, when we had hard gales from W. by S. S. by W. and S. and we continued our courſe N. W. till the 10th; between that time and the 20th, we had very copious dews, like ſmall ſhowers of rain.

On the 21ſt, we ſaw a great number of tropic and egg birds, and ſhot two of the former, which had a very beauteous plumage, being a fine white, mingled with a moſt lively red: their tails were compoſed of two long red feathers; and their beaks were of a deep red. We found ourſelves at this time in latitude 25° 21′ S. and longitude 120° 20′ W. having fair weather, with a dry, ſerene, and ſalubrious air.

Con-

Continuing our courfe N. wefterly, between the Dolphin's firft and fecond track, on the 4th of April, about three o'clock in the afternoon we difcovered land; and after two hours failing we approached near to it. It is a flat ifland, extending a great length from E. to W. defcribing the form of a crefcent; and has a fand-bank joined to it, on which the furf ran very high. In the middle of the ifland, there is a large falt lagoon, or lake; and at the eaft end of it are many palm trees. We faw clouds of fmoke afcend from different parts, proceeding, as we apprehended, from fires kindled by the natives, and defigned as fignals to us. Night came on before we could difcover the weft end of the ifland; and not knowing but there might be more iflands, we lay-to all night, and the next morning we faw another in latitude 18° 23', which, on account of a great falt lagoon in the middle of it, we called Lagoon-Ifle: Before noon we made another low ifland, which we called Thumb-cap Ifland. It ftretched a long way, and is made up of feveral parcels of land joined together by reefs: it has alfo a lagoon inclofed with a reef, upon which we difcovered many canoes; fome having ten people in them, and others a leffer number. As we failed along, the natives followed us, fome on the reef, others in canoes, and feemed defirous to have an intercourfe with us; but though we beckoned to them, they would not come off. They appeared to be very ftout men; their complexion almoft black, with fhort hair, and quite naked, having long lances, or poles, in their hands. Some of them waded up to the neck in water to look at us, but they did not difcover any hoftile intentions. Their canoes had out-riggers, with mat-fails: and when we put away from the land one of them followed us.

Upon thefe iflands we faw a variety of verdant trees, amongft which were fome palms; and upon the coaft, rocks of coral appeared above water. We difcovered fome of their huts, and feveral fires burning around them. The land formed a large femicircular bay, and the reef before it the fame figure; and the water was as fmooth as a mill-pond, and abounded with flying-fifh; but, to our furprife, we could not reach the bottom of it with 130 fathom of line, at one mile diftance from the fhore.

This

This day we alſo diſcovered another low iſland, which we called Chain Iſland: It is of an oval figure, conſiſting of a ridge of coral and ſand, with a few clumps of ſmall trees, and had a lagoon in the middle of it.   Theſe iſlands were dedicated to the Royal Society.

In the morning of the 10th, we ſaw Oſnabrug Iſland, bearing N. W. by W. half W. about ſix leagues diſtant, and, leaving it to the northward, at noon we diſcovered George's Iſland from the main-top maſt head, and ſtood toward it.

The 12th, the ſea being moſtly calm in the forenoon, we could get very little nearer land ; but many of the Indians came off to us in canoes (one of which was double, and had much carved work upon it) bringing with them cocoa nuts, and apples, to truck for nails, buttons, and beads.   Theſe canoes were but juſt wide enough for one perſon to ſit in the breadth : to prevent them from overſetting, they place out riggers, upon the top of which is fixed a bamboe fiſhing rod.   The people in the canoes were of a pale, tawny, complexion, and had long black hair. They ſeemed to be very good-natured, and not of a covetous diſpoſition ; giving us a couple of cocoa nuts, or a baſket of apples, for a button, or a nail.

While we lay before theſe iſlands, we had ſqualls of wind, ſome calms, and heavy ſhowers of rain.   Toward night we opened the N. W. point, and diſcovered the iſland named by the Dolphin's people, York Iſland, and called by the natives, as we afterwards learned, Eimayo.   A breeze ſpringing up, we lay off and on all that night ; and, on the 13th, we made the iſland of Otaheite, called by the Dolphin's people George's Iſland, which is oppoſite to York Iſland.   We entered Port Royal harbour, called by the natives Owarrowarrow, and anchored in nine fathom water, within half a mile of the ſhore.   The land appeared as uneven as a piece of crumpled paper, being divided irregularly into hills and valleys ; but a beautiful verdure covered both, even to the tops of the higheſt peaks.   A great number of the natives came off to us in canoes, and brought with them bananas, cocoas, bread-fruit, apples, and ſome pigs ; but they were errant thieves; and, while I was buſied in the forenoon in trucking with them for ſome of their cloth, (an account of which will be given hereafter,) one of them pilfered an earthen veſſel out of my c bin.   It was very diverting to fee the different emotions which the natives expreffed at the manœuvres of our fhip. They were very focial, and feveral of them came on board; fome of them remembered fuch of our people as had been there in the Dolphin, and feemed highly pleafed at our arrival. The captain and Mr. Banks went on fhore; but they returned greatly difappointed, as they could not find the principal inhabitants, and perceived that many of their houfes had been taken down fince the Dolphin left them.

On the 14th, in the morning, a great number of the natives came to us, round a reef point towards the fouth, and were very troublefome, attempting to fteal every thing they could lay their hands upon : they brought with them only two or three hogs, which they would not exchange for any thing but hatchets. Among the reft who vifited us, there were fome people of diftinction in double canoes : their cloaths, carriage, and behaviour evinced their fuperiority. I never beheld ftatelier men, [fee pl. III.] having a pleafant countenance, large black eyes, black hair, and white teeth. They behaved very courteoufly, and expreffed fome un-eafinefs at the conduct of the reft. We entertained them in the cabin, and then bent our fails, taking them with us for guides, till we had doubled the point, where we found a fine bay to anchor in. In the afternoon, a fmall party of us made an excurfion into the country, and the inhabitants followed us in great num-bers. At length, being fatigued, we fat down under the fhade of fome lofty trees, the undulation of whofe leaves rendered it very cool and pleafant. The high cocoas, and the low branching fruit trees, formed an agreeable contraft; while the cloud-topt hills, appearing between them, added to the natural grandeur of the profpect. The inhabitants ftood gaping around us while we feafted on the cocoa-nut milk, which afforded us a pleafing repaft.

On the 15th, in the morning, feveral of the chiefs, one of which was very cor-pulent, came on board from the other point, and brought us fome hogs; we pre-fented them with a fheet and fome trinkets in return; but fome of them took the liberty of ftealing the top of the lightening-chain. We went afhore, and pitched the markee: Mr. Banks, the captain, and myfelf, took a walk in the woods, and were afterwards joined by Mr. Hicks, and Mr. Green. While we were walking,

and

Plate III.

S. Parkinson del. *R. B. Godfrey Sc.*

A Native of Otaheite, in the Dress of his Country.

and enjoying the rural fcene, we heard the report of fome fire-arms, and prefently faw the natives fleeing into the woods like frighted fawns, carrying with them their little moveables. Alarmed at this unexpected event, we immediately quitted the wood, and made to the fide of the river, where we faw feveral of our men, who had been left to guard the tent, purfuing the natives, who were terrified to the laft degree; fome of them fkulked behind the bufhes, and others leaped into the river. Hearing the fhot rattle amongft the branches of the trees over my head, I thought it not fafe to continue there any longer, and fled to the tent, where I foon learned the caufe of the cataftrophe.

A centinel being off his guard, one of the natives fnatched a mufket out of his hand, which occafioned the fray. A boy, a midfhipman, was the command-ing officer, and, giving orders to fire, they obeyed with the greateft glee imagin-able, as if they had been fhooting at wild ducks, killed one ftout man, and wounded many others. What a pity, that fuch brutality fhould be exercifed by civilized people upon unarmed ignorant Indians!

When Mr. Banks heard of the affair, he was highly difpleafed, faying, " If we quarrelled with thofe Indians, we fhould not agree with angels;" and he did all he could to accommodate the difference, going acrofs the river, and, through the mediation of an old man, prevailed on many of the natives to come over to us, bearing plantain-trees, which is a fignal of peace amongft them; and, clapping their hands to their breafts, cried Tyau, which fignifies friendfhip. They fat down by us; fent for cocoa nuts, and we drank the milk with them. They laughed heartily, and were very focial, more fo than could have been expected, confidering what they had fuffered in the late fkirmifh. — Have we not reafon to conclude, that their difpofitions are very flexible; and that refentment, with them, is a fhort-lived paffion?

The horizon not being clear, we could not make any aftronomical obfervations; and therefore did not attempt to go round the point to the other bay. The wea-ther, however, fince we arrived here, has generally been clear, with now and then a flight fhower of rain, and the wind E. N. E.

Mr.

Mr. Buchan was feized with an epileptic fit this morning, and remained infenfible all day.

On the 16th, but few of the Indians came to us in their canoes, being, we apprehended, fomewhat alarmed at what had happened the day before. We got the fhip moored; and Mr. Banks and the captain went afhore to confer with the natives, and to prevail on them to traffic with us again.

On the 17th, early in the morning, Mr. Buchan died, and we went out in the pinnace and long boat to the offing, and buried him.

Two of the chiefs came on board this morning, bringing with them a prefent of hogs, fowls, plantains, bananas, cocoas, bread-fruit and a fort of yams. At this feafon the cocoas are young, many of them yielding a quart of fine milk, and the fhell is eatable, but they have no kernel.

We pitched one of the fhip's tents †, and went into the valley, where an Indian invited me to his hut, and fent his fon up a tall cocoa-tree to gather nuts: he climbed it very dexteroufly, by tying his feet together with a withe, then clafping the tree, and vaulting up very fwiftly. They admired every thing they faw about me, and I gave them a few trinkets.

On the 18th, in the night, we lay on fhore, and were much incommoded with a fpecies of flies with which the ifland fwarms; infomuch that, at dinner time, it was one perfon's employ to beat them off with a feather fly-flap, the handle of which is made of a hard brown wood, rudely carved, and fomewhat refembles a human figure.

---

† As we were to make the obfervation of the tranfit on this ifland, we built a temporary fort for our accommodation on fhore: [fee pl. IV.] It had a foffé, with palifadoes, next the river: guns and fwivels mounted on the ramparts; and within, we had an obfervatory, an oven, forge, and pens for our fheep. Centinels were alfo appointed as ufual in garrifons, and military difcipline obferved. The fandy ground, on which the fort ftood, was very troublefome when the wind was high.

On

Plate IV.

S. Parkinson del.

J. Walkman sculp.

Venus Fort, Erected by the Endeavour's People, to secure
themselves during the Observation of the Transit of Venus, at Otaheite.

On the 20th, one of their chiefs, named Tubora Tumaida, whom we called Lycurgus, with his wife and fon, came to vifit and dine with us: While we were at dinner, one of his attendants made up a difh with fome garbage which they brought with them, mixing it with cocoa nut liquor in a fhell, and it tafted like fowens ‡. This feemed to be a favourite difh with them, but we could not relifh it. They have alfo a kind of food like wheat flour in appearance, of which Lycurgus brought a fmall quantity, and mixed that alfo with cocoa nut liquor ; and, dropping two or three hot ftones into it, he ftirred it about till it formed a ftrong jelly : on tafting it we found it had an agreeable flavour, not unlike very good blanc-mange. Thefe people make up various kinds of pafte, one of which, called Makey Poe Poe, is made of fermented bread-fruit, and a fubftance called Meiya, mixt with cocoa-nut milk, and baked, taftes very fweet. In making thefe paftes, they ufe a peftle made of a hard black ftone, a kind of bafaltes, with which they beat them in a wooden trough. See pl. XIII. fig. 10.

The mode of dreffing their food too is very fingular : they make a hole in the ground, and, placing ftones in it, kindle a fire upon them ; and when they are fufficiently heated, they fweep off the afhes, and then lay their food upon them. At their meals the married women ate apart from the men, and we could not prevail on them to join us. The men, efpecially, feemed to like the manner of our eating, and handled knives and forks very well. Hogs and fowls are not very plentiful amongft them ; yams, and the beft bananas, are very fcarce in this ifland ; the natives bring down but few of either fort, and eat of them very fparingly. When the natives want to make a fire, they take a piece of light wood, make a groove in it, and rub along that with another piece till the fmall duft catches fire : This is very laborious, and requires a confiderable time to effect it.

On the 21ft, we went round the point, and met with Lycurgus fitting on the ground, with his wife by his fide, having a canoe covering, which he brought there on purpofe to be near us : he gave us a hearty welcome ; and, to divert us, ordered two of his boys to play on their flutes, while another fang a fort of melan-

‡ A kind of flummery made of oatmeal.

choly

choly ditty, very well suited to the music. Lycurgus is a middle-aged man, of a chearful, though sedate, countenance, with thick black frizzled hair, and a beard of the same kind: his behaviour and aspect had something of natural majesty in them. I shewed him some of my drawings, which he greatly admired, and pronounced their names as soon as he saw them. These people have a peculiar method of staining their garments: a girl that was present shewed me the whole process, which is as follows:——She took the young leaves of a convolvulus unfoliated, and then broke off the tops of a small fig, of a reddish hue, and squeezed out of it a milky fluid, which she spread on a leaf, rubbing it gently to mix it with the juice of the leaf, and then it became red; this she soaked up with the leaf of a solanum, and then daubed it upon some cloth: the colour is good, but whether it will stand, I am unable to determine. They make a variety of neat basket-work [see a figure of one of their baskets, pl. XIII. fig. 6.] for holding of their colours; the simplest of all is made of the leaf of a cocoa-nut, which they plait together, and gather up on each side: they also make a kind of bonnet [see pl. VIII. fig. 4.] of the same materials. They do not seem very fond of their cloaths, of which they have a variety of colours, but wear them sometimes one way, and sometimes another, as their humour is. Persons of distinction amongst them wrap a number of pieces of cloth about them; and that which is of a carmine colour is only worn by the superior class. The people in general are very fond of ear-rings, and will exchange for them what they deem the most valuable of their effects. Some of their ear-rings [see pl. XIII. fig. 13 and 14] are made of mother-of-pearl cut into various figures, which are tied to their ears by human hair, curiously plaited by the women. They also tie three pearls together with hair, and hang them on their ears. [See ibid. fig. 26.]

The cloth, worn by the natives of this island, is of a very singular kind, being made of the bark of a small tree which contains a glutinous juice, some of which we saw in our excursions. The mode of manufacturing it is very simple, though very laborious, and is mostly performed by women. After the bark has been soaked in water for a few days, they lay it upon a flat piece of timber, and beat it out as thin as they think proper with a kind of mallet of an oblong square, [see pl. XIII. fig. 5.] each side of which is cut into small grooves of four different sizes: they begin with that side where they are the largest, and end with the finest, which

leaving

leaving longitudinal ftripes upon the cloth, makes it refemble paper. Thefe people have garments alfo made of matting, [fee pl. IX.] which are chiefly worn in rainy weather.

The rates, or terms, on which we trafficked with the natives, were a fpike for a fmall pig; a fmaller for a fowl; a hatchet for a hog; and twenty cocoa-nuts, or bread-fruit, for a middling-fized nail.

When the natives beckon to any perfon at a diftance, contrary to our mode they wave their hands downwards; and when they meet a friend, or relation, whom they have not feen for fome time, they affect to cry for joy, but it feems to be en-tirely ceremonial.

The tide rifes and falls fcarce a foot in the harbour; but the furf runs high. The inhabitants are very expert fwimmers, and will remain in the water a long time, even with their hands full. They keep their water on fhore in large bam-boos, and in them they alfo carry up falt-water into the country. The boys drag for fifh with a fort of net made of convolvulus leaves; and fometimes catch them with hooks made of mother of pearl oyfters, large pinna marina, and other fhells; and the fhapes of them are very fingular. They have alfo fome made of wood, which are very large; [fee figures of feveral of them, pl. XIII. fig. 18, 19, 20, 21, 22, 23, 24, 25.] They fifh without bait, but the fifh are attracted the fooneft by fuch hooks as are made of glittering fhells. When they throw their hooks, they row their canoes as faft as poffible: fometimes they make ufe of a decoy made of the backs of cowries, and other fhells, which are perforated, and tied together in the fhape of a fifh, making a head to it with a fmall cowrey; and the tail is formed of grafs ingenioufly plaited. At a little diftance under this decoy, hangs the hook: [fee pl. XIII. fig. 15 and 25.] To fink their lines, they make ufe of bone, or a piece of fpar, which they fometimes carve. See ibid. fig. 16, 17.

The chief food of the natives is the bread-fruit and bananas, which they peel and fcrape with a fharp fhell; but they eat fparingly of flefh, and of fifh in general; but of the latter, fometimes alive, or raw; and, as they have no falt, they dip their meat into falt water. The natives, it feems, are very fubject to the itch, and other

cuta-

cutaneous eruptions, which is the more to be wondered at as their diet confifts principally of vegetables. They often move from one part to another in their canoes, carrying with them all their houfehold ftuff. Sometimes they fleep all night in their canoes *, but thofe ufed for that purpofe are made double, and have thatched awnings over them.

Tobiah, Obereah's favourite, being at dinner with us, and not feeming to like our provifion, which was pork-pie, remembering that we had a large cuttle-fifh, we ordered it to be brought ; Tubora Tumaida coming in the mean time, although he faid his belly was full, immediately feized on it as if it had been a dainty morfel, and, with another man, ate much of it quite raw ; and having the reft roafted, he ate the greateft part of it ; the remainder he put into two cocoa nuts, and fent it home with great care ; fo that, to all appearance, they value this fifh, as much as fome Englifhmen do turtle, or a haunch of venifon. When this fifh was dreffed it ate like ftewed oyfters, but not fo tender. I have been told that this fifh makes excellent foup. Thefe people alfo are fond of dog's-flefh, and reckon it delicious food, which we difcovered by their bringing the leg of a dog roafted to fell. Mr. Banks ate a piece of it, and admired it much. He went out immediately and bought one, and gave it to fome Indians to kill and drefs it in their manner, which they did accordingly. After having held the dog's mouth down to the pit of his ftomach till he was ftifled, they made a parcel of ftones hot upon the ground, laid him upon them, and finged off the hair, then fcraped his fkin with a cocoa fhell, and rubbed it with coral; after which they took out the entrails, laid them all carefully on the ftones, and after they were broiled ate them with great goût ; nor did fome of our people fcruple to partake with them of this indelicate repaft. Having fcraped and wafhed the dog's body clean, they prepared an oven of hot ftones, covered them with bread-fruit leaves, and laid it upon them, with liver, heart and lungs, pouring a cocoa-nut full of blood upon them, covering them too with more leaves and hot ftones, and inclofed the whole with earth patted down very clofe to keep in the heat. It was about four hours in the oven, and at night it was ferved up for fupper : I ate a little of it ; it had the tafte of coarfe beef, and a ftrong difagreeable fmell ; but Captain Cook, Mr. Banks, and Dr. Solander, commended it highly, faying it was the fweeteft meat they had ever tafted ; but the reft of our people could not be prevailed on to ate any of it. We have invented a new difh,

which

* The women fometimes row the canoes.

which is as much difliked by the natives, as any of theirs is by us. Here is a fpecies of rats, of which there are great numbers in this ifland; we caught fome of them, and had them fried; moft of the gentlemen in the bell-tent ate of them, and commended them much; and fome of the inferior officers ate them in a morning for breakfaft.

On the 27th, we faw a very odd ceremony performed; Tiropoa, one of Tubora Tumaida's wives, after weeping, and expreffing fome emotions of forrow, took a fhark's tooth from under her cloaths, and ftruck it againft her head feveral times, which produced a copious difcharge of blood; then, lamenting moft bitterly, fhe articulated fome words in a mournful tone, and covered the blood with fome pieces of cloth; and, having bled about a pint, fhe gathered up as much of it as fhe could, threw it into the fea, and then affumed a chearful countenance, as if nothing had happened. This, it feems, is a ceremony generally performed by widows after the deceafe of their hufbands.

This morning a woman, a fat, bouncing, good-looking dame, whom we found the queen, having a great quantity of their cloth of all colours, made us a vifit, and a prefent.

Tootahau, the king of the ifland, whom we called Hercules, too, and all his family, came and brought us prefents, which we kindly accepted.

On the 30th, the weather being fair, we made a tour in the country, which was very pleafant, and met with feveral rare plants, which afforded much agreeable amufement to our botanical gentlemen.

On the 2d of May, we miffed the aftronomical quadrant, it having been brought on fhore the day before, in order to make obfervation of the tranfit of Venus : feveral men were immediately difpatched into the country to fearch for it; and they were informed, by fome of the natives, that it had been carried through the woods to the eaftward. The captain, Mr. Banks, and Mr. Green, with fome other of our men, Tubora Tumaida, and a few of the natives, all armed, fet out in purfuit of it. Tootahau, the king, and feveral canoes, were detained till they returned. While they were on this expedition, I walked out to the eaft, in the evening, and

was

was almoſt ſtunned with the noiſe of the graſhoppers, with which this iſland abounds. At length I came to a large open place, on the ſide of which I ſaw a long houſe; and in the area many of the natives aſſembled, having brought with them large baſkets of bread-fruit: ſome of them were employed in dividing them, and others carried away whole baſkets full; ſo that it had the appearance of a market of bread-fruit. Near to this opening, there was another long houſe, where, it ſeems, they coloured their cloth, of which I bought a few pieces, and returned to the fort. About eight o'clock in the evening, the party, that went out in queſt of the quadrant, came back, having happily obtained it by the aſſiſtance of Tubora Tumaida. Some of the natives had taken it to pieces, and divided it amongſt them, but had done it no material damage. It was ſtolen by a man named Moroameah, ſervant to Titaboreah, one of their chiefs. They alſo found a piſtol, which one of the natives had ſtolen ſome time before. Tootahau wept while the party was abſent, and was much alarmed on the occaſion, apprehending that he ſhould be killed if the quadrant could not be found; and had ſent for two hogs to appeaſe us. Oboreah, the queen, fled from us; nor would any of the natives come to market. When Tubora Tumaida, and his party, who accompanied Mr. Banks, returned, and ſaw Tootahau confined, they ſet up the moſt doleful lamentation imaginable; but they were ſoon pacified by the aſſurances made them that we deſigned them no injury.

On the 4th, very few people came to market with proviſions, having been intimidated by the detention of their king Tootahau.

Some of the natives gave us an account of many neighbouring iſlands, to the number of nineteen, and ſhewed us one of them from a hill, which was Yoole Etea.

Moſt of the natives of this iſland ſmell ſtrong of the cocoa oil, and are of a pale brown complexion, moſtly having black hair, and that often frizzled; black eyes, flat noſe, and large mouth, with a chearful countenance; they all wear their beards, but cut off their muſtachios, [ſee pl. VIII. fig. 1.] are well made, and very ſturdy, having their bellies in general very prominent; and are a timorous, merry, facetious, hoſpitable people. There are more tall men among them than among any people I

have

Plate 1

S. Parkinson del.

T. Chambers Sc.

A Woman & a Boy, Natives of Otaheite, in the Dress of that Country.

have feen, meafuring fix feet, three inches and a half; but the women in general are fmall compared with the men. [See pl. V.] They muft be very honeft amongft themfelves, as every houfe is without any faftening. Locks, bolts, and bars, are peculiar to civilized countries, where their moral theory is the beft, and their moral practices too generally of the worft; which might induce a celebrated writer to conclude, though erroneoufly, that mankind, upon the whole, are neceffarily rendered worfe, and lefs happy, by civilization, and the cultivation of the arts and fciences. Nature's wants, it is true, are but few, and the uncivilized part of mankind, in general, feem contented if they can acquire thofe few. Ambition, and the love of luxurious banquets, and other fuperfluities, are but little known in the barbarous nations: they have, in general, lefs anxious thought for the morrow, than civilized; and therefore feel more enjoyment while they partake of heaven's bounty in the prefent day. Unaccuftomed to indulgences in cloathing and diet, which Europeans have carried to an extreme, they are lefs fubject to difeafes; are more robuft; feel lefs from the inclemencies of the feafons; and are, in conftitution, what the ancient Britons were before their civilization. Unhappily for us, the athletic conftitution of our anceftors is not to be found amongft us, being enervated by exceffes of various kinds; while difeafes, the effect of intemperance and debaucheries, contaminate our blood, and render them hereditary amongft our offspring.

The natives huts are inclofed by a low fence made of reeds; and the ground within them is very neatly bedded with a kind of ftraw, upon which they lay mats to fleep on; and, for a pillow, they have a four-legged ftool, joined at the bottom, which is made out of a folid piece of wood; and the only tools they have to work with are made of ftones, or fhells, as they had no iron upon the ifland until the Dolphin arrived. [See pl. XIII. fig. 7.]

Thefe huts are built at a confiderable diftance from each other; fo that the ifland looks like one continued village, and abounds with cocoa*, bread-fruit, and appletrees; the fruit of which drops, as it were, into their mouths; and may be the caufe that they are an indolent people: Were they inclined to induftry, provifions might

* I faw fome ftalks of cocoa-nuts which were as heavy as I could lift, which furprifed me the more as the ftalks were very flender.

be

be found in greater plenty amongſt them ; and, by proper cultivation, the fruits of the iſland would not only be increaſed, but their qual:ty might be improved. They ſeem, however, as contented with what is ſpontaneouſly produced, as if they had attained to the ne plus ultra, and are therefore happier than Europeans in general are, whoſe deſires are unbounded. When the men are at work, they wear only a piece of cloth round their middle, which they call maro: at other times they wear garments which they call purawei, and teepoota about their bodies, with a kind of turban on their heads; and, in walking, they carry a long white ſtick in one of their hands, with the ſmalleſt end uppermoſt.

Theſe people go to war in large canoes, at one end of which there is a kind of ſtage erected, ſupported by four carved pillars, and is called tootee. Their weapons are a kind of clubs, and long wooden lances. They have alſo bows and arrows. The former are made of a ſtrong elaſtic wood. The arrows are a ſmall ſpecies of reed, or bamboes, pointed with hard wood, or with the ſt'ng of the ray-fiſh, which is a ſharp-bearded bone. [See pl. XIII. fig. 13.] They alſo make uſe of ſlings, [ſee ibid. fig. 1.] made of the fibres of the bark of ſome tree, of which, in general, they make their cordage too : ſome of them, as well as their ſlings, are neatly plaited. Their hatchets, or rather adzes, which they call towa, are made by tying a hard black ſtone, of the kind of which they make their paſte-beaters, to the end of a wooden handle; and they look very much like a ſmall garden hoe: and the ſtone part is ground or worn to an edge. [See pl. XIII. fig. 9.] The making of theſe ſtone-inſtruments muſt be a work of time, and laborious, as the ſtone of which they are made is very hard. The natives have maros, or pieces of cloth, which reach up from the waiſt, to defend them from the lances, or bunches of hair curiouſly plaited. They alſo wear teepootas upon their heads, and taowmees, or a kind of breaſt-plate, hung about their necks; [ſee pl. XI.] large turbans too, in which they ſtick a ſmall bunch of parrot's feathers ; [ſee pl. XIII. fig. 12.] and ſometimes uſe what they call a whaow, which is a large cap of a conical figure. In their heivos, or war-dances, they aſſume various antic motions and geſtures, like thoſe practiſed by the girls when they dance taowree whaow,* playing on a clapper made of two mother-of-pearl ſhells ; and make the ephaita, or wry mouth, [ſee pl. VII. fig. 2.] as a token of defiance : they alſo join their hands together, moving them at the ſame time, and clap the palms of their hands

* A kind of diverſion.

Plate VI.

S. Parkinson del.   House and Plantation of a Chief of the Island of Otaheite.   R. B. Godfrey Sculp.

Plate VII.

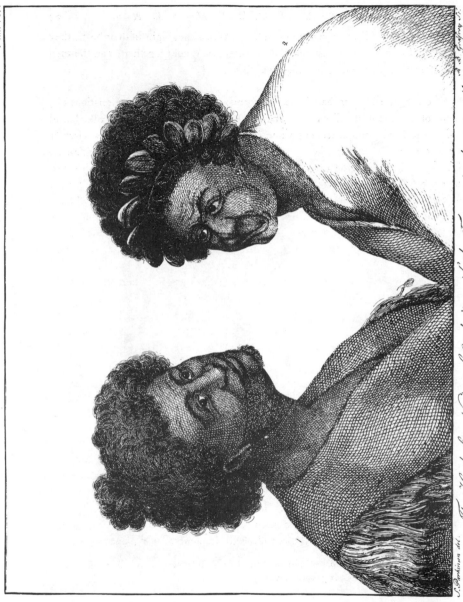

S. Parkinson del.

The Head of a Native of Otaheite, with the Face curiously tataow'd;
And the very Mouth, or manner of displaying their Enemies as practised by the People of that, & the neighbouring Islands.

hands upon their breafts near their fhoulders. When they fight in their boats, they generally throw a ftring to one another to faften the canoes together; and the men who are employed in doing this are never ftruck at †.

The natives cut their hair in various forms. When their neareft relations die, fome of them cut it off entirely, and go bare-headed; others leave a border all round the head; and others cut it into circles; while fome have only a circular piece cut off the crown like a prieft's tonfure; others ftill prefer another mode, leaving the hair upon the crown of the head, and cut off all the reft. All this they perform with a fhark's tooth, which cuts it very clofe: they alfo fhave with a fhark's tooth fitted to a piece of coarfe fhell. The natives are accuftomed to mark themfelves in a very fingular manner, which they call tataowing; [fee pl. VII. fig. 1.] this is done with the juice of a plant; and they perform the operation with an inftrument having teeth like a comb, dipped in the juice, with which the fkin is perforated. [See pl. XIII. fig. 2, 3, and 4.] Mr. Stainfby, myfelf, and fome others of our company, underwent the operation, and had our arms marked: the ftain left in the fkin, which cannot be effaced without deftroying it, is of a lively bluifh purple, fimilar to that made upon the fkin by gun-powder. Thefe people have invented a mufical inftrument, fomewhat like a flute, [fee pl. XIII. fig. 8. and pl. IX.] which they blow into through their nofes; but their notes, which are but very few, are rude and ungrateful. Their dances are not lefs fingular than their mufic; for they twift their bodies into many extravagant poftures, fpread their legs, fet their arms a-kimbo, and, at the fame time, diftort the mufcles of their faces, and twift their mouths diagonally, in a manner which none of us could imitate. [See pl. VII. fig. 2.]

Polygamy is not allowed amongft them; but the married women have not a very delicate fenfe of modefty: their hufbands will allow you any liberty with their wives, except the laft, which they do not approve. Moft of our fhip's company procured temporary wives amongft the natives, with whom they occafionally cohabited; an indulgence which even many reputed virtuous Europeans allow themfelves, in uncivilized parts of the world, with impunity; as if a change of place

† We faw two men who had been pierced through the fkull by ftones from a fling; the wounds were healed up, but had left a large operculum.

altered

altered the moral turpitude of fornication : and what is a fin in Europe, is only a·
fimple innocent gratification in America; which is to fuppofe, that the obligation
to chaftity is local, and reftricted only to particular parts of the globe.

It is cuftomary for the women to wear garlands of flowers on their heads, [fee pl.
VIII. fig. 1, 2.] which are compofed of the white palm-leaves gathered from the
fpathas from which the flower proceeds.   They alfo gather a fpecies of gardenia, as
foon as they open, and put them in their ears.   Both fexes are very cleanly ; they
wafh themfelves in the river three times a day ; and their hands and teeth after
every meal.

The children of both fexes are remarkably kind to one another, and, if any thing
be given them, will, if poffible, equally divide it amongft them.

On the fifth, the captain and Mr. Banks, with fome others, went to the weft,
and waited upon Tootahau, and fome other of the chiefs, who, it was fuppofed,
had taken affront, as the people did not bring fruit, as ufual, to market.   They
received them kindly, and entertained them with wreftling and dancing: when
they returned to the fhip, Tootahau, their king, came along with them, brought a
barbecued-hog, and the captain made him a prefent.

On the fixth, being the next day, the natives brought their fruits to market as
ufual.

In walking through the woods we faw the corpfe of a man laid upon a fort of
bier, which had an awning over it made of mats, fupported by four fticks ; a fquare
piece of ground around it was railed in with bamboos, and the body was covered
with cloth.   Thefe burial places are called Morai.

This day we alfo faw them polifhing their canoes, which was done with the ma-
drepora fungites, a fpecies of coral, or fea mufhroom, with which they alfo polifh
the beams of their houfes.

On

Plate VIII.

S. Chambers sc.

S. Hopkinson del.

Heads of divers Natives of the Islands of Otaheite, Huaheine, & Oheiteroah.

On the 8th, Mr. Mollineux went in the long-boat to the eaſt to buy ſome hogs, but could not get any: the people told them that they belonged to Tootahau, which evinced the ſuperiority of that man.

We ſaw a man this day of a very fair complexion, with ruddy noſe and cheeks, having the hair of his head, beard, eye-brows, and eye-laſhes, quite white; inſomuch that he was a luſus naturæ amongſt them.

On the 13th, as Mr. Banks ſat in the boat, trading with them as uſual, we ſaw a very odd ceremony performed: — Some ſtrangers came up, to whom the reſt gave way, making a lane for them to paſs through: the firſt perſon in the proceſſion preſented Mr. Banks with a ſmall bunch of parrot's feathers, with ſome plantain, and malape-leaves, one after another. A woman paſſed along the next, having a great many clothes upon her, which ſhe took off, and, ſpreading them upon the ground, turned round, and expoſed herſelf quite naked: more garments being handed to her, by the company, ſhe ſpread them alſo upon the ground, and then expoſed herſelf as before; then the people gathered up all her clothes, took leave, and retired.

On the 14th, we ſaw a perſon who had the appearance of an hermaphrodite.

On the 15th, we had but a ſlight ſea breeze, and the weather was very ſultry, though the clouds hung upon the mountains, and we expected ſome rain; we had ſome puffs of wind from the mountains, that raiſed the ſand in little clouds, which covered every thing, and rendered our ſituation ſtill more diſagreeable. In the evening we ſaw a remarkable large ring round the moon.

On the 16th, it rained very hard, and there were two rainbows. We hauled the Sein in ſeveral diſtant places, but caught no fiſh.

On the 17th, the centinel fired at one of the natives, who came before it was light with an intent to ſteal ſome of the caſks, which was the ſecond offence; but the powder flaſhed in the pan, and the man eſcaped with his life.

On

On the 20th, but few of the natives came to market, having been prevented by the rain.

On the 22d, it rained very hard, accompanied with thunder and lightening, more terrible than any I had ever heard, or seen, before. It rained so hard that the water came through the markee, and wetted every thing in it; and we were much afraid the ship would have suffered by the storm, but she providentially escaped.

On the third of June, it being very fair, the astronomers had a good opportunity of making an observation of the transit. Mr. Banks, and a party, went to Eimayo; and another party to the east, to make observations at the same time. Mr. Banks returned with two hogs, which he got from the king of Eimayo.

₊ The following calculation of the Transit, being found amongst Sydney Parkinson's papers, as also a table of the rising and falling of the Thermometer, between the 27th of April, 1769, and the 9th of July following, they are here subjoined for the information of the curious.

CALCULATION

CALCULATION of the TRANSIT.

8 no Error.

Sun's Meridian Altitude on the 2d of June   50   7
3d ditto   49 59
June the 3d, 1769.   Error of   16

H. M. S.	Sun's Altitude before the first external Contact.	D. M.	H. M. S.	Sun's Altitude.	D. M
	First Set.			First Set.	
8 48 9		28 42	2 45 18		32 47
50 10		29 5	46 31		32 34
51 41		29 21	47 35		32 22
	Second Set.			Second Set.	
8 53 19		29 36	2 48 39		32 12
55 7		29 57	49 44		31 56
56 19		30 13	50 33		31 49
	Third Set.			Third Set.	
8 57 36		30 27	2 51 33		31 39
58 37		30 37	52 28		31 29
59 44		30 47	53 35		31 16
	Before the first Internal Contact.			Before the second external Contact.	
	First Set.			First Set.	
9 25 48		35 20	3 13 39		27 35
27 46		35 34	14 36		27 24
28 23		35 47	15 35		27 14
	Second Set.			Second Set.	
9 29 15		35 55	3 16 33		27 3
29 46		36 2	17 25		26 53
30 29		36 9	18 19		26 43
	Third Set.			Third Set.	
9 31 13		36 13	3 19 14		26 34
32 4		36 23	20 14		26 21
32 43		36 29	21 1		26 12
	After the first Internal Contact.			After the second external Contact.	
	First Set.			First Set.	
9 42 56		38 9	3 32 3		24 5
43 52		38 25	33 14		23 51
45 25		38 31	34 32		23 36
	Second Set.			Second Set.	
9 46 32		38 42	3 35 31		23 25
47 59		38 54	36 33		23 11
49 27		39 8	37 30		23
	Third Set.			Third Set.	
9 50 27		39 17	3 38 29		22 55
51 9		39 25	39 58		22 31
52 6		39 32	41 5		22 21

	′ ″ ″				
2d internal Contact } 1st external }	0 23 10				
1st internal	0 39 30				
2d ditto -	3 10 57				
2d external	3 29 58				

Altitude in the Morning.

Time H. M. S.	Sun's Altitude	D. M.
7 42 29		15 51
0 45 26		16 25
0 46 38		16 40

The

The RISING and FALLING of the THERMOMETER.

April, 1769.		M.	N.	A.
Thurſday	27	68	82	60
Friday	28	68	84	70
Saturday	29	70	85	68
Sunday	30	69	86	70
May.				
Monday	1	70	85½	77
Tueſday	2	79	91	79
Wedneſday	3	78	91	80
Thurſday	4	70	91	79
Friday	5	72	91	79
Saturday	6	69	86	80
Sunday	7	72	91	80
Monday	8	71	86	77
Tueſday	9	70	85	78
Wedneſday	10	70	85	78
Thurſday	11	70	86	81
Friday	12	74	87	79
Saturday	13	75	86	78
Sunday	14	77	87	78
Monday	15	74	85	80
Tueſday	16	74	85	79
Wedneſday	17	72	87	79½
Thurſday	18	73	89	79
Friday	19	72	82	76
Saturday	20	72	73	73
Sunday	21	72	85	74
Monday	22	70	72	75
Tueſday	23	69	86	77
Wedneſday	24	70	87	79
Thurſday	25	72	82	78
Friday	26	73	83	81
Saturday	27	75	85	81
Sunday	28	71	86	80
Monday	29	71	86	78
Tueſday	30	70	84	76
Wedneſday	31	70	84	78
June				
Thurſday	1	71		

June.		M.	N.	A.
Friday	2			
Saturday	3			
Sunday	4			
Monday	5	74	84	78
Tueſday	6	74	86	78
Wedneſday	7	74	86	77
Thurſday	8	73	87	76
Friday	9	7-	83	79
Saturday	10	69	81	78
Sunday	11	74	77	77
Monday	12	72	82	79
Tueſday	13	72	83	78
Wedneſd.	14	72	87	81
Thurſday	15	74	87	79
Friday	16	72	83	77
Saturday	17	70	81	77
Sunday	18	72	83	68
Monday	19	72	82	74
Tueſday	20	70	83	76
Wedneſd.	21	69	86	77
Thurſday	22	70	86	76
Friday	23	69	86	76
Saturday	24	67	85	74
Sunday	25	74	84	76
Monday	26	67	79	75
Tueſday	27	70	84	76
Wedneſd.	28	71	85	77
Thurſday	29	67	80	78
Friday	30	76	82	78
July.— Sat.	1	70	78	78
Sunday	2	70	85	80
Monday	3	74	84	78
Tueſday	4	70	88	78
Wedneſday	5	70	88	77
Thurſday	6	2	83	78
Friday	7	76	83	78
Saturday	8	73	83	76
Sunday	9	72	83	70

Dr.

Dr. Solander, Mr. Banks, and feveral others, went to vifit Tootahau, to fee if they could obtain any hogs ; and, after going much farther than where he ufually refides, they met with him, and queen Oboreah : they treated them with fair promifes, and invited them to ftay the night with them, which they accepted ; but, in the morning, fome miffed their ftockings, others their jackets and waiftcoats ; amongft the reft, Mr. Banks loft his white jacket and waiftcoat, with filver frogs ; in the pockets of which were a pair of piftols, and other things : they enquired for them, but could get no account of them ; and they came away greatly diffatiffied, having obtained but one pig.

On the 12th, we received an account from the natives refpecting two fhips that had been on their coaft ; and we gathered from them that the crew were Spaniards, and that they had introduced the lues venerea amongft them ‡.

On the 15th, the oven-rake was ftolen, which, joined to the other things that had been pilfered from us by fome of the natives, and the infolent treatment Mr. Monkhoufe met with, determined the captain to feek redrefs ; he feized twentyfeven double canoes, with fails, which happened to be at the point, in the morning, fome of which came from another ifland ; and he threatened to burn them if the ftolen things fhould not be returned. Before noon they brought back the rake, but we had no account of the reft ; and the canoes were ftill kept in cuftody. Tootahau was much difpleafed, and would not fuffer any of the natives to fupply us with bread-fruit, cocoa-nuts, or apples. At this time the weather was very wet ; P. Brifcoe, one of Mr. Banks's fervants, was very bad of a nervous fever, and we had but little hopes of his recovery, having been, by a long courfe of ficknefs, reduced to very great weaknefs ; and, in this hot climate, it is a long time before an European recovers his ftrength, as I have known by experience.

On the 19th, in the evening, after dark, Oboreah, the queen, and feveral of her attendants, came from Opare, Tootahau's palace, in a double canoe, laden with plantains, bread-fruit, and a hog ; but brought none of the ftolen things with

‡ Thefe fhips, we afterwards learned at Batavia, were fitted out by the French, and commanded by M. Bougainville.

them,

them, pleading, that Obade, her gallant, had ſtolen them, and was gone off with them. Mr. Banks received her very coolly; nor would ſuffer them to lie in the markee, he being already engaged; and the captain refuſed their preſents, at which the queen appeared very ſorrowful. Mr. Banks and the reſt, went to-bed; and the whole tribe of the natives would have lain in the bell-tent, but I would not ſuffer them, and ſent them away. The next morning they returned to the tent, and captain Cook altered his reſolution, and bought ſome of their fruit. The queen behaved very haughtily, yet Mr. Banks agreed they ſhould lie in his markee in the day-time. Two of her attendants were very aſſiduous in getting themſelves huſbands, in which attempt they, at length, ſucceeded. The ſurgeon took one, and one of the lieutenants the other: they ſeemed agreeable enough till bed-time, and then they determined to lie in Mr. Banks's tent, which they did accordingly: but one of the engaged coming out, the ſurgeon inſiſted that ſhe ſhould not ſleep there, and thruſt her out, and the reſt followed her, except Otea Tea, who whined and cried for a conſiderable time, till Mr. Banks led her out alſo. Mr. Monkhouſe and Mr. Banks came to an eclairciſſement ſome time after; had very high words, and I expected they would have decided it by a duel, which, however, they prudently avoided. Oboreah, and her retinue, had gone to their canoe, and would not return; but Mr. Banks went and ſtaid with them all night.

This day, the princeſs Tetroah Mituah's canoes were taken, laden with preſents for us; but, as captain Cook knew ſhe was innocent, he let her have her canoes again.

On the 21ſt, in the morning, many of the natives came to us with preſents of various kinds; but, though called preſents, they were all paid for. Our tent was nearly filled with people; and, ſoon after, Amoa, who is chief of ſeveral diſtricts on the other ſide of the iſland, alſo came to us, and brought with him a hog. As ſoon as he appeared, the natives uncloathed themſelves to the waiſt; which mark of obeiſance to their ſuperiors we had not obſerved before, but judged it was uſually ſhewn to every perſon of diſtinguiſhed rank amongſt them. This man Oboreah called her huſband, and Toobaiah his brother; but there is little regard to be paid to what they ſay. A woman, called Teetee, came from the weſt, and preſented a very fine garment to the Captain, of a bright yellow in the ground,

bordered

bordered with red : in the middle of it were many croffes, which we apprehended they had learned from the French.

On the 23d, in the morning, we miffed one of our men, a Portugueze, whom we had taken in at Rio de Janeiro ; enquiring among the Indians, we learned that he was at Opare with Tootahau ; and one of them offered to go and bring him back to us, which he accordingly did the fame night. The account which he gave on his return was, That three men came to him crying Tyau, which is the watch-word, amongft them, for friendfhip, and then carried him from the fort, and dragged him to the top of the bay, where they ftripped him, forced him into a boat, and took him to Opare, where Tootahau gave him fome cloaths, and perfuaded him to ftay with him. This account we believed to be true, for, as foon as is was known amongft the natives that he was refcued, all of t he min the bell-tent moved off, and went to Opare in great hafte, being apprehenfive that we fhould reck our revenge on them.

On the 26th, the captain and Mr. Banks fet out to make a furvey of the ifland, and began with the weft fide.

On the 27th, we faw a favourite game, which the young girls divert them-felves with in an evening ; dividing themfelves into two parties, one ftanding oppo-fite to the other, one party throws apples, which the other endeavours to catch. The right of the game I am not acquainted with ; but now-and-then one of the parties advanced, ftamping with their feet, making wry mouths, ftraddling with their legs, lifting up their cloaths, and expofing their nakednefs ; at the fame time repeating fome words in a difagreeable tone. Thus are they bred up to lewdnefs from their childhood, many of them not being above eight or nine years of age.

The 28th ; this evening the captain and Mr. Banks returned from their weftern excurfion. And,

On the 29th, early in the morning, they fet out for the eaft part of the ifland, to make a furvey of it.

Provifions

Provifions of all kinds were, at this time, very fcarce ; and fome of the inhabitants almoft famifhed. This fcarcity was principally occafioned by fupplying us
too liberally with bread-fruit, which obliged the inhabitants to eat ehee, roafted,
in its ftead, which taftes much like our chefnut : but, as the bread-tree was full of
young fruit, we were in hopes that they would foon have another crop to relieve them.

On the firft of July, in the evening, the captain and Mr. Banks returned from
furveying the ifland, which they found to be larger than they expected, and brought
with them feveral hogs, and could have obtained more with more hatchets. In
their tour round the ifland, they difcovered that it confifts of two peninfulas, connected by a low marfhy ifthmus, through which Mr. Banks fuppofed canoes might
be drawn. From Port-Royal, which is fituate at the weft end, the coaft extends
E by S. about nineteen miles to a reef of three fmall iflands, forming a bay, called
Society-Bay. From this the land inclines into a deep bay, at the ifthmus or junc-
ture of the two divifions, of which the fmalleft is nearly oval, and furrounded by a
reef, which runs parallel to the fhore at about two miles diftance : This has feveral
apertures, or paffages, which afford fafe anchorage within. The north fide of the
ifland is likewife defended by a fimilar reef; but the ground within is foul, and
unfafe for veffels of burthen. The whole length of the ifland is about fifteen
leagues ; and its circumference forty leagues. Befides the above-mentioned, they
faw feveral other bays ; fome of them very good, and one, in particular, in which a
large fleet might have rode with eafe and fafety : the name the natives give it is
Papara.

They alfo learned, that the ifland is divided into two principalities, one of which,
comprehending the largeft peninfula, is called Otaheite Nooa, or Great Otaheite ;
the other, comprehending the fmalleft peninfula, is termed Otaheite Eetee, or
Little Otaheite. The former of thefe divifions is alfo called Oboreano, in honour of
of queen Oboreah, who is regent of it. The other divifion is alfo governed by a
woman named Teideede ; fhe is younger than Oboreah. The people of the two
divifions do not feem to be upon good terms, having but little communication with
each other.

In

In their voyage they also saw a large monument, of a pyramidal form, of polished stone, which they were told was the morai of Oboreah and Oamo, and the people there said they were brother and sister.

On the 6th of July, in the evening, a young woman came to the entrance of the fort, whom we found to be a daughter of Oamo. The natives complimented her on her arrival, by uncovering their shoulders. We invited her to the tent, but she did not accept of it.

On the 9th, two of our marines being enamoured with a girl, one of the natives deserted from the fort, and fled to the west part of the island, and intended to have staid there. On the same day one of the natives stole a knife from one of our sailors, and wounded him with it in the forehead, almost through his skull:— a fray ensued, and the Indians ran away.

On this day, Mr. Banks and Dr. Monkhouse went many miles to a valley toward Orowhaina: at length they came to a waterfall, and could proceed no farther. At this spot the mountains were almost perpendicular; and from several parts of them hung some ropes, designed, as was apprehended, to assist those who should attempt to ascend them in times of scarcity, to get fayhee, or wild plantain. The stones and soil, on some of the highest mountains, appeared as if they had been burnt, or calcined: and, on the lower ones, where I have been, the earth is a sort of red-ochre covered with various plants, but chiefly with fern.

Most of the materials which composed the fort having been taken down, and put on board the ship, we prepared to set sail.

On the 10th, hearing no tidings of the two men who deserted us, we resolved to seize several of the principal people, and detain them till we could recover them: we also sent a party in the pinnace who apprehended Tootahau, and brought him to the ship; upon which Oboreah, and several other of the chiefs, sent out their servants, who returned in the evening with one of them, and re-

ported

ported that the Indians had detained one of our officers who commanded the party
fent out after him; alfo one of the men who accompanied him, and, having feized
their arms, ufed them very roughly; upon which the marines were difpatched in
the long-boat after them, taking with them fome of the natives. In the mean
time, the natives, whom we had made prifoners, not knowing what would be
their fate, were much alarmed; but the next morning the marines returned with
the men that had been detained, with the others that had deferted; and the natives,
whom we had imprifoned, were releafed. After making ftrong profeffions of
friendfhip, they left us; and, as foon as they reached the fhore, bent their
courfe, as faft as poffible, to Opare, fhewing tokens of difpleafure as they went
along.

During our ftay here, Mr. Banks and Dr. Solander were very affiduous in collecting whatever they thought might contribute to the advancement of Natural
Hiftory; and, by their directions, I made drawings of a great many curious trees,
and other plants; fifh, birds, and of fuch natural bodies as could not be conve-
niently preferved entire, to be brought home.

The following catalogue exhibits fome of the principal botanical fubjects, natives
of this place, made ufe of by the inhabitants.

PLANTS

※※※※※※※※※※※※※※※※※※※※※※※※※※※※※

PLANTS of Use for Food, Medicine, &c. in OTAHEITE.

Native Name.	Latin Name.
Teatea-maowa,	*Jasminum-didymum,*

Grows upon the hills; has a very sweet-smelling white flower, which the natives admire much.

| E ava. | *Piper-inebrians.* |

The expressed juice of this plant they drink to intoxicate themselves.

| E to. | *Saccharum-dulcis.* |

Of this cane they make no sugar, but content themselves with sucking the juice out of it.

| E mohoo. | *Cyperus-alatus.* |

The stalks of this plant, stripped of their pulp, which they perform with a sharp shell, make a sort of thread used for several common purposes.

| Taihinnoo. | *Tournefortia-sericea.* |
| E tow. | *Cordia-sebestena.* |

The leaves of these two plants are ingredients in their red dye, or mattee, for their cloth.

| E marra. | *Nauclea-orientalis.* |

Of the timber of this tree they build their large canoes.

| E teea-ree. | *Gardenia-florida.* |

This was original v brought from some other island to Otaheite, and there planted on account of is most flagrant flower, which they crop as soon as grown and stick in their ears, calling it E teea-ree, that is, the flower, by way of eminence.

| Taowdeehaow. | *Convolvulus-alatus.* |

The stalks of this plant they give young children to suck.

E oomarra,,

E oomarra,   *Convolvulus-chryforizus,*

Planted and cultivated by the natives, on account of its root, which is the fweet potatoe of the South-fea Iflands.

Pohooe.   *Convolvulus-Brafilienfis.*

Of this plant they make a fort of feine, which they ufe in fuch ground where they cannot ufe another.

E maireeo.   *Galaxa-oppofiti-folia.*

The leaf of this plant is one of the ingredients in their manoe.

E deva, or E reva.   *Galaxa-fparfa.*

This plant has a pretty large white flower like that of an oleander. Of the wood of this tree they make their pahaoos, or drums.

E booa, or E pooa.   *Solanum-latifolium.*

The leaves of this plant they ufe in making their red dye or mattee.

Pouraheitee.   *Solanum-viride.*

The leaves of this plant, baked, are eaten as greens.

E nono.   *Morinda-citri-folia.*

The root of this tree they ufe to dye their garments yellow, and eat the fruit of it.

E tee.   *Draccana-terminalis.*

Of this plant there are five different forts, yielding a large root, which is eaten, and counted very good food, by the iflanders of the South-feas.

Tootaoopa.   *Loranthus-ftelis.*

This plant is remarkable for nothing except its name, which fignifies the Oopa, or pigeons dung ; that bird feeds on the berries, and voids the ftones on the trunk of trees, where it grows.

E peea.   *Chaitea-tacca.*

The root of this plant, properly prepared, makes an excellent ftrong jelly, like to blanc-mange, of the nature of falop, for which it is very juftly admired by thefe iflanders.

                                             Tawhannoo.

Tawhannoo.   *Guettarda-fpeciofa.*

The timber of this tree, which grows pretty large at Toopbai, and other low iflands near Otaheite, ferves to make ftools, chefts, pafte-troughs, and various other utenfils ; they alfo build canoes of it.

E àwaow.   *Daphne-capitata.*

This plant is ufed to poifon fifh, in order to catch them; and, for this purpofe, they beat or mafh it together and throw it into the rivers and fea within the reefs.

E owhe.   *Arundo-bambos.*

This is the common bamboe, of which thefe iflanders make great ufe; the large joints they keep to hold water and oil; of the fmall they make arrows, flutes, cafes to hold fmall things; and, when cut into flips, they ferve them for knives, and cut tolerably well.

E motoo.   *Melaftoma-malabathrica.*

This plant is one of thofe which they hang upon their whatta-note-toobapaow, or burial-ftand, to be eaten by the foul of the deceafed.

E hee, or E ratta.   *Aniotum-fagiferum.*

This is a tall and ftately tree which bears a round flat fruit, covered with a thick tough coat, and, when roafted and ftripped of its rind, eats as well as a chefnut.

E avee.   *Spondias-dulcis.*

This is a large ftately tree, and often grows to the height of forty and fifty feet: the fruit, which, I believe, is peculiar to thefe ifles, is of an oval fhape, yellow when ripe, and grows in bunches of three or four, and is about the fize of a middling apple, with a large ftringy core: it is a very wholfome and palatable fruit, improving on the tafte, which is neareft that of a mangoe ; it is ftrongly impregnated with turpentine, and makes excellent pies when green. The wood ferves for building canoes, and for feveral other purpofes.

Pouraoo, and epooataroorroo.   *Cratæva-frondofa.*

The fruit of this fhrub they lay upon their corpfes, and hang it upon their burial whattas,

whattas, it having an agreeable bitter fmell : it is one of thofe which are facred to their god Tané, and, for that reafon, is generally planted in, or by the fmall Morais, called Morai Roma Tané, which are a fort of altar near the houfes, upon which they offer victuals.

E peereepeeree.   Euphorbia-develata.

This plant is full of a milky juice, with which they dye their garments of an indifferent brown colour.

E aowiree.   Terminal'a-glabrata.

This tree, which grows to a large fize, is often planted in their Morais, and near their houfes, for the fake of its agreeable fhade; the wood ferves to build canoes, make chefts, ftools and drums : the kernel of the nut which is in the fruit, though fmall, has a very pleafant tafte. [See pl. X.]

E ratta, or e pooratta.   Metrofideros-fpectabilis.

This tree, or fhrub, grows upon the Tooaroa, or Lower-hills, and is much reforted to by the venee, or fmall blue parrot, which feeds upon the flowers, and is often caught here, by means of a glewy juice which iffues out from the tops of the ftalks, when broke by their feeding upon them, and catches them like bird-lime: the flowers are full of beautiful fcarlet ftamina; the natives ftick them in their ears by way of ornament; and the leaves are put in their monoe, when they can get nothing fweeter.

E arrarooá.   Pfidium-myrtifolium.

The only ufe they make of this tree, which has a flower like a myrtle, is to make their totos or clubs, and ewha's, or a fort of lances, being very tough: they call it an eraow paree, or the cunning tree.

E heiya.   Eugenia-mallaccenfis.

This tree grows upon the lower-hills, having great clufters of crimfon flowers, full of ftamina of the fame colour, much like an almond-bloffom, but more brilliant: the fruit, when ripe, is red, and as big as one's fift; fweet, very agreeable to the palate, and full of feeds : it is very well known in the Eaft-India iflands, where it is efteemed delicious fruit.

Tamanno.

Tamanno.   *Calophyllum-inophyllum.*

This is a moft beautiful verdant tree, that grows to a large fize, bearing fpikes of white flowers : with the juice of the fruit and leaves they dye their garments a pale yellow, which, at the fame time, gives them a rich perfume. The wood is greatly valued by them on account of its beauty and duration. They build canoes, make ftools, and other utenfils of it : it is moft likely planted in the Morais, being facred to their god Tané.

E poo-aiho.   *Saccharum-fatuum.*

With bundles of this grafs, lit up, they allure the fifh to the edges of the reefs, carrying them in their hands at night.

E atoorree.   *Portulacca-lutea.*

This fort of purflain grows very common in the low iflands, where the inha- bitants bake and eat it, and account it very good food.

E hootoo.   *Betonica-fplendida.*

This beautiful tree grows to a confiderable height, and bears a very large and fpecious white flower, full of long purple ftamina, with which they fometimes deck their heads, and fometimes ftick them in their ears : the fruit, powdered, they throw into the water to kill fifh ; and of the wood they build fmall canoes.

E pooamattapeepee.   *Befleria-laurifolia.*

The flower of this tree is much admired on account of its fweet fcent, for which reafon they ftick them in their ears and hair, and put them among their garments, and into their monoe. The wood is very tough and lafting, and of it they make drums, and thwarts acrofs their canoes.

E neearohettee.   *Stachys-dentata, or ruellia-fragrans.*

The juice of this plant, mixed with feveral others, they ufe as a plaifter to cure any fort of wounds.

E noonanoona.   *Boerhavia-procumbens.*

The ftalks of this plant are eaten when they have no better food.

E ava-

E ava-váidái. *Piper-latifolium.*

The juice of this plant has not the intoxicating quality of the other, fo that they prudently make an offering of it to their Eatooas, on whofe altars they hang bunches of it.

E pooraow. *Hibifcus-cufpidatus.*

The bark of this tree yields an excellent ftuff for making all forts of twine, cord, and ropes. Of the wood they make their bows, beams and pillars of their houfes, fmall canoes, ftools, and various other utenfils. Of the bark of the plant, when young, they weave a fort of matting, which is very neat, and is called by the fame name as the tree. The wood that remains after the bark is taken off, being very light, ferves, inftead of cork, to float their feins, and for handles to their fifgigs ; and to rub together to get fire.

E pooraow-toro-ceree. *Hibifcus-tricufpis.*

This plant is pretty much like the laft, and is ufed for the fame purpofes, but is inferior in quality.

E aiowte. *Hibifcus-rofa-finenfis.*

This tree is admired on account of its beautiful fcarlet flower, of which the young people make garlands for their hair, ftick them in their ears, and rub their lances with them to make them look red.

E wawei. *Goffipium-religiofum.*

This is a fpecies of cotton of which they have not yet found out the ufe.

E meerio. *Thefpefia-populnea.*

This beautiful tree is planted in all Morais, being held facred to Tané: they alfo make ufe of it as an emblem of peace; and always bring it in their hands when they meet with ftrange people. It yields a middling fort of timber, and is made ufe of for feveral purpofes.

E peereeperee. *Urena-lobata.*

The feeds of this plant are of the nature of a burr, from whence its name, to glue or ftick to any thing. The boys play the fame tricks with it as the children in Europe with the burr. They alfo make maro's, or a fort of mat of the bark.

Berdees.

Berdeebeedeeo.   *Abrus-pricatorius.*

The feed of this plant it the well-known Indian pea with a black fpot: of thefe they form ear-rings, and alfo ftick them on a fillet which they wear on their head.

E atai, erythoina.   *Corallodendron.*

This is a large tree, and remarkable for its bright fcarlet flower, making a moft beautiful fhow. The venee feeds upon its flowers, and is caught with the clammy juice that iffues out of it; the women make garlands of them, and put them round their heads.

E owhaee.   *Æfchynomene-fpeciofa.*

This fhrub grows wild, in great abundance, on the ifland of Toopbai; and is planted on the other iflands to fhade their houfes; and the flower of it, which is very beautiful, they often ftick in their ears.

E hora.   *Galega-pifcatoria.*

With this plant, beaten fmall, they poifon or ftupify fifh, throwing it into the water, by which means they are caught.

E peepee.   *Phafeolus-amœnus.*

The ftalks of this plant make a very good thread for weaving nets and feins. Of the flowers, which are very pretty, they make garlands for their heads.

E vaeenoo.   *Cotula-bicolor.*
E tooho.   *Epipactis-purpurea.*

Both thefe plants, bruifed, are ingredients in their Erapaow-mai, or plaifter to cure fores.

Taro.   *Arum-efculentum.*

The roots of this plant, of which there are feveral varieties, are as good as Ignames, and are reckoned very wholefome common food in the South-fea iflands. The leaves, when baked, tafte as well as greens.

E ape.   *Arum-coflatum.*

The root of this plant is as good as the laft, but confiderably larger: the leaves, which are very fmooth and extremely large, are ufed to wrap up, or lay any fort of victuals upon.

E toa-

E toa-caſuarina.   *Equiſetifolia.*

This is one of the beſt woods they have; it is very hard and heavy, and coloured like mahogany. They make their clubs, lances, cloth-beaters, and ſeveral
other knick-nacks and utenſils of it.

Tooneenna.   *Hernandia-ovigera.*

Of the wood of this tree they make a ſort of very ſmall canoes, and ſeveral other
neceſſary utenſils.

E hooe-rorro.   *Cucurbita-pruriens.*

The fruit of this tree is about the ſize of a ſmall orange, very hard, and quite
round, ſerving them, inſtead of bottles, to put their monoe or oil in.

Moemoe.   *Phyllanthus-anceps.*

The only thing remarkable about this plant is the leaves, which ſhut up at
night, from whence its name, which ſignifies ſleepy.

E aowte.   *Morus-papyriferus.*

This is the ſhrub from which they make their fineſt and moſt beautiful cloth;
and is probably the ſame with that of which they make paper in China. They
never let it grow old, but cut it down when it is about a man's height, ſtripping
the bark off, and laying it to ſoak in water. Of this they make their cloth either
thick or thin as they pleaſe. They plant it in beds, and take great pains in the
cultivation of it.

E roa.   *Urtica-argentea, or Urtica-candicans.*

Of the ſtalks of this nettle, beaten out, they make their beſt lines for their fiſh-
hooks, which has the quality of not rotting with ſalt-water; they alſo make belts,
or girdles of it, but very ſeldom garments; their beſt ſeins are alſo made of it.

E tootooe.   *Telopæa-perſpicua.*

Of the bark of this tree, ſoaked in water, they make that gummy ſubſtance
which they put upon their dark-coloured cloth to make it gloſſy, and keep out the
rain. The fruit of this tree is a ſort of nut, which yields a very fat kernel, of
which they make their black dye, uſed in Tataowing, by burning them and receiving the ſmoke. Strung upon a reed or ſtick they ſerve inſtead of candles, and
give a very good light.

E ooroo.

E ooroo.   *Sitodium-altile.*

This tree, which yields the bread-fruit fo often mentioned by the voyagers to the South-feas, may juftly be ftiled the Staff-of-life to thefe iflanders ; for from it they draw moft of their fupport. This tree grows to between thirty and forty feet high, has large palmated leaves, of a deep grafs-green on the upper-fide, but paler on the under ; and bears male and female flowers, which come out fingle at the bottom or joint of each leaf. The male flower fades and drops off ; the female, or clufter of females, fwell and yield the fruit, which often weighs three or four pounds, and is as big as a perfon's head when full grown. It is of a green colour ; the rind is divided into a number of polygonical fections ; the general fhape a little longer than round, and white on the infide, with a pretty large core. The fruit, as well as the whole plant, is full of a white clammy juice, which iffues plentifully from any part that is cut : it delights in a rich foil, and feldom grows, if ever, on the low iflands : it is a very handfome tree to look at, of a beautiful verdure, and well cloathed with leaves, bearing a vaft quantity of fruit, which appears to hang in bunches, and, by its great weight, bends down the branches : it bears fruit a great part of the year, and there are feveral forts of it, fome fmaller and others larger, which are ready to pluck at different feafons. They generally pluck it before it is ripe, ufing a long ftick with a fork at the end of it for this pur-pofe ; and, before they roaft it, fcrape all the rind off with a fhell ; and then, when large, cut it in quarters ; and, having prepared one of their ovens in the ground, with hot ftones in it, they lay the fruit upon thefe, having previoufly put a layer of the leaves between, and then another layer over them, and, above that, more hot ftones, covering up the whole clofe with earth, and, in two or three hours time, it is done ; it then appears very inviting, more fo than the fineft loaf I ever faw ; the infide is very white, and the outfide a pale brown ; it taftes very farinaceous, and is, perhaps, the moft agreeable and beft fuccedaneum for bread ever yet known, and, in many refpects, exceeds it. When thus baked, it only keeps three or four days ; another contrivance being ufed for keeping it ; they take the baked fruit, cut out all the cores, and, with a ftone-mallet, mafh it to a pulp in a wooden trough, or tray. This pulp they put in a hole that is dug in the ground and lined with leaves ; this is clofe covered up, and left a proper time till it ferments and becomes four, at which time they take it up, and make it into little loaves, which they wrap up in the leaves, and, in this ftate, it is baked, and called by them mahe,

and.

and will keep several months, being eaten when bread-fruit is out of season, and carried to sea with them; and of it they form several sorts of paste, such as pepe, popoee, &c. which are used by them at their meals. The leaves of this tree are very useful to wrap fish and other eatables in, when put into the oven to be baked. Of the wood they build canoes, and make several other sorts of utensils; and, of the bark of young plants of it, which are raised on purpose, they make very good cloth, which is but little inferior to that made of Eaowte, only somewhat more harsh and harder.

E awharra. *Pandanus-tectorius.*

This tree generally grows on the sandy hillocks by the sea-side, and is found in great plenty on all the low islands; the leaves are long, like those of sedge, sawed on the edge; the flowers are male and female, growing upon different trees; those of the male-flower smell very sweet; and, of the bractea of them, which are white, they make a sort of garlands to put round their heads; the fruit is orange colour, and as big as one's head, consisting of a congeries of small cones, like those of the Anana, or Pine-apple, which they much resemble: the bottom of these cones, sucked when full ripe, yield a flat insipid sweetness; and are eaten by the children; but the chief use of this tree is in the leaves, which, when plucked and dried, make excellent thatching for their houses, and various sorts of mats and baskets. This is the Palmetto of the eastern voyagers.

E mattee. *Ficus-tinctoria.*

The figs of this tree are one of the chief ingredients in their red-dye for their garments: when they use them they nip or bite off the stalk close to the fruit, at which time a small drop of milky juice issues out; this they either shake upon the tow-leaves, used in this dye, or else into a cocoa-nut shell, with a little water, or cocoa-nut milk; and then dip the leaves into it, which they roll up in a small bundle, and work or squeeze them between the palm and their fingers, till the red colour is produced by the mixture of the two juices; but, what is very odd, these leaves being beaten in a mortar, and the juice taken from them and mixed with the fig-milk, will not produce the same colour. Of the bark of this tree very good twine is made, which is of particular use for making of seins, and other nets.

E aowa.

E aowa. *Ficus-prolixa.*

This tree is remarkable on account of its trunk, which grows to an enormous fize, by the branches hanging down, and taking root again, which makes a very grotefque figure. Of the bark of young plants, raifed on purpofe, they make a fort of cloth, naturally of a ruffet-hue, which they call Ora, being worn in the mornings, and much valued by them, efpecially that which is beaten very fine and thin.

E toee. *Zezyphoides-argentea.*

The wood of this tree they make ufe of for various purpofes, fuch as fterns of canoes, heightening boards for ditto, and beams to beat their cloth upon.

E apeeree. *Dodonæa-vifcofa.*

The wood of this tree, which is very tough, ferves to make a particular fort of weapon, which they carry in their hand when they dive after fharks, and other large fifh.

E tive. *Dracontium polyphyllum.*

The root of this is ufed to make a jelly like the Peea, but is not near fo good.

Meiya. *Mufa-paradifaica.*

This is the well-known tropical fruit called Plantains, and Bananas, of which there is a great variety in thefe iflands: they reckon more than twenty forts which differ in fhape and tafte; fome of thefe are for eating raw, and others beft boiled, and will ferve inftead of bread: they plant them in a rich foil, and take great pains, in their cultivation.

Faihe. *Mufa-bihai.*

This is another fort of Plantains, which generally grow wild in the mountains, and fometimes are planted by them; they are far inferior to the laft, have a confiderable aftringency, and eat beft boiled or roafted. There are four different forts, and the leaves of this and the laft, ferve to put victuals upon; and the rind of the trunk to make a fort of bafkets called Papa-meiya.

E aree. *Coccus-nucifer.*

This palm, the fruit of which is fo well known in all places within the tropics, feems to be a native of thefe iflands, being found every where in the greateft plenty,

and

and in the greateſt perfection, eſpecially on the two low iſlands, called by them Motoos : theſe are many of them uninhabited, and are reſorted to for the ſake of the cocoa-nuts, which grow to a very great ſize on theſe iſlands; they love a ſandy ſoil, and thrive much near the ſea-ſide on the riſing of the hills : they are ſmaller, and later in growth; they begin to bear when they are about ten feet high, and yield fruit ſeveral times in the year, and continue growing till they are ſo very tall, that they, by far, overtop all the reſt of the trees: the leaves grow all at the top, from which the fruit hangs in ſeveral cluſters of twenty or thirty, ſo enormouſly heavy, it is amazing how the ſlender ſtem of this tree can ſupport them : when they have a mind to gather any for preſent uſe, they ſend up a boy who ties his feet together with a ſtring, and vaults up to the top with great eaſe; when there, he gets them off the ſtalk by ſcrewing them round, and then flings them down, taking care to give them a twirl firſt, otherwiſe they would fall to the ground with ſuch force, from ſuch a height, as would ſplit them, and loſe all the liquor. When they have a mind to gather the whole bunch, they cut it off, and lower it down with a rope; the way of opening them for preſent uſe is with their teeth, with which they pull off the outer rind, and then break the ſhell with a ſtone; but when they have many to peel, they do it by driving them upon a pointed ſtick, which is fixed in the ground for that purpoſe. Some ſorts of theſe nuts will not keep at all; and other ſorts, when pulled ripe, and properly dried and cured, will keep good a whole year : upon theſe racemi, or bunches, are ripe fruit, thoſe that are half ripe, and others juſt ſet at the ſame time. The uſes of this tree are many to the iſlanders of the ſouth ſeas; the fruit, when half ripe, yields about a pint to a quart of one of the moſt refreſhing and agreeable liquors in nature : this delicious beverage they often put amongſt their paſtes and puddings, and delight much to waſh their mouth and hands with a little of it; the ſhell is, at this time, very ſoft, and is often eaten together with a little of the rind, but in no great quantities, it being apt to occaſion coſtiveneſs; as the fruit grows older, the milk turns thicker, more luſcious, and waſtes away; the kernel begins to form round the edge, like a white tranſparent jelly, and is very nice eating in this ſtate. When it is ripe, the kernel is hard and white, about half an inch thick, and eats as well as a good nut; but the liquor is very indifferent, and, in a little time, waſtes away intirely; of the kernel they make two ſorts of puddings, called Poe, and Etooó, and eat it roaſted alone; they alſo make a ſauce for fiſh of it, called Taiyero, by

ſleeping

steeping the kernel in sea-water, and often shaking it, till it is almost dissolved; but the greatest quantity is used in making monoe, or oil, to anoint their hair; for this purpose they grate the kernel very small, then put it into a wooden tray, or trough, cover it, and set it in the shade, and, as the oil falls to the edges, they take it up with a shell, and put it into a calabash for use; it smells very rank, for which reason they put it into a quantity of scented woods and plants; but after all it smells very heavy, and is apt to give an European the head-ach. The shell is used for their drinking cups, vessels to hold water, and to put their victuals in; and, for this purpose, they make them smooth by rubbing them with coral. The shell of the ripe ones is black, and the others brownish white; the outer-rind, after being soaked in water, and well beaten, is drawn out into threads, of which they make variety of plaited-line for girdles, to frap their flutes, for slinging their calabashes, and has the quality of not rotting with salt-water: with this stuff they also calk their canoes; and, in the East-Indies, they make cables of it; of the leaves they make bonnets, and baskets to put their bread-fruit and apples in: the liber of the young leaves, which are very thin and transparent, they tie up in bunches, and stick in their hair by way of ornament: the brown skin, which covers the leaf, before it is unfolded, serves also for various purposes; and the wood of this tree answers all other common purposes very well.

E papa.

Of the leaves of this tree, which are very white and glistering, when dried, they make their evanne-matting, much admired for its beauty.

E howira.

This grows chiefly in the low islands; of the split leaves they make their best mats for garments, to sit, and sleep upon.

E yeiyei.

This plant is of the nature of osier; of the stalks of it they work their round baskets, which they call Heenei, and in which they keep their victuals, and all their utensils.

Doodooe-awai & Oheparra.

With these they dye their poowhirre, or brown cloth.

Patarar,

Patarra.

An eatable root, which I did not fee.

E nioee.

A fine eatable fruit, of a red colour, which I did not fee.

E apatahei.

An elegant flower, which I alfo did not fee.

Oowhe note Maowa.   *Diofcorea-alata.*

This plant produces the root fo well known by the name of Ignames, all over the Eaft and Weft-Indies: they have feveral forts of it, but that which grows upon the hills is the beft.

E nahae.

This is a fern, which has an extraordinary fweet fmell, and, for this reafon, it is ufed by the better fort of people to fleep on.

E ahei.

The wood of this tree, has a very rich and delicious fmell; is of a yellow colour, and is the principal ingredient ufed in perfuming their monoe, being grated fmall, and put to foak amongft it; as it is very fcarce, it is in great requeft amongft them; we could never get a fight of the tree, but were told it grew on the mountains. They have various other vegetables with which they perfume their monoe, and likewife their cloaths: the names of thefe are, Pooeva, Maiteeraow, Annee, Noonna, Ehaee, Amea, and Matehooa.

E atoo.

A plant of which they make mat garments.

A VOCABULARY.

A VOCABULARY of the LANGUAGE of OTAHEITE.

Aree,	*A chief.*
To aree,	*A secondary chief.*
Toomeite,	*A superior officer.*
Taowaa,	*A priest.*
Eiya,	*A centinel.*
Tootuai,	*A trader.*
Teine,	*A dependant, or tenant.*
Tatta màòwreèa,	*A poor man that gets his livelihood by labour, as a fisherman.*
Taow taow,	*A menial servant.*
Tata,	*People.*
Midee,	*A child.*
Earee,	*A boy.*
Aheine,	*A woman.*
Mituatane,	*Father.*
Mituaheine,	*Mother.*
Tooboonah,	*A grand-father.*
Teine,	*A brother.*
Tooaheine,	*A sister.*
Tooanah,	*An elder brother, or sister.*
Teine,	*A younger brother, or sister.*
Tane,	*A husband.*
Huaheine,	*A wife.*
Eeàpeèttèe, taowa, or tyau,	*A friend.*
Midya,	*A widow.*
Opareemo,	*A skeleton, or bones.*
Eeree,	*The flesh.*

Ewey,

Ewey, or aèe	*The skin.*
Matee,	*Blood.*
Ewaowa,	*The veins.*
Eraowroo,	*The hair.*
Erowroo,	*The head.*
Eto,	*The top of the head.*
Eboo,	*The temples.*
Irai,	*The brow.*
Matau,	*The eyes.*
Eahoo,	*The nose.*
Paparia,	*The cheeks.*
Tareeha,	*The ears.*
Ewauha,	*The mouth.*
Eooto,	*The lips.*
Eneeho,	*The teeth.*
Treero,	*The tongue.*
Maomee,	*The beard.*
Eaee,	*The neck.*
Trapooa,	*The gullet.*
Etapona,	*The shoulders.*
Erimau,	*The hands and arms.*
Aiai,	*The arm-pits.*
Wateea,	*The elbows.*
Aboorima,	*The palms of the hands.*
Epai,	*The thumb.*
Meyoooo,	*The nails.*
Eoma,	*The breasts.*
Eoo,	*The nipples.*
Eobco,	*The belly.*
Pito,	*The navel.*
Etooa,	*The back.*
Etohai,	*The hips.*
Ehoorai,	*The anus.*
Oowhau,	*The thighs.*

Etooree,

Etooree,	*The knees.*
Eawy,	*The legs.*
Edeai,	*The calf of the leg.*
Moa moa,	*The ancles.*
Etapooai,	*The foot.*
Oütoo,	*The heel.*
Matiyo,	*The toes.*
Eyoare,	*A rat.*
Eairo,	*The tail of a quadruped.*
Manoo,	*A bird.*
Mato manoo,	*A bird's eye.*
Eneèhote manoo,	*A bird's beak.*
B-haòw pè,	*The tail.*
Maniaow,	*The claws.*
Eroòppe,	*A pigeon, or dove.*
Ohaa te manoo,	*A bird's nest.*
Hooira moa,	*An egg.*
Aa,	*A green parrot.*
Veene,	*A blue parroquet.*
Morai,	*A duck.*
Eiya,	*A fish.*
Ewhai, or ephai,	*A cuttle-fish.*
Ehoomè,	*A seal.*
Ehoona,	*A turtle.*
Emahoo,	*A shark's skin.*
Eiyoo,	*Shagreen.*
Porahaaw,	*Shell-fish.*
Mapeehee,	*A limpet.*
E boòboo,	*A wilk.*
Aupuhua,	*Muscles.*
E ròrree,	*An actinia, or pisser, [a marine insect]*
Peeyaow,	*A libella, or dragon-fly.*
Ootooròhonnoo,	*A spider.*
Qatoo,	*A louse.*

E reemo,

E reemo,	*Sea-weed.*
Ewawaow, or erao,	*A leaf.*
Eramaiya,	*A plantain-leaf.*
Meiya,	*Plantains.*
Meiya èpé,	*Ripe plantains.*
Eaow,	*A tender green stalk.*
Epeea,	*A woody stalk.*
Ehooai,	*A calabash.*
Eboo,	*A cocoa-nut shell.*
Po-ooroo,	*The bark of the bread-fruit tree.*
Hoora-ooiro,	*Fruit.*
Ooroo,	*Bread-fruit.*
Ooroo epé,	*Bread-fruit kept till it is half rotten, which is, nevertheless, sweet when roasted.*
Bidibidio,	*Small red Indian pease.*
Etoomoo,	*Wood.*
Hanooa,	*A sort of wood like crab-tree wood.*
Whanooa,	*Land.*
Ewha,	*An opening in the land.*
Maowa,	*Mountains and hills.*
Te Maowa, tei tei,	*Steep or perpendicular hills.*
Orowhaina,	*A high peaked hill in Otaheite.*
Hiahia,	*Level or flat country.*
E ràpao,	*Mud.*
E àrahow,	*Ashes.*
Owhai,	*A stone.*
Owhai mamòe,	*A soft or splintery stone.*
Owhai maowree,	*A hard or flinty stone.*
Tatteiaowra,	*A transparent crystal.*
Wahaa, or eahei,	*Fire.*
Eahei,	*Light.*
Avy,	*Water.*
Eàrroe,	*The swell of the sea, and the surf.*

Oròmàtooa,

Oròmàtooa,	The air, or breath.
Hiamòorre,	Light puffs of air.
Matai,	Wind.
Eata,	The clouds.
Eohco,	Smoke.
Anooa nooa,	The rainbow.
Manaha,	The fun.
Toobatoora,	The fetting-fun.
Marama,	The moon.
Efedeea,	A ftar.
Taowruah,	The planet Venus.
Nataihieah,	The planet Saturn.
Eparai,	The horizon.
T'Oheèttee-otera,	The eaft.
T'Otera,	The weft.
Oàpitoaraow,	The north.
Tahèaweira,	The fouth.
A fale,	A houfe *.
E taòwteea,	The rafters of a houfe.
E ahaow,	The beams.
E toorroo tooròo,	The pofts.
Kipoo a meenìhee,	A chamber-pot.
Ebupau,	A ftool.
Tota, alfo Eeno,	A looking-glafs.
Mayo,	A fmall rail.
Ithee dee,	A wooden image.
Eiei,	A mallet for cloth.
Mahai,	An oven for baking bread.
Oorè dehaiya,	A large nail.
Oorè oorè,	A middling-fized nail.
Oore eeteea,	A fmall nail.

---

* Tootahau's houfe is one hundred and twenty yards long, and twenty yards broad : the roof is fupported by twenty pofts, each nineteen feet high.

Ueoi,

Utoi, or towa,	*An axe, or hatchet.*
Itee,	*A fly-flap.*
Whata,	*Sticks raised to hang baskets upon.*
Eitai,	*A straw-bag.*
Edevai,	*An open-wrought bag.*
Moean,	*Mats.*
Iteehahào,	*Red paint or dye.*
Matee,	*Red dye for cloth.*
Paee,	*A ship.*
Paee,	*A large canoe.*
Ewaha,	*A small canoe.*
Ewhàrraow,	*A boat-house.*
Taoda,	*A th`ck rope.*
Eaha,	*A plaited line, and thread for making nets.*
Ehow,	*A fishing-line.*
Oopeia,	*A seine.*
Hobuhoa,	*White cloth.*
Tuorloo,	*Thick white cloth.*
Ahao apau,	*Buff-coloured thin cloth.*
Habau,	*Thin buff-coloured cloth spotted with red.*
Poohiree,	*Reddish cloth.*
Ahao ora,	*Russet thin cloth.*
Haowaraia,	*Gummed cloth.*
Eiboo,	*Cloth made of old cloth.*
Pooroaw,	*A sort of stuff, taken from some tree, like hemp, of which they make cloth and girdles.*
Aihoo,	*A garment.*
Parawei,	*A shirt, or under garment.*
Maroa,	*A piece of cloth worn round the middle.*
Evane,	*A garment made of fine matting.*
Tumataw,	*A bonnet.*
Opaitea,	*A mat-girdle.*

Tamoou,

Tamoou,	*Wreaths of plaited human hair, which they set great value upon, worn as an ornament, chiefly on the head.*
Poe,	*Ear-rings.*
Poe oole oole,	*A yellow bead.*
Poe meedee,	*A green bead.*
Poe ere ere,	*A blue bead.*
Ewhahana,	*A bow.*
Eahe,	*An arrow.*
Epanoo,	*A drum.*
Paraow,	*A pair of clappers.*
Vivo,	*A flute.*
Mama,	*Child's pap.*
Poe,	*A paste, or pudding, made of the roots of arum.*
Peea,	*A strong jelly, or paste, made of the roots of arum.*
Mahei,	*A kind of sour paste, made of fermented bread-fruit.*
Opepe,	*A sort of paste.*
Monoe,	*Cocoa-oil.*
Toonoah,	*A mole in the skin.*
Ehaow,	*Sweat.*
Hooàre,	*Spittle.*
Hoòpe,	*Snot.*
Paiya,	*Fat.*
Matàiree tona,	*The stye in the eye.*
Trapaou,	*A scab.*
Ewhàiwhai,	*The elephantiasis.*
Eowhàoo,	*The windy dropsy.*
Opeepee,	*The numbness in the feet when they sleep.*
Màtte noa,	*A natural death.*
Heiva,	*A ceremony performed by the deceased's relations.*
Poohira,	*A place, or residence.*

Morai,

Morai,	*A burying-ground.*
Morino Tootahau,	*The burying-ground of Tootahau.*
Morai natówa,	*Our burying-place.*
Whata,	*The edifice they lay their dead upon.*
E peènei,	*An echo.*
E paeèna,	*The sound or noise which forms the echo.*
Ahoo,	*A fart.*
Mahana,	*A day.*
Poa,	*A night.*
Po oore,	*A dark night.*
Otaowa,	*Yesterday.*
Aouna,	*To-day.*
Oboboa,	*To-morrow.*
Obabadura,	*The day after to-morrow.*
Itopa de mahano,	*Sun-set.*
Otooe te po,	*Late in the night.*
Hàmanee,	*The temper or will.*
Tatta te Hàmannee màitài,	*A good-natured person.*
Tatta marè,	*A contradictory person, one that will not allow another to know as well as he.*
Tatta maowra, & tatta whattaow,	*A great lazy, idle, or loitering person.*
Tatta taowra,	*An industrious man, also an active, clever, stirring man.*
Amawhàttoo,	*A shrew, or scold.*
Maheine eawaow,	*An housewife.*
Niaowniaow,	*The stench of a carcase.*
Ehaowa,	*A smell.*
Motoo & puta,	*A hole.*
Epehe,	*A song.*
Tetooa,	*A title usually given to their women of rank, though every woman will answer to it.*
Teà,	*White.*
Amawhàttoo,	*Industrious, pains-taking.*
Peèo,	*Bent, bending, crooked, turning, winding.*
	Téeahaòwratea.

Téeahaòwratea,	*Strait, even.*
Epàceya,	*Smooth.*
Anànnà,	*Transparent or clear.*
Po-eèrree,	*Opake or dull.*
Eawhà,	*Brittle.*
Orroo, òrroo,	*Limber, or pliable.*
Eoròee,	*Tapering to a point.*
Oëöë, teres,	*Long, small, or slender.*
Toòmmoo,	*Blunt, opposed to oëöë.*
Mènne, mènne,	*Thick, short, and round.*
Tàrra tàrra,	*Crumpled or creased.*
Verra verra,	*Hot, applied to victuals.*
Marroowhai,	*Dry.*
Emàioèeya,	*Lame, or crippled.*
Oohàmmama,	*Open, expanded wide.*
Ooa-peèrree,	*Shut, fastened, or glued together.*
Hoònnehoònne,	*Swelled.*
Nooè,	*Large, grand, or chief.*
Etee,	*Little, or lesser.*
Nìnnoo nìnnoo,	*Juicy.*
Ewàwa,	*Hard and dry.*
Opàrirreè,	*Blown down, or blown away.*
Etooa,	*Under.*
Earo,	*Upper.*
Mona,	*Deep.*
T'joota,	*Ashore.*
Whattata,	*Near at hand.*
Oeta,	*Yonder, or without.*
Epapa tahei,	*Single.*
Niteeya,	*Double.*
Ataowa,	*Together.*
Woreede,	*Stolen.*
Ooapa,	*Given away.*

Tei

Teí moòa,	*Before.*
Tei moòrree.	*Behind.*
Tei ròtto poo,	*In the middle, or between,*
Tei ròtto,	*Within.*
Tei wahao,	*Without.*
Nehàia,	*When.*
Tèiene,	*Just now.*
T'èna,	*This.*
Ehai,	*When, where.*
Pahà,	*Perhaps, may be, very likely.*
No reira,	*From their.*
Paraow, peès,	*Rough or hard speech or tongue.*
Paraow teeahaowratea,	*Soft speech.*
Paraow ohoòmmoo,	*Low or soft talking.*
Paraow tooirro,	*Loud or high talk.*
Taowna,	*A word of great contempt.*
Myty,	*Good.*
Maw myty,	*Good victuals.*
Manamanatey,	*Very good, or sweet.*
Eena,	*Middling, or so-so.*
Porai,	*To talk.*
Meetee, & ehioèe,	*To kiss.*
Woradee,	*To be angry.*
Mataow,	*To be affronted, or indisposed.*
Eàwow,	*To scold.*
Emòto,	*To box, or fight.*
Mareere,	*To be cold.*
Eporiree,	*To be hungry.*
Eei,	*To eat.*
Eotte,	*To suck.*
Norothoe dé adee t'avai,	*To drink cocoa-nut liquor.*
Amama,	*To yawn.*
Iraòwai,	*To dose, slumber, or be drowsy.*
Màtte roah,	*To die, or be dead.*

Edoodbo,

Edoodoo,	*To make cloth.*
Eaow,	*To swim.*
Toobàipai,	*To knock.*
Toataow,	*To anchor.*
Heapoonnè,	*To encompass, or encircle.*
Ooawhèwhè,	*To entangle.*
Ehoòtè te Oops,	*To pull one by the hair.*
Eninnei,	*To squeeze, or press one.*
Pattòe,	*To jostle, or shake one.*
Ewhàttoe,	*To jog, or shuffle against a person.*
Oòmohaooa,	*To cram, or thrust into one.*
Taweèrree,	*To twine or whirl any thing about; to wring; also to pluck or gather cocoa-nuts, by twirling them round.*
Hiaree,	*To pluck or gather fruit.*
Taowra,	*To twine, cord, or line.*
Eàee niea te màtto,	*To climb up rocks.*
Epèe niea,	*To go up with a rope.*
Tìrai te pàhee,	*To build, or make a ship, or large canoe.*
Whainaow,	*To beget.*
Eeraira,	*To jump, or leap over.*
Eheèya,	*To tumble.*
Etoòrài,	*To drive, throw, or push down.*
Emàiroo,	*To sting.*
Ephàow,	*To smell.*
Eoòma,	*To nip.*
Tootoòà,	*To spit.*
Eetoò,	*To stand.*
Ehèhe,	*To buz like a fly.*
Mèamèa, & èrea èrièa,	*To shrink or shudder at any thing.*
Airareè,	*To fly.*
Emàow,	*To stick or adhere to any thing.*
Taimòradee,	*To reel to and fro.*
Ehò,	*To buy, exchange, or barter.*

Manoo—

Manooaheènnee,	*To depend or hang upon.*
Etoò,	*To lower, or set down upon the ground.*
Eàma,	*To carry on the shoulders.*
Madàidài,	*To look at, handle, or touch; to view.*
Epa,	*To give.*
Evaha,	*To be carried over the water.*
Mayneenee, or myneerea,	*To tickle.*
Itopa,	*To fall.*
A wharr awai,	*To go or pass away.*
Wahoee & ehaòe,	*To turn, or go back again.*
Eheèro harre ehòe,	*To come and go.*
Toòiro,	*To shout or halloo at one.*
Aiwee,	*To understand, or comprehend; to listen, or give ear.*
Ewhàro,	*To believe.*
Emàro,	*To disbelieve.*
Hoòna haòwnna,	*To deny, or disbelieve.*
Ewa, or ooai,	*It rains.*
Eoeffra,	*It lightens.*
Patiree,	*It thunders.*
Whaow whaow,	*It stinks.*
Eho mai, & harre mai,	*Come to me.*
Ehòee mai,	*Row to me.*
Paraow mai,	*Speak to me.*
Aremina,	*Come with me.*
Eeyaha, or Ihaya,	*Get away, or get you gone.*
Hareioota,	*Go you there or yonder.*
Harenaow,	*Do you go with me.*
Ara mai,	*Follow me, or come hither.*
Atira,	*Stop.*
Area,	*Stay.*
Parahei,	*Sit down.*
Ainao,	*Take care.*
Eeyo, or tirara,	*Look you.*

Titara,

Titara,	*Let me look, or shew me.*
Mamoo,	*Hold your tongue.*
Tehai,	*Where is he?*
Oewai,	*What is your name?*
Noa oie tehai,	*Where is such a person?*
Harehiea,	*Whither do you go?*
Wahoèe,	*What is it?*
T'ahoe t'eha,	*Of what is this garment made?*
Eha,	*What? or What say you?*
Eha t'oe, tirree eetee,	*What would you please to have?*
Tai poe etee noòw,	*Pray give me a little bead?*
Ooàteea te tirre n'oe,	*You shall have what you want.*
Eaoòwha te matai,	*The wind has changed.*
Mate,	*My sickness.*
Neeheeo,	*Good night.*
Waow,	*I.*
Naow,	*Myself.*
Tooanahoe & tooanahahow,	*You and I.*
Nat'owa,	*Ours.*
Potohe,	*Firstly.*
Aiba, aim, aipa, aita, & aiya,	*Are all negatives, and pronounced with the tongue thrust a little way out of the mouth.*
Nata,	*An article which signifies of.*
Taipara, tideo, tidoo,	*Words used in their songs.*

An OTAHEITEAN SONG.

TAOWDEE waow, tetatta waow, t'eva heinéa waow, te tanè a waow, teinai ye waow, e tottee era waow, e moo era waow, e pai era waow, e tei moore era waow, e tei whattee era waow, é tei niea era waow, e doo doo wai too mahioee, tootromaoo tooaipai toowaiwhatta too te whainè toota pèà tooaimooa e tootre deeree too wai doeo.

MENS NAMES.

Arabo.	Teetee.	Tooaoo.
Oaiyo.	Tiaree.	Toobaiah.
Obade.	Tirooduah.	Toobairoo,
Otapairoo.	Tirooroo.	Toopuah.
Otee.		

WOMENS NAMES.

Aidada.	Matai Irowhoa.	Oteateah.
Deaiyo.	Otapairoo.	Tirahaow diea.

Names of Islands near Otaheite.

Aiteah.	Maowrooah.	Tabuahmanoo.
Atiarabo.	Matea.	Taha.
Bola-bola.	Mopipahau.	Taheeree.
Bimayo.	Oheiteroah.	Tetiroah.
Huaheine.	Onooahaora.	Toopbai.
Maitoo.	Otahau.	Yoolee-Etea.

NUMERATION.

Tohe,	*One.*
Rooa,	*Two.*
Torhoo,	*Three.*
Ha,	*Four.*
Illemei,	*Five.*
Whaine,	*Six.*
Hitoo,	*Seven.*
Walhoo,	*Eight.*
Iva,	*Nine,*
Hoolhoo,	*Ten.*
Matohe,	*Eleven.*

Marooa,

Marooa,	*Twelve.*
Matorhoo,	*Thirteen.*
Maha,	*Fourteen.*
Maillemei,	*Fifteen.*
Mawhaine,	*Sixteen.*
Mahitoo,	*Seventeen.*
Mawalhoo,	*Eighteen.*
Maiva,	*Nineteen.*
Arooato,	*Twenty.*

REMARKS *on the Otaheitean Language.*

The language is very foft, having a great number of vowels, diphthongs, and triphthongs.

Every word, almoft, begins with a vowel, which they moft commonly drop.

It is alfo very metaphorical, as I have obferved in many inftances; as Matapoa, a perfon blind of an eye, which literally is Night-eye. Mataavai, the name of the bay we anchored in, literally fignifies Watery-eye; which appellation is not unapt from the great quantity of rain which falls in the bay. Tehaia, a woman's name, who being loft when a child, her friends went about, crying Tehai ? which means, Where is fhe ?

The natives could not repeat, after us, the founds of the letters, Q, X, and Z, without great difficulty; G, K, and S, they could not pronounce at all.

Many of the names of the people of our fhip having the G, K, or S, in them, they could not approach nearer the found of them than as follows:

Toote,	for	Cook.	Matà	for	Monkhoufe.
Opane	——	Banks.	Petrodero	——	Pickerfgill.
Tolano	——	Solander.	Tate	——	Clark.
Treene	——	Green.	Poline	——	Spoving.
Hite	——	Hicks.	Taibe	——	Stainfby.
Towara	——	Gore.	Patine	——	Parkinfon.

They

They have various founds peculiar to themfelves, which none of us could imitate; fome of them they pronounced like B and L mingled together; others between B and P, and T and D. Some like B h, L h, and D h.

When they mean to fpeak of a thing fomewhat fmall, they often double the word, as Oorè oorè, a fmallifh nail.

They alfo double the word for the fuperlative, as Teá teá, very white.

Mai, when placed after a verb, fignifies that the action was done to you.

Mai, when added to an adverb, fignifies feveral things, as Mai Maroo, fome-what foft, or inclining to be foft.

They have a whoop, when they call after any perfon, which they pronounce like Ahu ! raifing their voice very high at the laft fyllable.

On the 11th, the tents were ftruck, and we got every thing on board; but, on examining the anchor-ftocks, we found them very much worm-eaten, and were obliged to wait till the carpenter had made new ones, which detained us two days longer. None of the Indians came near us till the next day, except Toobaiah, who is a fort of high-prieft of Otaheite; and he defigned to fail with us; however, feveral of the principal natives fent their fervants on board with prefents; we fent them others in return, and left them tolerably well reconciled to us.

On the 13th, feveral of the natives came on board to take leave of us, to whom we made fome prefents; and, at parting with us, they appeared very forrowful. In the forenoon we weighed anchor, and failed, with a fine breeze, from the weft, fteering our courfe W. by N. having Toobaiah, and his little boy Taiyota, on board with us. [See pl. IX.] On our leaving the fhore, the people in the canoes fet up their woeful cry, Awai, Awai; and the young women wept very much. Some of the canoes came up to the fide of the fhip, while fhe was under fail, and brought us many cocoas.

Toward

Plate IX.

The Lad Tuiyota, Native of Otaheite, in the Dress of his Country.

Toward night we faw an ifland called, by Toobaiah, Tetiroah, and altered our courfe a little to the weftward, fteering for the ifland of Yoolee-Etea, the native place of Toobaiah.

On the 14th, we difcovered the ifle of Huaheine, which is high land, but the wind being againft us, we could not reach it; we therefore tacked about, and took a ftretch toward an ifland that we faw at a diftance, which Toobaiah told us was Yoolee-Etea.

In the afternoon of this day it was almoft calm; and we had but little wind till the next day, being the 15th: at noon we had a fine breeze; and at five in the afternoon were within fix leagues of the ifland of Huaheine. It was made up of feveral peaks of high land, and divided, like Otaheite, by fome lower land intervening. The ifland appeared to be almoft as large again as Eimayo; and, from the maft-head, we could difcover the tops of the mountains of Yoolee-Etea, over thofe of Huaheine.

Toobaiah praying in the afternoon, in the ftern-windows, called out, with much fervor, O Tane, ara mai, matai, ora mai matai; which is to fay, Tane (the god of his Morai) fend to me, or come to me with a fair wind; but his prayer proving ineffectual, he faid, *Wooreede waow*, I am angry. However, he told us that we fhould have wind when the fun arrived at the meridian, and fo it happened, though we did not impute to him the gift of prophecy or forefight.

Toobaiah told us they often had wars with the natives of Atiarabo, a neighbouring ifland; and that, when they take any of them prifoners, they cut off their under-jaws, and hang them up. Several of thefe trophies of victory Mr. Banks faw hung up in a man's houfe at Atiarabo, in one of his excurfions among the people of Oboreano, at a time when they had made prifoners Oroamo's four brothers, and two of Oboreah's, and had taken all her canoes.

Early

Early on the 16th, we were clofe to the fhore of the ifland of Huaheine; but, meeting with no fafe place to anchor in, we doubled the point, and went to the N. W. fide of the ifland, where we anchored, in a pretty little bay, clofe by the fhore in eleven fathom water : the water was very fmooth, and the banks fhoaled fo fteep, that we might have rid' fafe within forty yards off the fhore. Several canoes came off to us as we failed along the coaft, and fome of the natives came on board, amongft whom was a king, who was the firft that adventured to come up the fhip's fide, and he approached it trembling. Toobaiah converfed with them very freely.

This country affords a more pleafing profpect than Otaheite, being more pic-turefque. Some of the hills are very high ; and, from this bay, we can fee the iflands Yoolee-Etea, Otahau, and Bolabola; which laft appears like a hill of a conical form, forked at the top. Before the bay, and a good way farther on, runs a reef which opens at the two ends, but has no opening in the front. The Captain, Toobaiah, and fome others, went on fhore with the aree, or king ; and, as foon as he landed, he immediately repaired to an adjacent morai, and returned thanks to Tane for his fafe paffage, whom he prefented with two handkerchiefs, and fome other trifles ; and, to the furgeon who affifted him, he prefented a hog.

On the 17th, feveral of the inhabitants came on board, and brought with them fome cocoa-nuts ; and one of them, a friend of mine from Otaheite, brought a bafket of pafte or pudding, baked in bread-fruit leaves, which was made of the roots of Taro and cocoa-nuts: they call it Etaoo, and it taftes very much like the poe of Otaheite, and is very good food. The cuftom of changing names prevails much in this ifland, and is deemed a mark of great friendfhip.

During the fhort time we were upon the coaft of this ifland, we purchafed twenty-four hogs and pigs, befides fowls, fruits, and roots, at reafonable rates ; but they raifed the price of their commodities before we left them.

This

This ifland, the extent of which we had not time to learn, is confiderably longer than broad; and, to all appearance, very fruitful in cocoas, bread-fruit, plantains, and eatable-roots, fuch as taro, eape, and the fweet potatoe. Thefe roots, with different forts of pafte, are their principal food when there is no bread-fruit. They have a plenty of cuttle-fifh, but not fo many of other kinds as are to be found at Otaheite. Their cloth-tree is planted very neatly, and cultivated with great care, having drains made through the beds of earth to draw off the water; and the fides neatly built up with ftones: and, in the drains, they plant the arum which yields the yam they call Taro.

We found great quantities of a baftard fort of fhagreen upon the ifland, and many pearls of an indifferent fort.

The natives of this ifland are not of fuch a dark complexion as thofe of Otaheite, and the other neighbouring iflands; and the women are, in general, as handfome, and nearly of the fame colour, as Europeans; [fee pl. VIII. fig. 3 and 4.] from which we may draw a reafon for the name of this pretty ifland ||, which I left regretting that I did not fee more of it.

On the 19th, in the afternoon, we fet fail for Yoolee-Etea, and the next morning, being the 20th, we caft anchor in a bay, which is formed by a reef, on the north fide of this ifland. Two canoes of people came to us from the fhore, and brought with them two fmall hogs; they took but little notice of us, and expreffed as little furprize at any thing they faw. The captain went on fhore and took poffeffion of the ifland for the king; he faw but few inhabitants, and fcarce any of diftinguifhed rank amongft them. They behaved fo coolly that the captain did not know what to make of them. Toobaiah, who was with him, feemed to be quite difpleafed. We did not know the occafion of their refervednefs; but conjectured that the Bolobola people had been amongft them.

|| Huaheine, the name of this ifland, means alfo a wife.

On the 21ſt, ſome of us went on ſhore, and bought many plantains, and cocoa-nuts. The plantains were moſtly green, and, boiled or roaſted, ate as well as a potatoe.

In the afternoon we went on ſhore again, and ſaw but few of the natives in the country, which, though very pleaſant, looks like an uninhabited or deſerted place. We ſaw ſome morais, [ſee pl. X.] or burial places, which are ſimilar in all theſe iſlands; and went into one of them, in which there was a whatee, or altar, with a roaſted hog, and fiſh upon it, deſigned as an offering to the Ethooa, or god. Near to the whatee, or altar, there was a large houſe, which contained the coong-drums uſed at their ſolemnities: and, adjoining to this houſe, were ſeveral large cages of wood, having awnings of palm-leaves upon them. Theſe cages are called Oro, and reſted upon beams laid upon others that ſtood upright, and ſeemed in-tended for the reception of the birds ſacred to Ethooa, of which there are two that fly about their morais, the grey heron, and a blue and brown king-fiſher. Theſe morais are paved, or rather covered with a ſort of coral, and planted with various ſorts of flowering ſhrubs, ſuch as nonoah, etoa, and hibiſcus. At the front of the morai, which faces the ſea, they have built a ſort of amphitheatre, of large rough ſtones; and, among theſe ſtones, there are a great many long boards ſet up, carved in various figures, according to their fancy. Every family of note has one of theſe morais ornamented as much as they can afford *. I have been told, that the inhabitants of theſe three iſles worſhip the rainbow, which they call Toomeitee no Tane.

On

* A kind of prieſt, [ſee pl. XI.] called heiva, attends theſe Morais, cloathed in a feather gar-ment, ornamented with round pieces of mother-of-pearl, and a very high cap on his head, made of cane, or bamboo; the front of which is feather-work; the edges beſet with quills ſtripped of the plumage. He has alſo a ſort of breaſt-plate, of a ſemicircular ſhape, made of a kind of wicker-work; on which they weave their plaited twine in a variety of figures: over this they put feathers of a green pigeon in rows; and between the rows is a ſemicircular row of ſhark's teeth. The edge of the breaſt-plate is fringed with fine white dog's hair.

This prieſt is commonly attended with two boys, painted black, who aſſiſt him in placing the hog and fiſh for the Ethooa; as alſo in ſtrewing the body of the defunct with leaves and flowers of bamboo; and,

Plate X.

J. Parkinson del.

Ja. Newton Sculp.

A Morai or Burial Place, in the Island of Yoolee=Etea.

Plate XI.

S. Parkinson del.   *T. Chambers Sculp.*

An Heiva, or kind of Priest of Yoolee=Etea, & the Neighbouring Islands.

Oɲ the 24th, in the afternoon, we went out at the weft end of the bay, which the natives call Opou, but found our paffage very difficult on account of the fhoals, one of which we narrowly efcaped: the man, who founded, crying out Two fathom, we wore fhip directly, or we fhould have been on a bank. At length, however, we cleared the fhoals; but not being able to get out in time, anchored over-againft a deep bay; and fome of our men went on fhore to look for hogs.

This ifland is, in many refpects, much like Huaheine, and the country as much variegated; but this fide of the ifland feems to have undergone fome revolution; the inhabitants are but few, and poor, and have no political diftinction of rank amongft them. The fhagreen is in greater plenty here, and at Huaheine, than at Otaheite, where it was a fcarce commodity. They have alfo great plenty of taro, and eape. As to the bread-fruit it was but young; and of apples I faw none.

On the 25th, we fet fail from the bay of Owhare, and fteered our courfe to the weftward, defigning to go to Bolobola, or round Otahau, to the fouth-fide of Yoolee-Etea; but, the wind blowing from the weftward, we could not double the point of Otahau; fo that we did nothing that day but traverfe the coaft of Bolobola.

The ifland of Bolobola is made up of one very high forked peak of land, with feven low hills round it.

In the evening, at fun-fet, we difcovered the ifland of Toopbai, making in low land.

and, for two or three days after, is conftantly employed in ranging the adjacent fields and woods, from which every one retires on his approach. The relations, in the mean time, build a temporary houfe near the Morai, where they affemble, and the females mourn for the deceafed, by finging fongs of grief, howling, and wounding their bodies in different places with fhark's teeth; after which they bathe their wounds in the fea or river, and again return to howl and cut themfelves, which they continue for three days. After the body is corrupted, and the bones become bare, the fkeleton is depofited in a fort of ftone pyramid built for that purpofe.

On

On the 28th, the wind blowing full from the weſt, and being often becalmed, we could not weather the point, the wind hauling round the iſland, and meeting us as we tacked about.

In the evening, Mr. Banks, Dr. Solander, and the Maſter, went on ſhore, in the pinnace, to Otahau, and, not returning ſo ſoon as expected, we fired a cannon at nine o'clock; and, ſtill neither ſeeing nor hearing of them, we fired another, and hung out a light in the ſhrouds. We were ſoon anſwered by them with a muſket, by which we found they had got out to ſea; and about ten they arrived, and brought with them three hogs, fifteen fowls, with a great quantity of plantains, cocoa-nuts, and taro.

This iſland is but thinly inhabited, and ſome parts of it very barren.—We had a great ſwell among theſe iſlands.

On the 30th, we went round to Bolobola, and beat up to windward, to get to the other ſide of Yoolee-Etea, and had a ſharp breeze from the S. E. all night. This day we ſaw the iſland of Maowrooah, conſiſting of a large round hill, with a ſmall one on the ſide of it.

On the 1ſt of Auguſt, after ſo long beating to windward, we at laſt got along-ſide of Yoolee-Etea; but even then we could not get into the bay which we deſigned to enter; and, the wind being againſt us, we were obliged to caſt anchor at the entrance of it, between two reefs. In the afternoon we attempted to warp the ſhip into the bay, but endeavouring to heave the anchor, we found it was faſtened to ſome rock, where we left it till the next morning. The natives came off to us in great numbers, and we bought of them ten hogs, for ten ſpikes each, with plenty of cocoas, and plantains, and they ſeemed very joyful at our arrival.

Early on the 2d, we attempted again to get up the anchor; with ſome difficulty happily ſucceeded; and, afterwards, warpt the ſhip into the bay, which is called Amameenee, and moored her in a proper ſtation, about a mile from ſhore. The natives flocked to us again; appeared highly delighted, and were ſo fond of

our

our commodities, that, for a few small nails, they gave us many things of confiderable value amongst them; and whatever we gave them, whether nails, pewter, watches, or other toys, were immediately hung upon their ears.

On the 4th, we went on shore, and took a walk up into the country, which is very pleasant, and saw a great quantity of Taro and Eape growing: We saw alfo a great quantity of the true Yam, which is so common in the West-Indies; and bread-fruit trees, which were nearly in perfection; though the crop of fruit upon them did not appear to be so large as I have seen.

There are several Morais in this part of the island; in one of which we saw a string of jaw-bones hung up on the Afale, or house, of the Ethooa, with several skulls laid in rows: and we met a man of a fair complexion, whose hair was white as milk; also their Aree Dehei, or king, who is called Oorea, and his son; the former appeared to be a very modest fort of a man, and the latter as handsome a youth as I ever saw. Opoone, who is king of Bolobola, stays in the next bay; they say he is a very old man, and we suppose the people of this island have submitted to him *.

The border of low land round the hills is very narrow here, and not very populous; but several of the inhabitants are comely, and in a much more flourishing

* Toobaiah informed us, that, some years past, the chiefs of Otaheite, and the neighbouring islands, banished such of their criminals as were convicted of thefts, and other crimes which they thought did not deserve death, to an adjacent island called Bolobola, which, before the commencement of that law, was almost barren and uninhabited; which practice continued several years. In procefs of time their numbers so greatly increased, that the island was insufficient for their subsistence. Being men of desperate fortunes, they made themselves canoes, turned pirates, and made prisoners such of the people of the islands near them as had the misfortune to fall in their way, and seized their canoes and effects. Opoone, who was one of the worst of these criminals, by artful insinuations so wrought on the rest, that he was admitted their chief, or king; and, growing still more powerful, by frequent acquisitions of prisoners, he adventured to make war on the people of Otahaw, a neighbouring island, who, not expecting so sudden an invasion, were not prepared for defence, and were obliged to submit to be tributaries to him. He afterwards conquered Yoolce-etea, and other islands, which he annexed to his dominion of Bolobola.

state

ſtate than thoſe on the other ſide of the iſland, who are men of Yoolee-etea, or men of Bolobola, we could not learn which.

There is a great number of boat-houſes all round the bays, [ſee pl. XII.] built with a Catanarian arch, thatched all over; and the boats kept in them are very long, bellying out on the ſides, with a very high peaked ſtern, and are uſed only at particular ſeaſons.

We had a great quantity of fiſh brought on board in the afternoon of this day, and three pounds and a half were ſerved to each man of the ſhip's company.

On the 7th, in the afternoon, Mr. Banks and myſelf went to ſee an entertainment called an Heivo. We paſſed over four bays E. and were carried, by the natives, till we came to the bottom of a bay called Tapeeoee, where a number of people was aſſembled. A large mat was laid upon the ground, and they began to dance upon it, putting their bodies into ſtrange motions, writhing their mouths, and ſhaking their tails, which made the numerous plaits that hung about them flutter like a peacock's train. Sometimes they ſtood in a row one behind another, and then they fell down with their faces to the ground, leaning on their arms, and ſhaking only their tails, the drums beating all the while, with which they kept exact time. An old man ſtood by as a prompter, and roared out as loud as he could at every change. Theſe motions they continued till they were all in a ſweat; they repeated them three times alternately, and, after they had done, the girls began. In the interval, between the ſeveral parts of the drama, ſome men came forward, who ſeemed to act the part of drolls; and, by what I could diſtinguiſh, they attempted to repreſent the Conqueſt of Yoolee-etea, by the men of Bolobola; in which they exhibited the various ſtratagems uſed in the conqueſt, and were very vociferous, performing all in time to the drum. In the laſt ſcene, the actions of the men were very laſcivious.

The people, in the part where this farce was performed, are chiefly Bolobola men, and they ſeem to be ſettled in the beſt part of the iſland, the low-land being wider here than in any other part near the harbour. On this coaſt there are many ſpits and ſhoals, formed of coral rocks; and, on the reef, the ſurf breaks very

high,

Plate XII.

S. Parkinson del.   T. Newton fec.

A Boat-House, in which the Natives of Yoolee-Etea, and the
Neighbouring Islands, preserve their Canoes of State from the Weather.

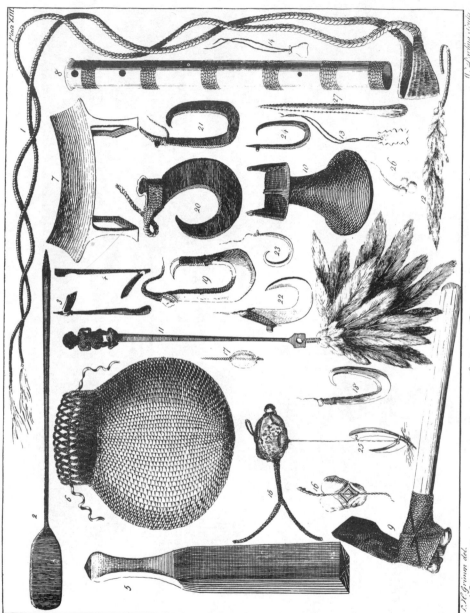

Plate XIII

R.B. Grimm del.   W. Darling Sculp

Various Instruments, & Utensils, of the Natives of Otaheite, &c of the adjacent Islands

high, and makes a noise as loud as thunder.   There are some plantations of pepper in this part of the island.

It is remarkable, that, notwithstanding the people of these islands cannot pronounce the sound of the letter K, yet I have met with a great number in Yoolee-etea, who, having a *bec* in their speech, continually substitute it instead of that of their favourite letter T.

The UTENSILS of the inhabitants of the island of Otaheite, and the neighbouring islands, being similar, we have here annexed a plate of some of them, to which we have occasionally referred ; but, as we have not mentioned the sizes of them, we shall here recapitulate those drawn in the plate, and shall give a particular account of each.   The number of the plate is XIII. of which,

No. 1. Is a Sling, about four feet long, made of plaited twine, formed from the fibres of the bark of a tree ; the part, which holds the stone, is woven very close, and looks like cloth, from which the string gradually tapers to a point.

2. The Paddle, made of wood neatly shaped, and worked very smooth, used to strike the instruments No. 3 and 4, wherewith they indent or mark their skins, which they call Tataowing.   It is about eighteen inches long.

3. and 4. Are their Tataowing Instruments, the handles of which are wood ; towards the end of which is a hollow made to lay the fore-finger of the hand in which holds it : the head is made of one or two flat pieces of bone, of various breadths, tapering to a point towards the handle, to which it is fastened very tight with fibres of the bark of a tree: the broad part, or bottom, is cut into many small sharp teeth.   When they mark any person, they dip the instrument, a small one or large one, according to the figure intended, into a black liquid, or juice, expressed from some plant, and, placing it on the part intended to be marked,

marked, give it a fmall blow with the paddle, which caufes a great deal of pain. Thefe inftruments are about five inches in length.

5. The Cloth-beater, about fourteen inches long.

6. One of their Bafkets; round the mouth is a kind of netting made of plaited twine, through which a ftring is put, which draws the plaiting together, and clofes up the mouth. It is eleven inches high, and three feet in circumference.

7. An Ebupa, or Stool, ufed as a pillow; they generally put a piece of their cloth on it before they lay their head on it. There are many fizes of them; the very large ones they ufe alfo as ftools to fit on. This, expreffed in the figure, was twelve inches and a half long; but fome are of the length of two feet.

8. Is one of their Flutes, made of Bamboo, and ornamented with the plaited twine, which alfo ftrengthens it; they are about one foot and a half long.

9. One of their Hatchets, the handle of this was fourteen inches and a half long; the head about four inches and a half in length, and the edge about two inches broad.

10. Is a figure of the Stone Pafte-beater: this was feven inches and a quarter high.

11. A Fly-flap, the handle made of a hard brown wood, is thirteen inches long.

12. The Feather-Ornament for the Head, fix inches long.

13, 14. Mother-of-pearl Ornaments for the Ears, about half an inch long.

15. The Decoy ufed in fifhing, made of fhells; the length, from the head to the extremity of the tail, feven inches and a half.

16. A Bone Plummet for their fifhing lines, carved, two inches and a quarter long.

17. Another Plummet, made of Spar, about one inch long.

18. A

18. A Mother-of-pearl Fish-hook, two inches long.

19. A Fish-hook made of wood, and pointed with a piece of shell, three inches and three quarters long.

20. A Fish-hook made of a large Pinna-marina shell, three inches and three quarters long.

21. Another Fish-hook, made of a large Pinna-marina shell, three inches and three quarters long.

22. Another ditto, made of Mother-of-pearl, two inches long.

23. Another ditto, three quarters of an inch in length.

24. Another ditto, made of Pinna-marina shell, one inch and half long.

25. Another ditto, made of two pieces of Mother-of-pearl, one for the shank, the other for the point. The line is fastened both at the top and bottom. The points of these hooks are sometimes barbed like ours; at the bottom they tie some hair.

26. Three Pearls tied together by plaited hair, worn as an ornament for the ears: each pearl was about the size of a small pea.

27. Sting of a Sting-Ray, used to point their lances and arrows, four inches and a half long.

A JOURNAL

A

J O U R N A L

O F A

V O Y A G E to the S O U T H   S E A S,

In his Majefty's Ship The E N D E A V O U R.

P A R T II.

O N the 9th of Auguft we weighed anchor, and proceeded from this bay to the fouthward, to fee what difcoveries we could make there, purfuant to the directions of the admiralty, and carried with us as many hogs from this ifland as we could ftow, with a great number of Plantains, Taro, Eape, and Yams, to ferve us inftead of bread.

On the 13th, at noon, having had a brifk wind for three days, we difcovered high land, and, toward night, approached near it. Toobaiah informed us that it was an ifland called Oheiteroah, being one of the clufter of nine, and bore the title of Oheite added to them.

We hauled in our wind, and, on the 14th, in the morning, bore down to the ifland, and hoifted out the pinnace, in which Mr. Banks and Dr. Solander went

on

on fhore to feek for an anchoring place in a large bay formed by two points of land. They returned with an account that they could find none, nor any good landing for the boat: and that, when they got near the fhore, feveral of the natives jumped into the pinnace, and attempted to feize on Mr. Banks, which obliged our people to fire, and fome of the natives were wounded. They were armed with long clubs, and fpears, made of the wood of a tree which they called Etoa; and their cloaths were red and yellow, made of bark, ftriped and figured very regularly, and covered with gum. They had alfo curious caps on their heads, and made a very martial appearance. Mr. Banks brought fome wooden-work on board, very ingenioufly wrought, and told us that they faw canoes which were carved with great ingenuity, and painted very neat.

Thefe people are very tall, well proportioned, and have long hair, which they tie up, [fee pl. VIII. fig. 5 and 6.] and are tataowed, or marked on different parts of their bodies, but not on their pofteriors, like the people of the other iflands. On one of our boats approaching them, they began to talk to Toobaiah, though they feemed very much intimidated, and begged that our people would not kill them; and faid they would not furnifh us with any eatables unlefs we came on fhore, which they intreated us much to do. They faw no women among them. From the fhip we obferved a few houfes.

This ifland does not fhoot up into high peaks, like the others, but is more even and uniform, divided into fmall hillocks, like England, which are here and there covered with tufts of trees. At the water's edge there are many clifts almoft per-pendicular. We faw no bread-fruit, and very few cocoas; but all along the edge of the beach was thick planted with Etoa, which ferved to fhelter their houfes and plantations of Meiya from the wind.

This ifland is fituate in 22° 23' fouth latitude, and 150° 5' weft longitude, and has no reef furrounding it, like the other iflands.

On the 15th, in the morning, we paffed the tropic of Capricorn, having a fine breeze from the north, with clear pleafant weather; and faw feveral tropic birds.

On

On the 16th, we faw the appearance of feveral high peaks of land, which deceived us all: we bore away for them, but, the fky clearing up, we found our miftake, and fo refumed our courfe to the fouth. Thermometer 72, and a cold air.

On the 17th, we were becalmed moft part of the day, and had a great fwell from the weft in latitude 26° 25′ S. Thermometer 70.

On the 20th, we had light breezes, and were often becalmed; but, toward night, we had a brifk breeze from the north, which increafing, we brought the fhip to, under the two topfails, and remained fo all night, and had a continual fwell, which made the fhip roll very much.

On the 21ft, we had a ftiff gale all day, with hazy weather, and fome thunder and lightening from the weft; we fcudded before the wind, having the forefail and two topfails clofe-reefed fet. The fwell was fo great that the fhip rolled pro-digioufly, and every thing was thrown down. We faw feveral Pintado birds, and Shear-waters.

On the 22d, we had fine clear weather, and the wind much abated. We faw fome Albatroffes, and feveral Pintado birds. This bird is barred on the wing with black and white, from whence the name in Spanifh, a Cheque-board. We alfo faw feveral parcels of fea-weed. Latitude 31° 3′ S. Wind S. W. and by W.

On the 23d, we had light breezes, and it was calm moft part of the day. To-ward night, it rained very hard, with the wind to the north. We faw a grampus, or young whale, and an albatrofs. Lat. 32° 5′.

On the 24th, we had heavy fqualls, with rain, from the fouth, and faw a water-fpout. The wind ftill continuing to blow very hard, we lay-to under our main-fail; and, in the night, the wind was exceffive cold.

On

On the 25th, we had fair weather, but the air was ſtill ſharp, though the wind was moderate, and came about to the S. W. Lat. 32° 3′. Thermometer 62.

On the 26th, we had variable weather, with a weſterly wind, and ſaw a grampus and an albatroſs.   Latitude 32° 15′.

On the 27th, we had clear weather, with the wind at north, but, toward the evening, it was ſqually.   We ſaw ſeveral albatroſſes, pintados, and ſhear-waters. Latitude 33° 35′.——On the ſame day we killed a dog, and dreſſed him, which we brought from Yoolee-Etea: he was exceſſively fat, although he had eaten nothing while he had been on board.

On the 28th, we had hazy weather, and a drizzling rain all day, with a faint breeze from the north, and ſaw a great many birds called Shear-coots.   This morning, John Raden, the boatſwain's mate, died.   His death was occaſioned by drinking too freely of rum the night before.   In the evening the wind came about to the weſt, and, the next morning, the 29th, the weather being clear, at about four o'clock we ſaw a comet, about 60 degrees above the horizon.   Latitude 37°.

On the 30th, we had a briſk breeze, and a great ſwell from the weſt, with fair clear weather, but very cold.   The Thermometer, in open air, was at 52. One of Mr. Banks's ſervants ſaw a bird of a fine green colour, and likewiſe ſome ſea-weed.   In the night, we had heavy ſhowers of hail, and ſudden guſts of wind, which were very piercing, and ſo violent, that we were obliged to lay the ſhip to under the foreſail.   The ſame weather continued all the next day, the 31ſt, accompanied with a high ſwell from the weſt, which made the ſhip run gunnel-to under water.   A vaſt number of birds, of different kinds, followed us all day, ſporting on the ſurface of the water.   Theſe were Pintados, (a bird of a ſilver colour, ſuch as we ſaw in the Atlantic ocean,) Albatroſſes, and various ſorts of Procellariæ.   Several parcels of rock-weed were alſo ſeen by ſome of our people.   Latitude 39° 25′ S.   Thermometer, in open air, 48.

Oa

On the 1st of September, we had hard piercing gales and squalls from the W. and N. W. with violent showers of hail and rain. The sea ran mountain-high, and tossed the ship upon the waves: she rolled so much, that we could get no rest, or scarcely lie in bed, and almost every moveable on board was thrown down, and rolled about from place to place. In brief, a person, who has not been in a storm at sea, cannot form an adequate idea of the situation we were in. The wind still increasing, we laid the ship to under the foresail. The heavens, however, being clear, at four in the morning, we saw the comet again between Aldebaran and Orion. Latitude, by account, 40° and odd; and Thermometer 44.

On the 2d, we had hard gales, and squally weather. About noon we set the mainsail, and bore away N. N. W. the captain having, pursuant to his orders, gone in search of the continent as far as 40° south latitude, and determined to stand to the southward, to see what discoveries he could make in that quarter, apprehending that, if we continued much longer in these high latitudes, we should not have sails enough to carry us home : besides, the weather was so tempestuous, that, had we made land, it would not have been safe to have approached near it.— The course which we have steered to the southward, has been mostly between 147 and 150 degrees, west longitude.

On the 3d, we had dark and gloomy weather, with a light westerly breeze, and the air was very cold.

On the 5th, we had variable weather, with some rain : we saw some Albatrosses with white beaks, and others all white, except the tips of their wings.

On the 6th, we had hard gales from the west, which obliged us to go under our courses; but the weather was clear, though cold.

On the 8th, we were becalmed most part of the morning; but, in the afternoon, the wind came about easterly, and brought with it some rain.

On

On the 9th, we had a fine breeze, all day, from the fouth, with clear weather; and, toward night, faw fome parcels of fea-weed.—This day a whole allowance of beef was given to the fhip's company.

On the 10th, we had fqually weather, with the wind at S. S. W. faw fome fea-weed, and had feveral white fqualls, which looked as if we had been near land.

On the 11th, we had fome fqualls, with light fhowers of rain, and the wind at S. W.

On the 12th, the wind varied between S. and W. and we had agreeable clear weather, with fome few fqualls. Latitude 33° 18′. Thermometer 57.

On the 14th, we had moderate, though variable, weather, with the wind at north. We faw feveral Albatroffes flying about the fhip, and two very large ones, quite white, fwimming upon the water.

On the 15th, we had hard gales of wind from the E. and S. E. the weather very hazy, with fome rain, and faw a few Pintados.

On the 16th, the weather was fqually, but clear, and the wind S. W.

On the 18th, we were becalmed moft part of the day; however, the weather was clear, and the wind S. W.

On the 19th, it was calm till the afternoon, and then we had a fhort breeze from the eaft. Mr. Banks went in the boat, and fhot fome Pintados, and caught fome Molufca, Doris, Phyllodore, and the fine purple Limax, which were fwimming upon the water. At night the water was full of flafhes of light, occafioned by the Molufca. Latitude 29° S. Longitude 159 W. and we had a great fwell from the S. W.

On

On the 21ft, we had a fmart breeze from the S. E. fuppofed to be the tail of the trade winds, with clear weather. This breeze continued till the 24th, with fair and moderate weather. We fteered S. S. W. in hopes of difcovering the continent. Latitude 31° 24′ fouth, and 162 weft longitude.

On that day the wind came about to the eaft: we faw fome fea-weeds, and a log of wood about three feet long.

On the 26th, we had a frefh breeze from the north, with the weather gloomy. We faw feveral parcels of fea-weed, of that kind called Leather-weed, in latitude 35° 53′ S. 162 longitude. In the night we had a very hard gale from the north, with heavy fhowers of rain.

On the 27th, early in the morning, the wind was moderate, but the fea ran very high, and the fhip rolled fo much that every moveable on board was thrown about; and it was with great difficulty that we faved ourfelves from being toffed out of our cots. The night came on while we were in this fituation, which proved very dark, and every thing confpired to make it difmal, and aggravate our diftrefs. The next morning, however, was fair; the heavens cloudlefs; the fun rofe peculiarly bright, and we had a fine breeze from the weft. In the afternoon the wind veered to the north, and we faw many parcels of fea-weed of different forts. We alfo faw a feal, and concluded that we were not far from land. Latitude 37° 30′ fouth.

On the 28th, we had a frefh gale from the weft, which continued till noon, and then chopped about to the S. W. We altered our courfe to W. N. W. having run to the fouth as far as 40° latitude, and longitude 166° weft; met with fome fea-weed; and faw feveral black-beaked Albatroffes and Shear-waters.

On the 29th, we had a fmart breeze from the fouth, with clear, though fharp weather; thermometer 54; — faw feveral parcels of fea-weed, and a land-bird that flew like a plover; with a great number of Pintados, Shear-waters, and large white Albatroffes, with the tips of their wings black. We founded, but found no bottom, with 120 fathoms of line. The captain apprehended that we were near
land,

land, and promifed one gallon of rum to the man who fhould firft difcover it by day, and two if he difcovered it by night; alfo, that part of the coaft of the faid land fhould be named after him.

On the 1ft of October, the weather was fair, but very cold, and almoft calm. In the morning, we faw a feal afleep upon the furface of the water, which had, at firft, the appearance of a log of wood; we put the fhip about to take it up, but it waked, and dived out of fight. Great flocks of Shear-waters flew about the fhip, and feveral parcels of fea-weed floated by the fide of it. We found, by this day's obfervation, that we had gone ten leagues farther to the northward, than what appeared by the log-account. The mafter was fent in queft of a current, but could find none. Latitude 37° 45' fouth, and 172° longitude, weft from London.

Though we had been fo long out at fea, in a diftant part of the world, we had a roafted leg of mutton, and French-beans for dinner; and the fare of Old England afforded us a grateful repaft.

This day we founded, and found no bottom at 120 fathoms.

On the 2d, the fea was as fmooth as the Thames, and the weather fair and clear. Mr. Banks went out in a little boat, and diverted himfelf in fhooting of Shear-waters, with one white Albatrofs, that meafured, from the tip of one wing to the other, ten feet, feven inches; and alfo picked up a great many weeds of various kinds: we faw alfo feveral forts of rock-weed; and the water looked as green as it does in the channel.

On the 4th, we had light breezes from the S. E. with clear fharp weather. In the morning we faw fome rock-weed; and, in the evening, a great fhoal of bottle-nofed porpoifes fwam along-fide of the fhip, with a great number of other porpoifes, having fharp white fnouts, and their fides and bellies of the fame colour.

On the 5th, we had light breezes from the N. E. and pleafant weather: about two o'clock in the afternoon one of our people, Nicholas Young, the furgeon's boy, defcried a point of land, of New Zealand, from the ftarboard bow, at about

nine

nine leagues diftance, bearing W. and by N. we bore up to it, and, at fun-fet, we had a good view of it. The land was high, and it appeared like an ifland. We regaled ourfelves in the evening upon the occafion; the land was called Young Nick's Head, and the boy received his reward. The fea, on this coaft, was full of a fmall tranfparent animal, which, upon examination, we called Beroe Coaretata. Latitude 38° 49' *.

On the 8th, we had light breezes and dead calms all day, and could not get in nearer the land than two or three leagues; but it appeared, at this diftance, to be of confiderable extent, with many fmall iflands around it; and had rifing hills like the coaft of Portugal. We faw fmoke afcend from different parts, and thence concluded that it was inhabited. The two extreme points of the land bore N. and S. S. W. We faw feveral grampuffes, but few birds.

On the 9th, early in the morning, the wind being favourable, we ftood in nearer land, where it feemed to open and form a deep bay; [fee pl. XIV.] but, on approaching it, we difcovered low land, and it was much fhallower than we expected. Upon entering we had regular foundings all the way, from twenty-fix to fix fathoms, and caft anchor on the eaft fide in ten fathoms water, about two or three miles from the fhore, over-againft the land on the right, where there was the appearance of a river. At the entrance of the bay, which is a very large one, being about three leagues in breadth, and two in depth, are feveral chalky cliffs, from which runs a low ridge of land that ends in a hillock: at a little diftance from the hillock, there is a fmall high ifland, and, on the top of it, an inclofure of pales. Abundance of white cliffs are feen all along the coaft; and the hills appear to be covered with fmall wood and bufhes, affording but an indifferent landfcape. We difcovered feveral houfes by our glaffes. They feemed to be thatched, and the eaves of them reached to the ground. Within the bay there are many hills one behind another; though moft part of the bay is furrounded by a valley in which is a number of trees; from whence, as well as other parts of the country, we faw fome fmoke arife. We alfo

* As we have, in pl. XXV. given a map of the coaft of New Zealand, in which the latitudes and longitudes, of the feveral places we explored, are correctly fet down, we fhall, in our account of that ifland, omit mentioning the fituation of places in that refpect, and, once for all, refer the reader to the map.

difcovered

Plate XIV.

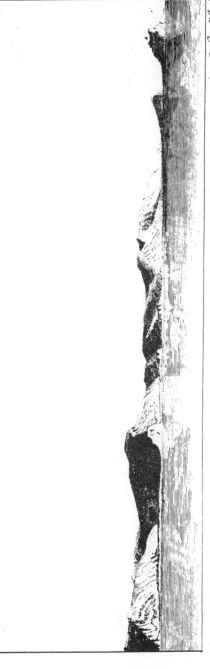

1. Young Nick's Head. 2. Morai Island.

View of the North Side of the Entrance into Poverty Bay, & Morai Island, in New-Zealand.

S. Parkinson del.

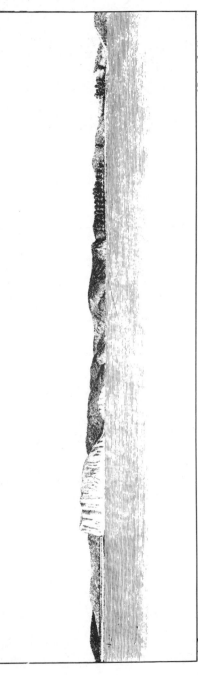

R. B. Godfrey Sc.

View of another Side of the Entrance into the said Bay.

discovered many of the natives (who seemed to be of a very dark hue) and several of their canoes hauled upon the beach. The natives, on approaching nearer to them, took but little notice of us. Having cast anchor, the pinnace, long-boat, and yaul, were sent on shore with the marines. As soon as the people who were in the pinnace had passed a little way up into the country, while the long-boat went up the river to see for water, some of the natives, who had hid themselves amongst the bushes, made their appearance, having long wooden lances in their hands, which they held up in a threatening posture, as if they intended to throw them at the boys in the yaul. The cockswain, who stayed in the pinnace, perceiving them, fired a musquetoon over their heads, but that did not seem to intimidate them: he therefore fired a musket, and shot one of them through the heart; upon which they were much alarmed, and retreated precipitately.

The water in the river was found to be brackish, in which we were disappointed; but they shot some wild ducks of a very large size, and our botanical gentlemen gathered a variety of curious plants in flower.

In the ensuing night, while we were all on board, the natives assembled on the shore, which was about three miles distance, talked loud, and were very clamorous. We ordered a strict watch to be kept all the night, lest they should come off in their canoes and surprise us.

Early on the morning of the 10th, the long-boat, pinnace, and yaul, went on shore again; landed near the river where they had been the night before, and attempted to find a watering place. Several of the natives came toward them, and, with much entreating, we prevailed on some of them to cross the river, to whom we gave several things, which they carried back to their companions on the other side of the river, who seemed to be highly pleased with them, and testified their joy by a war-dance. Appearing to be so pacifically disposed, our company went over to them, and were received in a friendly manner. Some of the natives were armed with lances, and others with a kind of stone truncheon; through the handle of it was a string, which they twisted round the hand that held it when they attempted to strike at any person. [See pl. XV.] We would have purchased some of their weapons, but could not prevail on them to part with them on any terms. One of them, however, watched an opportunity, and fnatched a hanger from us; our people refented the affront by firing upon them, and killed three of them on the fpot; but the reft, to our furprife, did not appear to be intimidated at the fight of their expiring countrymen, who lay weltering in their blood; nor did they feem to breathe any revenge upon the occafion; attempting only to wreft the hanger out of the man's hand that had been fhot, and to take the weapons that belonged to their other two deceafed comrades; which having effected, they quietly departed. After having taken poffeffion of the country, in form, for the king, our company embarked, and went round the bay in fearch of water again, and to apprehend, if poffible, fome of the natives, to gain farther information of them refpecting the ifland. They had not gone far before they faw a canoe; gave chace to it, and, when they came up with it, the crew threw ftones at them, and were very daring and infolent. Our people had recourfe to their arms: the Captain, Dr. Solander, and Mr. Banks, fired at them, and killed and wounded feveral of them. The natives fought very defperately with their paddles, but were foon overpowered: their canoe was taken, three of them made prifoners, and brought on board the fhip, and the reft were fuffered to efcape. They were, in perfon, much like the natives of Otaheite, and had their lips marked with a blue colour, but no other part of their bodies, in which they differed from the before-mentioned people. They talked very loud, but were rude in their addrefs, and more unpolifhed than the Otaheiteans. We were much furprifed to find they fpoke the Otaheitean language, though in a different dialect, fpeaking very guttural, having a kind of *hec*, which fome of the people of Yoolee-Etea have in their fpeech. Toohaiah underftood them very well, notwithftanding they make frequent ufe of the G and K, which the people of Otaheite do not. Their canoe was thirty feet long, made of planks fewed together, and had a lug-fail made of matting.

On the 11th, in the morning, the boats went on fhore again, and carried the three men whom we had taken, dreffed up very finely. The men did not feem willing to land, and when we left them, they cried, and faid that the people on that fide of the bay would eat them. While a party of our men went to cut wood, thefe men hid themfelves in the bufhes, and many of the natives appeared on the other fide of the river. We beckoned to them, and, at length, one man, of more courage than the reft, ventured over to us without arms, with whom we conferred,

by

Plate XV

S. Parkinson del. T. Chambers Sc.

A New Zealand Warrior in his Proper Dress, & Compleatly Armed, According to their Manner.

by our interpreter Toobaiah, for a confiderable time ; and, during the conference, about two hundred more, armed with lances, poles, and ftone bludgeons, made up to us, which the captain feeing, and being apprehenfive they intended to cut off our retreat to the boats, as they had got to the other fide of the river, he ordered us to embark, and return to the fhip; which we did accordingly, taking with us the three natives whom we had brought on fhore ; but, in the afternoon, we fet them on fhore again ; they parted with us reluctantly, and went into the woods; but, fome time after, we faw them, with our glaffes, come out again, make figns to us, and then go in again.

Thefe men, while on board, ate an immoderate quantity of every thing that was fet before them, taking pieces at one time into their mouths fix times larger than we did, and drank a quart of wine and water at one draught. They informed us, that there was Taro, Eape, Oomara, Yams, and alfo a peculiar kind of Deer, to be found upon the ifland.

The natives on this fide of the bay were tataowed, or marked, in various forms on their faces; and their garments, wrought of rufhes, reached down below their knees, and were very thick and rough. They tie their forefkins to their girdle with a ftring, and have holes pierced in their ears, which fhews that they fometimes wear fome fort of ear-rings : they have alfo fome bracelets ; neck-laces they well knew the ufe of; but they did not like our iron wares. We faw a piece of wood which looked as fmooth as if it had been cut with an axe ; but of what materials the inftruments are compofed, which they ufe for that purpofe, we could not learn. We went into fome of their houfes, which were very meanly thatched, having a hole in the center of the roof to let out the fmoke ; but we faw nothing in them except a few cockles, limpets, and mufcle-fhells.

We found here a fort of long-pepper, which tafted very much like mace ; a Fulica, or bald Coot, of a dark blue colour; and a Black-bird, the flefh of which was of an orange colour, and tafted like ftewed fhell-fifh. A vaft quantity of pumice-ftone lies all along upon the fhore, within the bay, which indicates that there is a volcano in this ifland.

On

On the 12th, early in the morning, we weighed anchor, and attempted to find'
fome better anchoring-place, as this bay (which, from the few neceffaries we could
procure, we called Poverty Bay) was not well fheltered from a S. E. wind, which.
brings in a heavy fea.. The natives call the bay Taoneroa, and the point of land,,.
at the entrance on the eaft fide, they call Tettua Motu.

In the afternoon we were becalmed, and fix canoes came off to us, filled with;
people; fome of them armed with bludgeons made of wood, and of the bone of
a large animal.. They were a fpare thin people, and had garments wrapt about.
them made of a filky flax, wove in the fame manner as the cotton hammocks of
Brazil, each corner being ornamented with a piece of dog-fkin. Moft of them:
had their hair tied up on the crown of their heads in a knot, and by the knot ftuck:
a comb of wood or bone. In and about their ears fome of them had white feathers, with pieces of birds fkins, whofe feathers were foft as down; but others had
the teeth of their parents, or a bit of green ftone worked very fmooth. Thefe
ftone ornaments were of various fhapes. They alfo wore a kind of fhoulder-knot,
made of the fkin of the neck of a large fea-fowl, with the feathers on, fplit in two
length-ways. Their faces were tataowed, or marked either all over, or on one
fide, in a very curious manner; fome of them in fine fpiral directions like a
volute, [fee pl. XVI.] being indented in the fkin very different from the reft: and
others had their faces daubed over with a fort of red ochre. The bottom of their
canoes was made out of a fingle tree; and the upper part was formed of two
planks, fewed together, narrowed both at head and ftern. The former was very
long, having a carved head at the end of it painted red, and the ftern ended in a
flat beak. They had thwarts to fit on, and their paddles were curioufly ftained
with a red colour, difpofed into various ftrange figures; and the whole together
was no contemptible workmanfhip. After we had given them a variety of beads
and other trinkets, they fet off in fo great a hurry, that they left three of their
people on board with us. We were at this time off a cape, which we named Table
Cape: we made but little way that night..

On the 13th, two canoes came off to us; and one of the natives came on board of
our fhip, but, being much intimidated, could not be prevailed on to ftay long.. He:
was;

Plate XVI

S. Parkinson del.   T. Chambers Sc.

The Head of a Chief of New Zealand, the face curiously tataow'd, or mark'd, according to their Manner.

was tataowed in the face, and wore a garment made of a fort of filky flax, wrought very ftrong, with a black and brown border round it, and a weapon in his hand made of the bone of a grampus. [See pl. XXVI. fig. 22.] There were feveral women in the canoe with uncommon long breafts, and their lips ftained with a blue colour.

In the afternoon, more canoes came to us. Some of the people in them were disfigured in a very ftrange manner; they brandifhed their arms, and fhewed figns of contempt, while the reft paddled hard to overtake us; and, at length, attempted to board us. The captain ordered one of the men to fire a mufket over them, which they did not regard. A great gun, loaded with grape fhot, was fired, which made them drop aftern; but whether any of them were wounded, we could not difcover. Several of the canoes had outriggers; and one of them had a very curious piece of ornamental carving at the head of it.

At this time we were doubling the weft point of the land, formed by a fmall high ifland, and got into very foul ground, the foundings being from feven to thirteen fathoms, and were afraid of running upon it; but we happily efcaped. After we had doubled this ifland, which was called Portland Ifle, or, according to the natives, Teahowray, we got into a fort of large bay, and, the night coming on, we thought it beft to drop anchor, defigning, next morning, to make for a harbour in the corner of the bay, where there was the appearance of an inlet. Moft of the country in view makes in flat table-hills, with cliffs of a white clay toward the fea. In the evening, feveral of the natives came, in two canoes, to vifit us: they feemed to be more friendly than the former; but were, however, fo frightened, that we could not perfuade them to come on board: we offered them various things, which they kindly accepted.

On the 14th, we made for the inlet, which we faw the night before, and, on coming up to it, found that it was not fheltered, having only fome low land at the bottom of it. Ten canoes, filled with people, chaced us; but our fhip failing too faft for them, they were obliged to give over the purfuit.

We

We failed round moft part of the bay without finding any opening ; and the foundings, all along the fhore, were very regular. The country appeared more fertile hereabout, and well covered with wood, the fea-fhore making in clayey cliffs, upon which the furf broke very high. This bay was called Hawke's Bay.

In the afternoon, a canoe followed us, with eighteen people in her, armed with lances ; but as they could not keep pace with us, they gave up their expedition.

In failing along, we could plainly diftinguifh land that was cultivated, parcelled out into fquare compartments, having fome forts of herbs growing upon them.

On the 15th, in the morning, we bent our courfe round a fmall peninfula, which was joined to the main land by a low ifthmus, on which were many groves of. tall ftrait trees, that looked as if they had been planted by art ; and, within-fide of it, the water was quite fmooth. We faw fome very high ridges of hills ftreaked with fnow ; and, when we had doubled the point of this peninfula, the low ifthmus appeared again, ftretching a long way by the fea-fide. The country looked very pleafant, having fine floping hills, which ftretched out into beautiful green lawns, though not covered with wood, as other parts of the coaft are.

In the morning, while we were on the other fide of the peninfula, nine canoes came to us, in which were one hundred and fixty of the natives : they behaved in a very irrefolute manner, fometimes feeming as if they would attack us ; then taking fright, and retreating a little ; one half paddling one way, and the other half paddling another, fhaking their lances and bone bludgeons at us, talking very loud and bluftering, [fee pl. XVII.] lolling out their tongues, and making other figns of defiance. We did all we could to make them peaceable, but to no purpofe, for they feemed, at length, refolved to do us fome mifchief ; coming along-fide of the fhip again, and threatening us, we fired one of our guns, loaded with grape-fhot, over their heads : they looked upon us for fome time with aftonifhment, and then haftened away as faft as they could. By this time two other canoes came toward us, but ftopped a little, and held a conference with thofe that were return-ing, and then made up to us, leaving the reft at fome diftance, who feemed to

wait

Plate XVII.

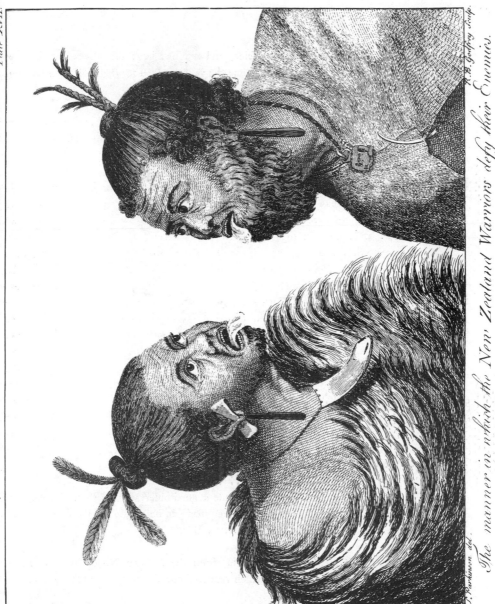

J. Parkinson. del.

R.B. Godfrey. Sculp.

The manner in which the New Zealand Warriors defy their Enemies.

Plate XVIII.

A War Canoe, of New Zealand.

S. Parkinson del.

R. B. Godfrey Sculp.

wait their deſtiny. We made ſigns to them that we meant them no harm, if they would behave peaceably, which they ſo well underſtood, that they took all their weapons and put them into a canoe, and ſent it off while they came cloſe to the ſhip. We threw them ſeveral kinds of things, but they were ſo timorous that they durſt not venture on board; nor would they ſend any thing to us. During this interview another canoe came up, threw a lance at the ſtern of the ſhip, and made off again. The lance fell into the water and ſunk immediately. There were ſome good-looking people in theſe canoes, others were disfigured, and had a very ſavage countenance. One old man, in particular, who ſeemed to be a chief, was painted red, and had a red garment, but the garments of ſome others were ſtriped. The principals amongſt them had their hair tied up on the crown of their heads; and ſome feathers, with a little bundle of perfume, hung about their necks. Moſt of them were tataowed in the face, and many of them quite naked, who ſeemed to be ſervants to the reſt. Several of them had pieces of a green ſtone * hung about their necks, which ſeemed to be pellucid, like an emerald. Their ſpears were not unlike our ſheriffs halberts, having red and yellow taſſels tied to them. In one of their canoes we ſaw a hatchet, made of the green ſtone, in ſhape like thoſe of Otaheite. Their canoes [ſee pl. XVIII.] had from eighteen to twenty-two men in them, and were adorned with fine heads made out of a thick board, cut through like filligree-work, in ſpirals of very curious workmanſhip. At the end of this was a head, with two large eyes of mother-of-pearl, and a large heart-ſhaped tongue. This figure went round the bottom of the board, and had feet and hands carved upon it very neatly, and painted red: they had alſo high-peaked ſterns, wrought in filligree, and adorned with feathers, from the top of which depended two long ſtreamers, made of feathers, which almoſt reached the water. Some of theſe canoes were between fifty and ſixty feet long, and rowed with eighteen paddles. They gave us two Heivos, in their canoes, which were very diverting. They beat time with their paddles, and ended all at once with the word Epaah ; at the ſame inſtant ſtriking their paddles on the thwarts: all which afforded a truly comic act.

* Pieces of this kind of ſtone were brought home in the Endeavour; on examination it appears to be a fine ſort of Nephritic ſtone. This remark will ſerve for all their ornaments hereafter mentioned, ſaid to be made of a green ſtone.

The

The weather was remarkably fine for some time before and after we came to this island, having light breezes, and clear weather, with some calms.

On the 16th, we had several fisher canoes come to us; and, after much persuasion, they gave us some fish for cloth and trinkets; but none of their fish was quite fresh, and some of it stank intolerably. They went away very well satisfied, and then a larger canoe, full of people, came up to us, having their faces shockingly besmeared with some paint. An old man, who sat in the stern, had on a garment of some beast's skin, with long hair, dark brown, and white border, which we would have purchased, but they were not willing to part with any thing. When the captain threw them a piece of red baize for it, they paddled away immediately; held a conference with the fishers boats, and then returned to the ship. We had laid a scheme to trepan them, intending to have thrown a running bow line about the head of the canoe, and to have hoisted her up to the anchor; but, just as we had got her a-head for that purpose, they seized Toobaiah's little boy, who was in the main-chains, and made off with him, which prevented the execution of our plan. We fired some muskets and great guns at them, and killed several of them. The boy, soon after, disingaged himself from them, jumped into the sea, swam toward the ship, and we lowered down a boat and took him up, while the canoes made to land as fast as possible.

The speech of these people was not so guttural as the others, for they spoke more like the Otaheiteans. Many of them had good faces; their noses rather high than flat; and some of them had their hair most curiously brought up to their crowns, rolled round, and knotted.

In the evening, we were over-against a point of land, which, from the circumstance of stealing the boy, we called Cape Kidnappers. On doubling the cape, we thought to have met with a snug bay, but were disappointed, the land tending away to a point southward. Soon after we saw a small island, which, from its desolate appearance, we called Bare Island.

On

On the 17th, we failed along the coaft, near as far as forty-one degrees, but, not meeting with any convenient harbour to anchor in, the land lying N. and S. when we came abreaft of a round bluff cape, we turned back, being apprehen-five that we fhould want water if we proceeded farther to the fouthward. We faw no canoes, but feveral villages, and, in the night, fome fires burning upon the land. The coaft appeared more barren than any we had feen before. There was clear ground, and good anchorage upon the coaft, two or three miles from the fhore; and from eight to twenty fathoms water. This cape we named Cape Turn-Again.

On the 19th, in the afternoon, we were off Hawke's Bay, which we could not enter, the wind being foul. A canoe came to us with five people in it, who feemed to place great confidence in us: they came on board, and faid they would ftay all night. The man, who feemed to be the chief, had a new garment, made of the white filky flax, which was very ftrong and thick, with a beautiful border of black, red, and white round it.

On the 20th, early in the morning, having a fine breeze, we made Table Cape, paffed Poverty Bay, and came to a remarkable point of land, being a flat perpen-dicular triangular-fhaped rock, behind which there appeared to be a harbour, but, on opening it, we found none: this point we called Gable-End Foreland. The country is full of wood, and looks very pleafant in this part; but, toward night, we faw fome land that appeared very broken and dreary, formed into a number of points, over which we could fee the back land.

On the 21ft, we anchored in a very indifferent harbour, in eight fathoms and a half water, about one mile and a half from the fhore, having an ifland on our left hand, which fomewhat fheltered us. Many canoes came off to us, and two old men, of their chiefs, came on board. Thefe people feemed very peaceably in-clined, and were willing to trade with us for feveral trifles which they had brought with them. We faw many houfes, and feveral tracts of land, partly hedged in and cultivated, which formed an agreeable view from the harbour, called, by

the

the natives, **Tegadoo**. Some of our boats went on fhore for water, and found a rivulet where they filled their cafks, and returned to the fhip unmolefted by the inhabitants, many of whom they faw near the rivulet.

On the 22d, in the morning, the boats went on fhore again for wood and water; and, a fhort time after, Mr. Banks and fome others followed them; and, while they were abfent, the natives came on board and trafficked with us; having brought fome parcels of Oomarra, and exchanged them with us for Otaheite cloth, which is a fcarce commodity amongft them. They were very cunning in their traffic, and made ufe of much low artifice. One of them had an axe made of the before-mentioned green ftone, which he would not part with for any thing we offered him. Several of them were very curioufly tataowed; and one old man was marked on the breaft with a large volute, and other figures. The natives, both on board and on fhore, behaved with great civility, and, at night, they began to heivo and dance in their manner, which was very uncouth; nothing could be more droll than to fee old men with grey beards affuming every antic pofture imaginable, rolling their eyes about, lolling out their tongues, and, in fhort, work-ing themfelves up to a fort of phrenzy.

The furf running high, the men who went on fhore found great difficulty in getting the water into the long-boat, and, in coming off, the boat was fwampt; we therefore enquired of the natives for a more convenient watering-place, and they pointed to a bay bearing S. W. by W. On receiving this information we weighed anchor; but, the wind being againft us, we ftood off and on till the next morning, the 23d, and then bore away to leeward, and looked into the bay which we had paffed before. About noon we dropped anchor, and one of our boats went into a little cove where there was fmooth landing and frefh water, and we moored the fhip about one mile and a half from the fhore. This bay is called, by the natives, Tolaga, and is very open, being expofed to all the violence of the eaft wind. Several canoes came along-fide of the fhip, of whom we got fome fifh, Oomarras, or fweet potatoes, and feveral other things; but the natives were very indifferent about moft of the things we offered them, except white cloth and glaffes, which fuited their fancy, fo that we found it difficult to trade with them. They had fome green ftone axes and ear-rings but they would not part with

them,

them on any terms; and as to their Oomarras, they fet a great value upon them.

The country about the bay is agreeable beyond defcription, and, with proper cultivation, might be rendered a kind of fecond Paradife. The hills are covered with beautiful flowering fhrubs, intermingled with a great number of tall and ftately palms, which fill the air with a moft grateful fragrant perfume.

We faw the tree that produces the cabbage, which ate well boiled. We alfo found fome trees that yielded a fine tranfparent gum: and, between the hills, we difcovered fome fruitful valleys that are adapted either to cultivation or pafturage. The country abounds with different kinds of herbage fit for food; and, among fuch a variety of trees as are upon this land, there are, doubtlefs, many that produce eatable fruit. Our botanifts were agreeably employed in invefligating them, as well as many other leffer plants with which the country abounds. Within land there were many fcandent ferns and parafaitic plants; and, on the fea fhore, Salicornias, Mifembrean, Mums, and a variety of Fucus's. The plant, of which they make their cloth, is a fort of Hemerocallis, and the leaves yield a very ftrong and gloffy flax, of which their garments and ropes are made. Adjoining to their houfes are plantations of Koomarra * and Taro † : Thefe grounds are cultivated with great care, and kept clean and neat.

The natives, who are not very numerous in this part of the country, behaved very civil to us: they are, in general, lean and tall, yet well fhaped; have faces like Europeans; and, in general, the aquiline nofe, with dark-coloured eyes, black hair, which is tied up on the crown of the head, and beards of a middling length. As to their tataowing, it is done very curioufly in fpiral and other figures; and, in many places, indented into their fkins, which looks like carving; though, at a diftance, it appears as if it had been only fmeared with a black paint. This tataowing is peculiar to the principal men among them: fervants and women content themfelves with befmearing their faces with red paint or ochre; and, were it not for this nafty cuftom, would make no defpicable appearance. Their cloth is white, and as gloffy as filk, worked by hands, and wrought as even as if it

had

* A fweet potatoe, which the Otaheiteans call Oomarra.

† Yams.

had been done in a loom, and is chiefly worn by the men, though it is made by the women, who alfo carry burdens, and do all the drudgery. Their cloathing confifts in a girdle of platted grafs, which they wear round their loins, having fome leaves hung upon it, and a kind of grafs-rug cloak thrown over their fhoulders. Many of the women, that we faw, had very good features, and not the favage countenance one might expect; [fee pl. XIX.] their lips were, in general, ftained of a blue colour, and feveral of them were fcratched all over their faces as if it had been done with needles or pins. This, with a number of fcars which we faw on the bodies of the men, was done upon the deceafe of their relations. The men have their hair tied up, but the womens hangs down; nor do they wear feathers in it, but adorn it with leaves. They feem to be proud of their fex, and expect you fhould give them every thing they defire, because they are women; but they take care to grant no favours in return, being very different from the women in the iflands who were fo free with our men.

The men have a particular tafte for carving: their boats, paddles, boards to put on their houfes, tops of walking fticks, and even their boats valens, are carved in a variety of flourifhes, turnings and windings, that are unbroken; but their favourite figure feems to be a volute, or fpiral, which they vary many ways, fingle, double, and triple, and with as much truth as if done from mathematical draughts: yet the only inftruments we have feen are a chizzel, and an axe made of ftone. Their fancy, indeed, is very wild and extravagant, and I have feen no imitations of nature in any of their performances, unlefs the head, and the heart-fhaped tongue hanging out of the mouth of it, may be called natural, [See pl. XXVI. fig. 16.]

The natives build their huts on rifing ground under a tuft of trees; they are of an oblong fquare, and the eaves reach to the ground. The door is on one fide, and very low; their windows are at one end, or both. The walls are compofed of feveral layers of reeds covered with thatch, and are of confiderable thicknefs. Over the beams, that compofe the eaves, they lay a net made of grafs, which is alfo thatched very clofe and thick. Their fires are made in the center upon the floor, and the door ferves them for a chimney. Their houfes, therefore, of courfe, muft be full of fmoke; and we obferved that every thing brought out of them fmelt ftrong of it; but ufe, which is a kind of fecond nature, makes them infen-

fible

Plate XIX.

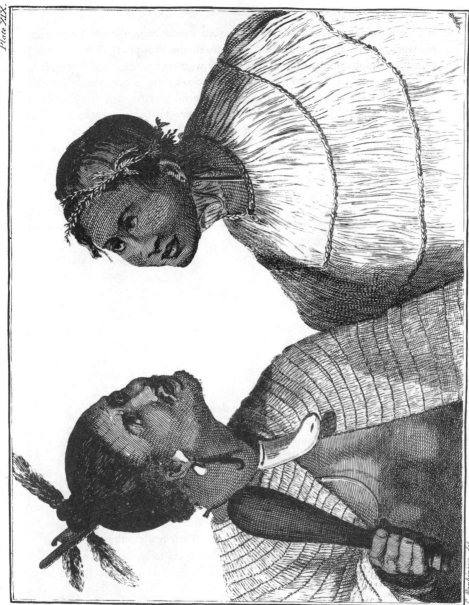

S. Parkinson del.

A New Zealand Warrior, & his Wife, in the Dress &c. of that Country.

W. Dowling Sculp.

Plate XX.

J. Banks del.

J. Newton sculp.

View of a curious Arched Rock, having a River running under it, in Tolago Bay, on the East Coast of New Zealand.

fible of the inconvenience, or they would have found out fome means to have removed it; for neceffity is the mother of invention. We faw but few of their houfes, and thofe few were moftly deferted, their inhabitants having forfaken them through fear of us, who, doubtlefs, appeared as ftrange kind of beings to them as they did to us.

We faw many beautiful parrots, and birds of various kinds, one in particular that had a note very much like our blackbird; but we found no ground fowl, or domeftic poultry. Of quadrupeds we faw no other than dogs, which were like thofe on the ifland of Otaheite, and of them but a few, though it cannot be fuppofed that fo large a country, as this appears to be, fhould be deftitute of deer, and other kind of four-footed animals.

This bay abounds in a variety of fifh, particularly fhell and cray-fifh; fome of the latter, which we caught, weighed eleven pounds; thefe are found in great plenty, and feemed to be the principal food of the inhabitants, at this feafon of the year, though they have a kind of fern, the roots of which, roafted, make a good fubftitute for bread, efpecially when their Koomarra is young and unfit for ufe.

Moft of the rocks, which are many on the fea fhore, are compofed of a fandy ftone, through which the furf had worn feveral paffages. One of them, in particular, was very romantic, it had the appearance of a large arch which led from the fea-fide into the vallies, and through it ran a ftream of water. The whole formed a very uncommon view, [fee pl. XX.] peculiarly ftriking to a curious fpectator.

From the view which we had of the coaft, and the obfervations made, we might judge that the country is well fituated, naturally fertile, and capable of great improvement by cultivation, efpecially as the climate is diftinguifhably mild and favourable.

We

We had clear and fair weather all the time we were upon the coaſt, excepting one day, and, though the weather was hot, yet it ſeemed, by what we obſerved, that a ſea breeze conſtantly ſet in about eleven o'clock in the forenoon, which moderated it.

On the 30th, having obtained a ſufficient quantity of wood and water, we left the bay, and, ſailing along the coaſt, about noon came up with a point of land before an iſland: this point we called Eaſt Cape; and the iſland, Eaſt Iſland, from which the land altered its direction, and tended away to the weſt. This day the land appeared to us conſiderably higher than the reſt. It was divided by fine deep valleys, and had all the appearance of a rich fertile country, being cloathed with large verdant trees, had ſome parcels of ground cultivated, and ſeveral rivulets among them which loſt themſelves in the ſea. We could alſo diſcover ſeveral villages, which ſeemed to have been fenced in by art. We paſſed a bay which we called Hicks's Bay, after our firſt lieutenant.

On the 31ſt, we ſailed along the coaſt, and had light breezes, and pleaſant weather. In the forenoon ſeven canoes came off to us in a hoſtile manner, brandiſhing their lances, and waving their paddles. One of theſe canoes was very large, and had between fifty and ſixty people in her; ſome of them gave us an heivo; and one of them, a prieſt, as we ſuppoſed, talked very much. They kept paddling about us, calling out to us *Kaka kee, no Tootwais, harre yoota patta pattoo*; that is to ſay, if we would go on ſhore they would beat us with their patta pattoos; and, being apprehenſive that if we ſuffered them to approach nearer to us, we might be obliged to offer violence to them, the captain ordered a gun, loaded with grape-ſhot, to be fired over their heads, the report of which terrified them ſo much, that they paddled away till they had got, as they ſuppoſed, out of our reach, and then they ſtopped, and held a conſultation; after which they ſeemed as if they intended to return, and we fired another gun loaded with ball, and then they made as faſt as poſſible to the ſhore. Theſe were the ſame ſort of people, and their canoes of the ſame kind with thoſe we had ſeen before. Being at this time off a cape, we named it, from the haſty retreat of the natives, Cape Runaway. This day we diſcovered land to the N.E. of us.

On

On the 1ſt of November, a great number of canoes came off to us, one of which had part of a human ſkull to throw out the water with. We prevailed on ſome of the natives to come along-ſide of the ſhip, and traded with them for cloth, cray-fiſh, and muſcles. They gave us ſeverl Heivos, but ſome of them ſeemed to threaten us. A breeze ſpringing up, we left them; and, a little farther on the coaſt, another ſquadron of fiſher-boats came off to us, with whom alſo we had ſome traffic. Theſe, as well as the reſt, were very ready to ſnatch any thing they could lay their hands on; and, watching an opportunity, they ſtole a pair of ſheets that were tied by a line at the ſhip's ſtern, and were going off with them, upon which we fired ſeveral muſkets, but they did not much regard them; we then fired ſome grape-ſhot amongſt them, and they paddled away ſomething faſter, till they ima-gined themſelves out of our reach, and then they held up their paddles, and ſeemed to defy us. We fired another gun loaded with round and grape-ſhot, which paſſed between two canoes, and narrowly miſſed them; on which they heſitated no longer, but repaired immediately to the ſhore.

Toward night, we were near a ſmall high iſland, called by the natives Mow-tohora, about three leagues from the land. In going between this and the main land, a canoe came off to us from the iſland. This canoe was double, and differed in other reſpects from thoſe we had ſeen before. After we had talked with the people which came in it a conſiderable time, they gave us ſeveral heivos, then looked at us very ſtedfaſtly, and, having threatened us, they ſtood off toward the main land. Oppoſite to this there is a high peaked hill, which we named Mount Edgecombe; and a ſmall bay, which we called Lowland Bay, and the two points thereof, from their ſituation, Highland Point, and Lowland Point; the latter of which ſtretches a great way, and is covered with trees; near it there are three ſmall iſlands, or rocks, and it was with difficulty that we ſteered clear of them in the night, and got into ſix fathoms water; ſoon after which we made a point of land, which we called Town Point: this was at the entrance of a little cove.

On

On the 2d, in the morning, we difcovered three forts of land; but, as the weather was hazy, could not make many obfervations. We alfo paffed three other iflands: one of them was rocky, high and barren, which we called White Ifland. The other two were lower; one of them we named Flat Ifland, in which which we faw a village. A canoe purfued us, but, having a brifk breeze, it could not overtake us. Toward night it blew pretty hard, right on fhore; we therefore tacked about, and failed backward and forward till the next morning, the 3d: then the canoe which we faw the night before gave us chace again; having a fail, they at length came up with us; failed along-fide of us for a confiderable time, and now and then gave us a fong, the tune of which was much like the chant which the popifh priefts ufe at mafs: they alfo gave us a heivo, but foon after threw fome ftones at us: we fired a mufket, loaded with fmall fhot, at a young man who diftinguifhed himfelf at the fport, and he fhrunk down as if he had been wounded. After a fhort confultation they doufed the fail, and ftood back for an ifland.

We failed along with a moderate breeze, and paffed an ifland, or clufter of rocks, which we called the Court of Aldermen: and, from the vicinity of one of the three laft mentioned iflands to them, we gave it the name of The Mayor.

This clufter of rocks lies off a point of land, and terminates the bounds of this large bay to the N. W. which, from the number of canoes that came off to us, bringing provifions, we named The Bay of Plenty.

The coaft hereabout appeared very barren, and had a great number of rocky iflands, from which circumftance we named the point, Barren Point. The land is very grotefque, being cleft, or torn into a variety of ftrange figures, and has very few trees upon it. About noon, feveral canoes came off to us, and the people in them were fo daring as to throw a lance into the fhip, but we fired a mufket, and they paddled away from us. Their canoes were formed out of one tree, and fhaped like a butcher's tray, without any ornament about them. The people, who were naked, excepting one or two, were of a very dark complexion, and made a mean appearance. We ftood in for a bay, and, at night, anchored in it, having feven fathoms water. Several canoes, like the former, followed us; the people in them cut a defpicable figure; but they were very merry, and gave us feveral heivos, or cheers.

This bay, which the inhabitants call Opoorangee, is the beft harbour we have found, being well land-locked; and we found good landing at the watering-place, in a falt-water river, which winds a great way up into the country. At the bottom of the bay there is another river, which alfo feems to extend very far within land. The name the natives gave to the country, about the bay, is Konigootaoivrao.

On the 4th, early in the morning. we were vifited by feveral canoes; the people in them, about one hundred and thirty-five in number, had a few arms, but feemed unrefolved what to do; fometimes ftaring at us in a wild manner, and then threatening us: but, at laft, they traded with us, exchanging the few trifles they had brought for cloth. They were very fly, and attempted to cheat us. We fired feveral mufkets at them, and wounded two of them; the reft, however, did not feem to be alarmed till the captain fhot through one of the canoes, which ftruck them with a panic; and, on firing a great gun, they made off to land.

On the 5th, in the morning, two of the natives came on board, and feemed to be very peaceably inclined: we made them fome prefents; they exchanged what trifles they had for fmall pieces of cloth, which they were very fond of, and went away highly pleafed, promifing to bring us fome fifh. Some people, it feemed, came to them now-and-then from the north, plundered them of every thing they could find, and carried their wives and children away captives; and not knowing who we were, nor our defign in vifiting their coaft, was the reafon that they were at firft fo fhy of us. To fecure themfelves from thefe free-booters, they build their houfes near together on the tops of rocks, which, it feems, they can eafily defend againft the affaults of their enemies; but, being fo fubject to the ravages of thofe ruffians, they are much difpirited, and that may be the principal caufe of their poverty and wretchednefs.

We

We fent the pinnace to haul the feine, and caught a large draught of mullets, and other kind of fifh. In the mean time the yaul drudged for fhell-fifh, and met with indifferent fuccefs.

On the 9th, a great number of the natives came in canoes about the fhip, and brought us a large quantity of fifh, moftly of the mackrel kind, with a few John Dories; and we pickled down feveral cafks full of them.

Some of thefe canoes came from another part of the country, which were larger, and of a better fort than the reft : the people in them, too, had a better appearance; among whom there were fome of fuperior rank, furnifhed with good garments, dreffed up with feathers on their heads, and had various things of value amongft them, which they readily exchanged for Otaheite cloth. In one of the canoes there was a very handfome young man, of whom I bought fome things: he feemed, by the variety of his garments, which he fold one after another till he had but one left, to be a perfon of diftinction amongft them: his laft garment was an upper one, made of black and white dog-fkin, which one of the lieutenants would have purchafed, and offered him a large piece of cloth for it, which he fwung down the ftern by a rope into the canoe ; but, as foon as the young man had taken it, his companions paddled away as faft as poffible, fhouting, and brandifhing their weapons as if they had made a great prize ; and, being ignorant of the power of our weapons, thought to have carried it off fecurely ; but a mufket was fired at them from the ftern of the fhip: the young man fell down immediately, and, it is probable, was mortally wounded, as we did not fee him rife again. What a fevere punifhment of a crime committed, perhaps, ignorantly ! The name of this unfortunate young man, we afterwards learned, was Otirreeoònooe.

The weather being clear all day, we made a good obfervation of the paffage of Mercury over the fun's difk, while Mr. Green made an obfervation on fhore. From this circumftance the Bay was termed Mercury Bay.

On the 11th, it blew very hard all day from the N. and N. by E. and a great fwell tumbled into the bay, which rendered our fituation a very favourable

one ;

one; for, had we been out at fea, we fhould have had a lee-fhore. The inhabitants did not venture out in their canoes this day; and, the night before, we
were almoft fwamped in coming off in the long-boat, being upon the fhoals, and
the fea running high.

While we lay in this bay the natives brought us a great number of cray-
fifh, of an enormous fize, which were very good. Thefe were caught by
women, who dived for them in the furf amongft the rocks. A long-boat full of
rock oyfters, too, were brought on board of us at one time, which were good
food, and tafted delicioufly. A little way up the river there were banks entirely
compofed of them. We alfo got abundance of parfley for the fhip's ufe; and, at
the place where we watered, we found a great quantity of fern, the root of which
partakes much of a farinaceous quality: the natives dry it upon the fire, then
beat it upon a ftone, and eat it inftead of bread.

On the 16th, in the morning, the weather being very fair, we weighed anchor,
and ftood out to fea, but, having a ftrong breeze from the weft, which was againft
us all this day and the next, being the 17th, we did nothing but beat to windward. The country in view appeared rather barren, and had but few figns of
inhabitants. We faw feveral iflands, which we named Mercury iflands.

On the 18th, in the morning, we paffed between the main and an ifland which
appeared to be very fertile, and as large as Yoolee-Etea. Two canoes came to us
from the main, having carved heads, like thofe we had feen in the bay of Opoorangee: one of them was longer than the other, and had fixty of the natives in
her: they gazed at us awhile, and then gave us feveral heivos; but the breeze
frefhening, they were obliged to drop aftern, and we foon left them. The coaft
hereabout is full of iflands: the name of the largeft is Waootaia; and one of the
fmall ones is called Matoo Taboo. After we had paffed this ifland, (the paffage
between which and the main we named Port Charles,) it feemed as if we were
in a large bay, the land furrounding us on every fide, excepting a-head, where
we could difcover none: we bent our courfe that way, and got, at length, inclofed
between two fhores, which feemed to form a kind of ftrait. Night coming on, we
anchored here, not daring to venture farther, as we knew not whether we were

in

in a ftrait or a bay. The land on both fides of us appeared very broken, and had
a high and bold fhore, tolerably well cloathed with verdure; but it appeared to be
thinly inhabited; nor did we fee any figns of cultivation. There are many fmall
iflands along the fhore, among which are fome good harbours.

On the 19th, in the morning, feveral of the natives came on board of us : their
canoes were the largeft we had feen, and the people in them behaved very friendly.
By what we could learn, they had got intelligence of us from the people that inhabit the country about Opoorangee Bay, which is not very diftant. They told us
this was not an entrance into the main, but a deep bay. Some of them prefented
us with a large parcel of fmoaked eels, which tafted very fweet and lufcious. We
obferved that the natives mode of falutation was by putting their nofes together.

We failed along till we came to fix fathoms water, and then let go our anchor.
The weather being hazy, we could not have fo good a view of the land upon the
coaft as we wifhed to have ; but it appeared to be well covered with wood, and
fome parts of it cultivated. This day we caught a confiderable quantity of fifh,
with hook and line, of the fcienna or bream kind. The natives call this harbour
Ooahaowragee.

On the 20th, early in the morning, the Captain, Mr. Banks, and Dr. Solander,
fet out, in the long-boat and pinnace, for the bottom of this gulph, to fee in what
manner it terminated : and, as it blew very frefh, and a great fwell rolled into the
bay all day, they did not attempt to return till the next morning, the 21ft ; then,
with fome difficulty, on account of the fwell, they reached the fhip again, and
reported, that they had been a confiderable way up a frefh-water river, at the end
of the gulph, in which they found three fathoms water. It was about half a mile
broad, and would make an excellent harbour. Near the entrance of this river,
which they named the Thames, there was a village, and a Hippa, or place of re-
fuge, erected to defend it, which was furrounded by piquets that reached above
water when the tide was up ; and, at low-water, it was unapproachable on account
of a foft deep mud. The inhabitants of the village behaved civil and obliging,
and promifed to bring fome provifions to the fhip; but, the weather proving unfavourable, they could not fulfil their engagement. On that day they alfo met

with

with the large tree of which we had feen fo many groves formed in different parts of the coaft. This tree has a fmall narrow leaf, like a juniper's, and grows to the height of ninety feet, and is nine feet in girth. It is generally found in low land, and has a very dark-coloured appearance at a diftance. The natives, it is thought, make their canoes of this tree. They alfo faw feveral young cabbage palm-trees, and a new fpecies of Pardanus, or palm-nut.

In the afternoon we weighed anchor, proceeded down the gulph with the tide, the wind blowing hard from N. N. W. and, toward night anchored pretty near the fhore.

On the 22d, in the evening, feveral canoes, full of people, fome of whom we faw the night before, came on board, brought us fome provifions, and parted very readily with their cloaths, and any thing they had about them, for pieces of wafte paper and Otaheite cloth, which they put about their heads and ears, and were very proud of their drefs.

The wind being ftill againft us, we were obliged to tide it down the river, and anchored between tides, and paffed a point of land which we called Point Rodney.

The next day, being the 23d, we had heavy rains, accompanied with thunder.

On the 24th, we had a fmart breeze from the S. W. and, failing along fhore, paffed between the main and a number of iflands of feveral fizes. The appearance of the coaft was very different at different places; well cloathed and verdant in fome parts, and barren in others; but we faw no figns of inhabitants in any. We anchored in an open bay, and caught a great number of large fifhes of the fcienna or bream kind; we therefore named this Bream Bay; and the two extreme points which formed it, Bream Head and Bream Tail. Off this bay lies a parcel of rocks, to which we gave the appellation of the Hen and Chickens.

On the 25th, we had clear weather, with the wind at S. W. The coaft we paffed along that day was moftly level, having but few figns of inhabitants: to-

ward

ward night feveral large canoes came off to us, filled with people, armed with a variety of weapons; they paddled round the fhip, finging and dancing; fometimes grinning, and then threatening: we trafficked with them for fome things; but they went off with fome others, meaning to take an advantage of us. While they were parlying among themfelves we fired feveral mufkets at them, loaded with fmall fhot, which they attempted to fkreen themfelves from with their ahavos, or cloaks. We fired again, and fplintered one of their canoes, which feemed to alarm them much, and they paddled away from us as faft as poffible, till they thought themfelves out of our reach, and then they ftopped and threatened us; but we fired a great gun, which fo thoroughly difconcerted them, that they made the beft of their way to the fhore. Thefe people were much like them we had feen heretofore, excepting that they were more tataowed: moft of them had the figure of volutes on their lips, and feveral had their legs, thighs, and part of their bellies, marked. One woman, in particular, was very curioufly tataowed. The tataow upon their faces was not done in fpirals, but in different figures from what we had ever feen before.

On the 26th, many canoes vifited us. The people in them were much the fame as the former. They had a variety of things on board, and about them, but were loth to part with any of them excepting fifh, of which we obtained a large quantity.

The coaft we failed along this day, was generally barren, and broke into a number of fmall iflands, among which we prefumed there might be fafe and good anchorage. We had calm and pleafant weather.

On the 27th, we were among a parcel of fmall broken iflands, which we called the Poor Knights; and many canoes came along fide of us, but the people in them feemed to be half mad. We afked them for fome fifh, and they took them up by handfuls and threw them at us, not regarding whether they had any thing from us in return: more canoes coming up, they began to behave very rudely, and heaved ftones at us. One man, in particular, more active than the reft, took up a ftick and threw it at one of our men on the taffel. A mufket loaded with fmall fhot was fired at him, upon which he clapped his hands to his face and fell flat in

the

Plate XXI.

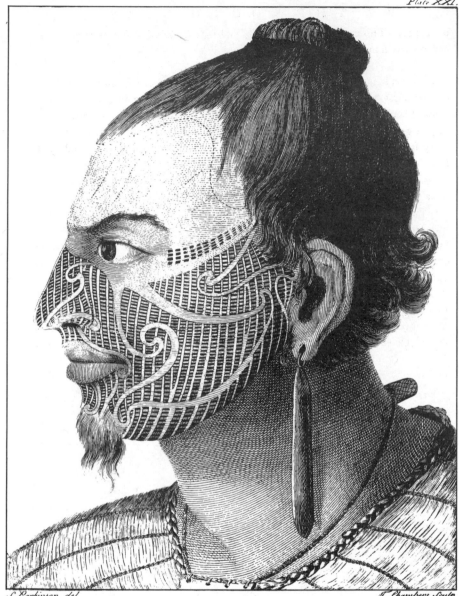

S. Parkinson del.   T. Chambers Sculp.

Head of Otegoongoon, Son of a New Zealand Chief, the face curiously tataow'd.

the canoe. This event alarmed the reft, and they made off as faft as they could, and we faw no more of them.

The wind having been againft us for feveral days, and as we could get no far-ther with our heavy fhip, on the 29th, in the morning, having weathered a long point of land, which we named Cape Brett, we bore away to leeward; got into a very large harbour, where we were land-locked, and had feveral pretty coves on every fide of us. We paffed a fmall ifland which we named Piercy Ifland, and foon after caft anchor. Many canoes came off to us; and the people in them, according to cuftom, behaved fomewhat unruly: while I faluted one of them, in their manner, he picked my pocket. Some of our people fired upon them, but they did not feem to regard it much. One of our boats went on fhore, and then they fet off all at once, and attempted to feize her, in which, however, they failed; but foon after Mr. Banks got on fhore, he had like to have been apprehended by one of the natives, but happily efcaped. The marines fired upon them; five great guns were fired from the fhip, and Otegoowgoow, [fee pl. XXI.] fon to one of their chiefs, was wounded in the thigh. The natives, affrighted, fled precipitately to a Hippa, where our people followed them; and, at length, they became very fubmiffive. Had thefe barbarians acted more in concert, they would have been a formidable enemy, and might have done us much mifchief; but they had no kind of order or military difcipline among them. They gave us fome large mackarel, which ate very delicioufly, and that was almoft the only article they would part with.

On the 5th of December, we weighed anchor, but were becalmed at the en-trance of the bay, which we called the Bay of Iflands, from the many iflands in it. However, as it frequently happens in life, a leffer evil fecured us from a greater; being detained here, we efcaped a fevere gale at fea, that might have proved very dangerous to us, as the wind blew a perfect hurricane, one day, ac-companied with heavy fhowers of rain.

The natives (being more fenfible of our power) behaved very civil, and brought us a great many fifh; and while we lay here, we caught fome ourfelves with hook and line.

A

A canoe came into the bay that had eighty people in her, moſt of whom pad-dled ; the chiefs wore garments of dogs ſkins, and were very much tataowed ; the men upon their hips, and the women on their breaſts, necks, and bellies. We ſaw many plantations of the Koomarra, and ſome of the Eaowte, or cloth trees.

At night, again, it was almoſt calm, and we were near the ſhore. We deſigned to tack about, but were hurried, by an eddy-tide, upon the breakers, off a point of land called, by us, Point Pococke, before we were aware of it, which threw us into a panic, and occaſioned great confuſion. Not having room to anchor, we hoiſted out the pinnace to tow her off: we thought we had ſeen a whale, but it proved to be a rock, and we ſtruck upon it twice. We got clear of it again, and ſtreamed the buoy, but luckily did not let go the anchor. Soon after we ſaw ſeveral ſmall iſlands, which we named Cavalle Iſlands. We paſſed two points of land which formed a bay, to which we gave the appellation of Doubtleſs Bay ; and the two points which formed it were called by us Bay Point, and Knuckle Point. We were now got into a very long open bay, which, from the appearance of the country, we named Sandy Bay.

We beat to windward four days, and made but little way, having continual breezes from the weſt ; and, on the 19th, many canoes came off to us, of which we bought a good quantity of fiſh. The land hereabout looked very barren, and tends away to the north.

On the 1cth, the wind was N. W. we beat to windward, and made but little way. The land in ſight was very low, and very barren, being moſtly ſandy, hav-ing here and there a few buſhes, but ſcarce a tree to be ſeen, yet it appeared to be inhabited.

On the 13th, the N. W. wind ſtill prevailing, we could do nothing but lie on and off the land, without making any way. It blew very hard, and we had ſome fierce ſqualls, attended with heavy ſhowers of rain, which drove us back to where we had been four days before.

On

On the 14th, we were quite out of fight of land ; the wind continued to blow very ftrong; we had great fwells from the weft; and our fails being very tender, many of them were much torn in the gale.

On the 17th, in the morning, we were near land again, which feemed to be the fartheft north, the land tending away from this point, which we called the North Cape to the South Weft. This land was pretty high, with a table top. We faw no canoes, nor any inhabitants; but, in the evening, we faw fome fmoke on the high land.

On the 20th, the wind ftill continuing wefterly, we got no farther than the laft bluff point. We had fome violent fqualls of wind, with heavy rains, thunder, and lightening.

On the 21ft, in the morning, the wind came about to the fouth ; but, as we were a confiderable diftance from fhore, we could only ftand to the weftward without being able to get near the land.

On the 24th, after having beat about for three days, we difcovered land, which we fuppofed was the ifland of the Three Kings, though we could not bring it to appear any thing like the defcribed figure of that ifland in Dalrymple's Book, having nothing of that broken appearance which that figure exhibits, forming one large clump of land, rather flat at the top, with eleven fmall rocks lying in a row from it. It being calm, Mr. Banks went out in the fmall boat; and we faw fome birds fo much like our ifland geefe, that we could not have diftinguifhed the difference. We caught feveral of them, made them into a pye, and they tafted excellently.

On the 27th, in the morning, it blew very hard from the eaft, all day, accompanied with heavy fhowers of rain, and we brought the fhip to under a reef main-fail.

On

On the 28th, the wind veered about to the S. W. and blew from that quarter fiercer than it had done the day before from the eaft; the fea alfo ran very high, and we brought to under a balanced mizen, and a mizen ftay-fail.

On the 30th, we difcovered land to leeward of us, which we took for Cape Maria Van Diemen; but as the wind continued ftill very boifterous, and the fea ran very high, we did not venture to approach near it; we therefore tacked about, and ftood to the N. W. intending to ftand backwards and forwards till the weather fhould be more moderate. In the evening, we difcovered the ifland of the Three Kings, on our lee-bow, and tacked about, without attempting to weather it.

On the 31ft, the wind blowing from the S. W. we did not approach the fhore, but, in the afternoon, we faw the land very plain, and difcovered a mountain which we had feen on the other fide of the land; we called it Mount Camel, from its likenefs to that animal: to the north of which it appears very fandy and barren, having only here and there a green plat. The fame neck of land we faw on the other fide, which reaches to Cape Maria Van Diemen, and this tends to the S. E.

On the 3d of January, 1770, in the forenoon, we faw the land again; this was high flat table land, and tended away to the S. E. where we loft fight of it; the wind ftill continued between the fouth and weft.

On the 4th, we ftood along fhore: the coaft appeared very low, fandy, and barren. About noon, the wind began to frifk and blow from the S. W. and fearing, if it fhould blow frefher, that we might get foul on a lee-fhore, we tacked about, and proceeded to the N. W. Before we tacked, we obferved a bending of the land which we thought might be a bay, but it proved otherwife, and we therefore named it Falfe Bay.

On the 7th, we had light breezes and calms for feveral days, with fair weather, and were out of fight of land. On that day we faw a fun-fifh, very fhort and thick, having fcarce any tail, but two large fins; it was as big as a fhark, and of the fame colour.

On

Plate XXII.

S. Parkinson del.

T. Mazell sculp

View of the great Peak, & the adjacent Country, on the West Coast of New Zealand.

On the 9th, we had a pleafant breeze from the N. E. the weather gloomy; the land in view low and level, tending away to the S. E. In the evening it appeared higher, and tended fuddenly to the weft; but we were not near enough to diftinguifh any thing upon it.

On the 10th, we had a fine breeze from the north, and paffed a high floping land, covered with wood, where we had feen fome fmoke. A few leagues farther from this point, which we called Woody Point, we faw a fmall flat ifland, or rock, which was almoft covered with gannets, or foland geefe; and therefore called it Gannet Ifland. Soon after we paffed a point of land, at which time, feeing a number of albatroffes on the fea, we named it Albatrofs Point: This point ftretched out a great way, and formed a fmall harbour. As we proceeded on our courfe, the land, though level, appeared much higher, and pretty well cloathed with verdure. We faw a point of land which we called, from its appearance, Sugar-Loaf Point, near which are feveral fmall iflands; and, from their vicinity to the point, we named them Sugar-Loaf Ifles. The weather being ftill gloomy, and the wind veering about to the S. W. we were obliged to ftand off and on the land.

On the 11th, in the evening, we difcovered a very peaked hill, which appeared to be as high as the peak of Teneriffe; [fee pl. XXII.] and all the bottom part of it was covered with clouds in the fame manner; we named it Mount Egmont.

The next morning, on the 12th, we approached nearer to it, but could not fee the top of it, which was loft in the clouds. From this peak the land declined gradually to a point on each fide, one ending in the fea, and the other ftretching to the coaft north of it, which was, in general, low and level, but covered with trees, as were alfo both fides of the peak. When we were abreaft of it we had very heavy fhowers of rain, with thunder and lightening; and, at length, the peak itfelf was totally inveloped in darknefs. In the night we faw a large fire. The point off this peak we called Cape Egmont.

On

On the 13th, early in the morning, we defcried the top of the peak, which was ftreaked with fnow, and, finding the land tended away to the eaft, we concluded that we were in a large bay.

On the 14th, we faw land ahead of us, and ftill apprehended we were in a large bay. We alfo difcovered feveral iflands and very deep breaks in the land : The coaft hereabout is very high, and the tops of the hills are covered with clouds; but, the weather being hazy, we faw nothing on the land excepting a fire lit up at night.

On the 15th, in the forenoon, having reached to the farther end of the fuppofed bay, we entered into a fmaller, or rather a harbour, it being land-locked on every fide. At the entrance of this harbour there are two iflands, on the fmalleft of which we difcovered a Hippa : we paffed very near it, and the natives flocked in crouds to gaze at us. We ftood in for a little cove, and anchored within two cables length of the fhore, oppofite to a fmall rivulet which ran into the fea. Some of our people went on fhore, and fhot fome birds : we alfo hauled the fein, and caught a large draught of fifhes, fome of which weighed twenty-one pounds ; and, on the fhore, we found mufcles, and other forts of fhell-fifh, in great plenty.

All the coves of this bay teem with fifh of various kinds, fuch as cuttle-fifh, large breams, (fome of which weighed twelve pounds, and were very delicious food, having the tafte of fine falmon,) fmall grey breams, fmall and large baracootas, flying gurnards, horfe-mackarel, dog-fifh, foles, dabs, mullets, drums, fcorpenas or rock-fifh, cole-fifh, the beautiful fifh called chimera, and fhaggs.

The manner in which the natives of this bay catch their fifh is as follows :—— They have a cylindrical net, extended by feveral hoops at the bottom, and contracted at the top; within the net they ftick fome pieces of fifh, then let it down from the fide of a canoe, and the fifh, going in to feed, are caught with great eafe.

The

The country, about the cove where we lay, is entirely covered with wood, and so full of a fort of fupple-jack, that it is difficult to pafs through it: there is alfo a little fand-fly which is very troublefome ; and the bite of it is venomous, raifing a bump upon the fkin which itches very much. The tops of fome of the hills, which at firft appeared to be bare, we found covered with the fern plant, which grows up to about a man's height. The hills decline gently to the water's-edge, and leave no flat land excepting one place.

The woods abound with divers kinds of birds, fuch as parrots, wood-pigeons, water-hens; three forts of birds having wattles ; hawks; with a variety of birds that fing all night. We alfo found a great quantity of a fpecies of Philadelphus, which makes a good fubftitute for tea. At one particular place we met with a fubftance that appeared like a kid's fkin, but it had fo weak a texture, that we concluded it was not leather ; and were afterward informed, by the natives, that it was gathered from fome plant called Teegoomme : one of them had a garment made of it, which looked like their rug cloaks.

The air of the country, one would imagine, is very moift, and endued with fome peculiar putrefcent qualities, as we found maggots in birds a few hours after they had been fhot.

The natives came to us fometimes, and behaved peaceably; but, to our furprife, we had adequate proofs that they are CANNIBALS. Some of our people, in the pinnace, went into a little cove, where one family refided, and faw feveral human bones which appeared to have been lately dreffed and picked ; and were told, that a little while before, fix of their enemies had fallen into their hands ; four they killed and ate; the other two jumped into the water and efcaped from them, but they were unfortunately drowned, and our people faw one of their bodies floating upon the water. The natives alfo brought us feveral human bones on board, and offered them to fale, fucking them in their mouths, and, by the figns which they made to us, evinced that they thought human flefh delicious food. One day, in particular, they brought four fkulls to fell ; but they rated

them

them very high. Thefe fkulls had their brains taken out, and fome of them their eyes, but the fcalp and hair was left upon them. They locked as if they had been dried by the fire, or by the heat of the fun. We alfo found human bones in the woods, near the ovens, where they ufed to partake of their horrid midnight re-pafts : and we faw a canoe the baler of which was made of a man's fkull. The natives feemed even to take pride in their cruelty, as if it was the moft laudable virtue, inftead of one of the worft of moral vices; and fhewed us the manner in which they difpatched their prifoners; which was to knock them down with their patta pattoos, and then to rip them up.

The natives, in this part of **New Zealand,** [fee pl. XXIII.] wear large bunches of feathers on their heads, and their garments in a fingular manner, juft as Abel Tafmen, the perfon who, about one hundred and fifty years ago, difcovered this land, has figured in his work. They were not defirous of any thing we had except nails, which they foon difcovered to be ufeful.

When thefe people are pleafed on any particular occafion, they exprefs it by crying Ai, and make a cluck with their tongues not unlike a hen's when fhe calls her chickens.

We heard a great cry, or howling, at the Hippa every night, and, moft likely, at that time they were cutting and flafhing themfelves, according to their cuftom, which is done with a piece of green ftone, fhell, or fhark's tooth, which they drive into their flefh, and draw it along, beginning at their feet and continuing it to their heads.

While we lay here, fome of our people went toward the Hippa in a boat; fe-veral of the natives came out to welcome them ; moft likely they took it to be a traverfe, and Mr. Monkhoufe fhot at them. An old man came in a few days after and told us one perfon was dead of a wound which he received. In this Hippa there are about thirty-two houfes, containing upwards of two hundred inhabitants. Some of our people faw the bones of a girl, the flefh of whi h, they faid, they ate the day before. Another party of our people, going to an ifle on the other fide of

the

Plate XXIII.

S. Parkinson del.   T. Chambers Sculp

The Heads of Six Men, Natives of New Zealand, ornamented According to the Mode of that Country.

JVSS-N

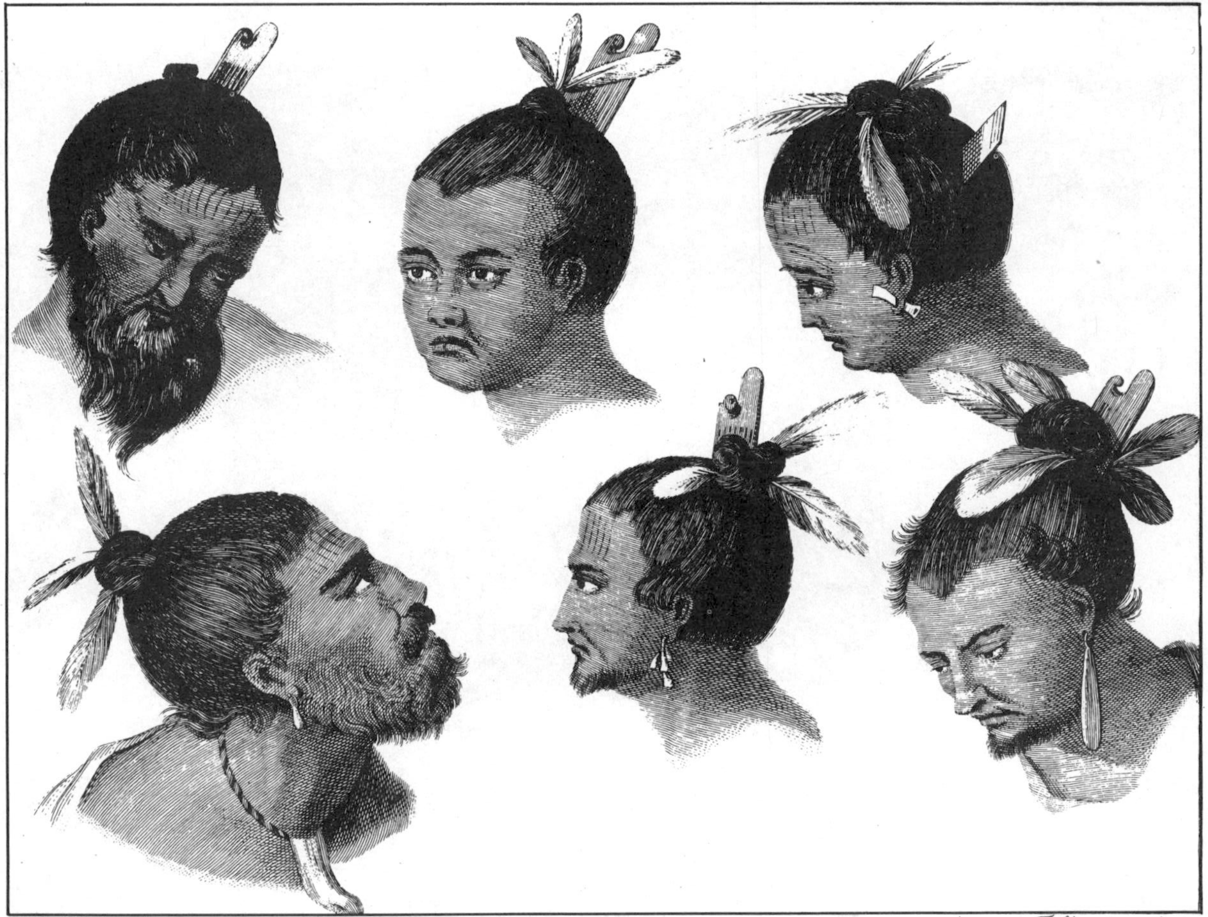

Plate XXIV.

S. Parkinson del.

J. Newton sculp.

View of an Arched Rock, on the Coast of New Zealand; with an Hippa, or Place of Retreat, on the Top of it.

the bay, met with a canoe, and were told, that a young girl had been taken from them.

There are many small islands around that appear to be entirely barren; and we saw no inhabitants upon this excepting those that belong to the Hippa; and they neither sow nor plant any thing, but live chiefly on fish, and on their neighbours when they can catch them.

We saw one of their Hippas which was situated on a very high rock, hollow underneath, forming a most grand natural arch, one side of which was connected with the land; the other rose out of the sea. Underneath this arch a small vessel might have sailed. [See pl. XXIV.] It was near a pleasant bay, and almost inaccessible: one of the natives came out and waved a large garment, or piece of cloth, to us as we passed along.

Their canoes were very stately ones: very few of the natives are tataowed: we asked them if their ancestors had not told them of such a ship as ours that they had seen in their time, but they appeared to be entirely ignorant of it. These cannibals told us, that the people, who belonged to those they had slain and eaten, were coming to them, over the hills, to kill them the next day, but it proved a false alarm.

On the 1st of February, we had a strong wind from the N. E. The hawser with which we moored the ship was broke by the strain of the sea, it being fastened on shore to a tree, and we were obliged to let go another bower. It rained all this day and part of the next, continuing, without intermission for thirty-two hours.

On the 6th, we left the bay, which we called Cannibal Bay, having been in it about three weeks. The captain called it Charlotte's Sound. The two points, which form the entrance, were named Cape Koomarroo, and Point Jackson. The natives call the land about it Totarranooe. We bent our course to an opening at the entrance of this bay, on the east, which we saw on our coming into it, concluding it a passage between the north and south part of this island. In the evening we were in the mouth of the straits, where we were becalmed. On

a

a fudden we were carried toward a parcel of broken iflands, or rather rocks, which
lie at the entrance of the ftraits; the two largeft we named the Two Brothers.
Being alarmed, we ran to the poop of the fhip, where we heard a great noife, and
faw the appearance of breakers, upon which we drove bodily aftern; neared
the iflands quickly; let go our anchor; and, before we had veered away
150 fathoms of cable, we found ourfelves amongft thefe fuppofed breakers, which
proved to be a ftrong tide that fet through the ftraits; it made a very great ripling,
efpecially near the iflands, where the water, running in heaps, bears, and whirl-
pools, made a very great noife in its paffage.   Thefe ftraits run nearly in a north and
fouth direction.

On the 7th, we weighed anchor, and proceeded along the ftraits with the tide
and a fine breeze, which fet us through with great rapidity.   At the entrance into
the ftraits, from the north, there is a fmall ifland on the north fide, near a point of
land on the main; this ifland we called Entry Ifland.   The land on the fouth fide is
very high, and but thinly cloathed, though we faw here and there a fine level.
At one part, in particular, the land was very low, and feemed to form an entrance.
We faw a very long row of high trees, like thofe at Hawke's bay, and at Ooahaowragee, or the river Thames; and it is probably the mouth of fome river.
We called this bay Cloudy Bay; oppofite to which, on the other fide of the
ftraits, is a cape or point of land which the natives of Cannibal Bay call Teera-
witte.   Here is alfo a great number of hills, and one much higher than the
reft, having its fummit covered with fnow, which we faw at a great diftance.   The
north coaft tended away eaftward; and the fouth to the S. S. W. which we followed till the night clofed in upon us; then the wind chopped about; and, being
willing to fatisfy ourfelves whether the north part of this land was an ifland, we refolved to fail as far north as Cape Turnagain.   Thefe ftraits, which we named
Cook's Straits, are about thirteen miles long, and fourteen broad.   The two eafter-
moft points of which we called Cape Campbell and Cape Pallifer.   The flood tide
comes ftrong in from the fouthward, and, on the days of new and full moon, it is
high water about eleven o'clock.

On the 8th, we failed along the fouthern coaft of this ifland: the weather was
hazy, but we difcovered many extenfive lawns, with fome high hills, the tops of
which

which were moftly flat. In the afternoon, three canoes came off to us; two of them were large and handfome.   The natives in them, who feemed to have been cut and mangled in feveral parts of their bodies, behaved peaceably; and, by afking for nails, we concluded they had heard of us from the people of fome other iflands where we had been.   They were much like the natives of Mataroowkaow, a village in Tolaga Bay; being very neatly dreft, having their hair knotted on the crown of their heads in two bunches, one of which was Tamoou, or plaited, and the wreath bound round them the fame.   In one of the canoes there was an old man who came on board; attended by one of the natives; he was tataowed all over the face, with a ftreak of red paint over his nofe, and acrofs his cheek.   His brow, as well as the brows of many others who were with him, was much furrowed; and the hair of his head and beard quite filvered with age.   He had on a flaxen garment, ornamented with a beautiful wrought border; and under it a petticoat, made of a fort of cloth which they call Aooree Waòw: on his ears hung a bunch of teeth, and an ear-ring of Poonamoo, or green ftone.   For an Indian, his fpeech was foft, and his voice fo low that we could hardly hear it.   By his drefs, carriage, and the refpect paid to him, we fuppofed him to be a perfon of diftinction amongft them.

We obferved a great difference betwixt the inhabitants on this fide of the land, north of Cook's Straits, and thofe of the fouth.   The former are tall, well-limbed, clever fellows; have a deal of tataow, and plenty of good cloaths; but the latter are a fet of poor wretches, who, though ftrong, are ftinted in their growth, and feem to want the fpirit or fprightlinefs of the northern Indians.   Few of them are tataowed, or have their hair oiled and tied up; and their canoes are but mean.

On the 9th, at noon, latitude fouth, we had a good view of Cape Turnagain. We hauled in our wind to S. W. to make the land on the other fide of Cook's Straits. The coaft we failed along was lower, and had many white clayey and chalky cliffs upon it.   We paffed two points of land to which we gave the names of Caftle Point and Flat Point.

On

On the 14th, we paſſed Cook's Straits, without ſeeing them, on the eaſt ſide of * Toaipoonamoo. The land conſiſts of high ridges of mountains, whoſe tops, ſtreaked with ſnow, had but little verdure upon them ; and, at the bottom of them, we ſaw but little low land.

In the afternoon, four double canoes, in which were fifty-ſeven people, came off to us ; they had ſome leaves about their heads, but few cloaths on their bodies, and ſeemed to be poor wretches. They kept aloof from us, nor could we perſuade them to traffic with us.

On the 16th, we ſailed along ſhore, and had frequent calms. About noon we paſſed a broad opening which ſeemed to divide the land; on the N. W. ſide of which is a ſmall bay, which we named Gore's Bay. In the evening the land tend-ed away to the S.W. and formed in various bluff points, and was, within, of a middling height, very broken, and ſomewhat bare. We ſaw ſome ſmoke, but were not near enough to make any accurate obſervations. We paſſed alſo the ap-pearance of ſeveral good harbours.

On the 17th, we ſaw more land which ſtill tended away to the S.W. and, it is pro-bable, the ſtraits we ſaw is a paſſage between the main or land we ſailed along the day before and the iſland or land we ſaw this day ; or this may, perhaps, be a con-tinuation of the larger. About the middle of this iſland, which we called Banks's Iſland, there ſeems to be a fine large bay. We hauled in our wind, and ſtood to the eaſt, one of the lieutenants being perſuaded that he ſaw land in that quarter ; but, in the evening, we bore away to the ſouth, and, on the 18th, Latitude 45° 16′, we hauled in our wind, and ſtood to the weſt, being certain that we could not miſs of land if there was any ſo far to the ſouth. In the evening we ſaw vaſt ſhoals of grampuſſes and bottle-noſed porpoiſes.

On the 19th, ſtanding ſtill to the weſtward, with a briſk breeze, in the fore-noon, we diſcovered high land ſouthward of us, being then, by our reckoning,

___

* Or the Land of Poonamoo, which is the name by which the natives diſtinguiſh the ſouthern divi-ſion of this iſland, and where the Poonamoo, or Green Stone, is found. The northern diviſion of New Zealand is called by them Eaheino-Mauwe.

thirty-

thirty-three leagues to the weftward, and eight fouthward of the land we had parted from when we failed to the eaft. We hauled in our wind and ftood for it.

On the 20th, in the morning, we were near the land, which formed an agree-able view to the naked eye. The hills were of a moderate height, having flats that extended from them a long way, bordered by a perpendicular rocky cliff next to the fea ; but, when viewed through our glaffes, the land appeared very barren, having only a few trees in the valleys, or furrows of the hills, and had no figns of inhabitants. The air was very fharp and cold.

Having beat to windward for feveral days without gaining any way, with the weather gloomy and very cold, on Saturday, the 24th, we had a frefh breeze from the north, which carried us round the outermoft point, which we called Cape Saunders : beyond which the land tended away to the S. W.

The next day, the 25th, we had variable winds and calms till the afternoon; and then we had the wind from the S. W. which was directly againft us : it blew very violently, and we were obliged to go under fore and main fails ; and tore our fore-fail in pieces. The land thereabout was pretty high, indifferently well covered with trees, but had no figns of inhabitants.

On the 27th, it continued blowing hard from the S. W. we lay to all day : at length the wind abated, but continued ftill in our teeth. Thermometer 46.

On the 4th of March, after having beat about near a week, by the favour of a breeze from the north, we got fight of land again, which tended away to the S. W. and by W. and appeared to be of great extent. We had a continual rolling fwell from the S. W. and faw the appearance of a harbour, which we named Mou-lineux's Harbour, after the name of the mafter of our fhip. We had light breezes and calms till the ninth ; and, at the dawn of that day, we narrowly efcaped running the fhip upon a ledge, or parcel of craggy rocks ; fome of which were but juft feen above water. They were luckily difcovered by the midfhipman's going to the maft head. The breeze being moderate, we put the helm a-lee, and were deli-vered from this imminent danger by the good providence of God. The land,

which

which we then faw at a confiderable diftance, feemed to be an ifland, having a great opening between it and the land which we had paffed before; but, the captain defigning to go round, we fteered for the fouth point, hoping it was the laft.   This large opening we named South-Eaft Bay; on the N. W. fide of which there is a fmall long ifland, that we called Bench Ifland.   We ftood out to fea, but, meeting with contrary winds, we beat to windward for a confiderable time: at length, the wind coming fair, we fteered wefterly, and, unexpectedly, found ourfelves between two large fhoals, which had fome rocks upon them; but we fortunately efcaped them. We called thefe fhoals The Traps.   Toward night, we got fo far round as to make the point bear N. N. E. and then we faw fome kind of ftuff upon it that glittered very much, but could not difcover what it was compofed of.   This day the weather was more moderate than it had been for many days; and being one of the inferior officers birth day, it was celebrated by a peculiar kind of feftival; a dog was killed that had been bred on board; the hind quarters were roafted; and a pye was made of the fore quarters, into the cruft of which they put the fat; and of the vifcera they made a haggis.

On the 1cth, we ftood out a confiderable way to fea; and, on the 11th, in the morning, fetched the land, and approached near it.   It had the appearance of a clufter of iflands, or a bay with a large break, being divided by a number of valleys and peaked hills, many of which were pretty well covered with wood, and had fome fnow on the tops of them; but we faw no figns of inhabitants.   We called this bay South-Weft Bay, near which lies a fmall ifland, that we named Solander's Ifle.   Having contrary winds we were driven back as far as 47° 45′ fouth latitude; but, the wind coming round again, we fteered north-wefterly, and made a point of land, which we named the Weft Cape.   We went round this cape; on the N. E. fide of which there is a fmall bay; we called it Dufky Bay; and the N. W. point of it we called Five Fingers Point, about which we faw feveral rocks.

On the 13th, we failed along the weftern coaft with a very brifk breeze from the fouth.   The land appeared very romantic, having mountains piled on mountains to an amazing height; but they feemed to be uninhabited.   We faw the appearance of fome good harbours, one of which, larger than the reft, we

called

called Doubtful Harbour; but night coming on we did not venture into any of them.

On the 14th, we failed along fhore with a pleafant breeze; the land rofe immediately from the water's edge to a very great height. Some of the higheft hills were covered with fnow, and the others with wood; but we faw no figns of inhabitants. We paffed feveral breaks in the land, which might be good harbours, but we did not enter into any of them. We faw, this day, a great number of albatroffes.

On the 16th, having a breeze, we failed along the fhore of the land we had paffed the day before, which appeared as wild and romantic as can be conceived. Rocks and mountains, whofe tops were covered with fnow, rofe in view one above another from the water's edge: and thofe near the fhore were cloathed with wood, as well as fome of the valleys between the hills, whofe fummits reached the clouds. We faw a break in the land which we thought might be a good harbour, but it proved only a fmall open bay, we therefore called it Miftaken Bay. As we failed along we paffed a broken point, that had a flat top, from which the water poured down into the fea, and formed three grand natural cafcades. This point we named Cafcades Point. On the N. E. fide of it there was a bay which we called Open Bay.

On the 20th, we met with contrary winds, which carried us away to the weftward; but, the wind coming favourable again, we refumed our former courfe, and came up with a head of land which we named Cape Foul Wind.

On the 24th, we faw a point of land which we called Rock's Point, and foon after met with a Cape; and, when we got round it, found ourfelves in a large bay, but did not anchor in it. The land tended away to the S. E. and, at the bottom of the bay, there is probably a river. We continued our courfe to the S. E. and came up with a large tract of land ftretching a good way from the main to a point, near which there is a fmall ifland. We named this point Cape Stephens; and the ifland Stephens Ifle. Having weathered the point we found ourfelves in a

large

large bay, which we called Admiralty Bay. In the mouth of this bay there are several small islands, which we named Admiralty Isles.

On the 26th, in the evening, we anchored in the Bay, which we found was about ten leagues N.W. of Charlotte's Sound, or Cannibal Bay, after having endured the dangers of foul winds, and the tedious suspense of many calms*. The inhabitants of Cannibal Bay, where we were on the 6th of February, told us, that we might sail round the south land in four days, but we had been near seven weeks in making the tour. There is no low land hereabout, the hills rising from the water's edge. Since we came from Charlotte's Sound, we saw no signs of inhabitants, except one smoke, which, perhaps, arose from some other than the hand of man; for it would seem that this land was almost entirely uninhabited, except Charlotte's Sound; and it has all the appearance of a cluster of islands, through which there are various straits, though we had no time to discover them. This second part of the land is about the size of the other, and the whole together is as large as Great-Britain.

In this bay we saw some deserted houses, but no inhabitants; and the land about it is more wild and not so flat as Charlotte's Sound; but the bay abounded as plentifully with fish, and we caught a great quantity with hooks and lines, which were distributed amongst the ship's company. We had now passed near six month, on the coast of New Zealand; had surveyed it on every side, and discovered it to be an island near three hundred leagues in length; inhabited by Cannibals, accustomed to the carnage of war from their infancy, and peculiarly undaunted, as well as insensible of danger.

The captain having fulfilled his orders, it was at his option to stay as much longer in these seas as the safety of the ship and provisions would admit; and to return home either by the East-Indies or Cape Horn. Considering that Cape Horn was at a great distance from this bay; that the season of the year was at hand which is the most unfavourable for going into so high a latitude; and that at the present time,

* The Map annexed, in which the ship's track is accur. ·ly marked, will give the reader an idea of the fatigue and danger which attended our traverse. [See ¦. XXV.]

Plate XXV

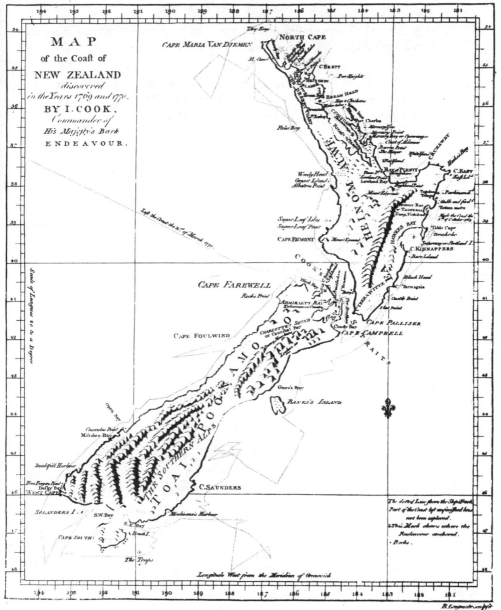

MAP
of the Coast of
NEW ZEALAND
discovered
in the Years 1769 and 1770.
BY I. COOK,
Commander of
His Majesty's Bark
ENDEAVOUR.

and for five months paft, the monfoons prevailed in the Chinefe feas; it was thought beft to proceed weft to the coaft of New Holland, and fo to the northward along it, in order to find a convenient refrefhing place; then to fearch for the fuppofed Straits between New Holland and New Guinea, (which, it is thought, admiral Torrey went through;) and along the north coaft of New Holland, to the ifland of Java; but, if thefe could not be found, it was propofed to proceed along the coaft to Dampier's Straits, which lie between New Guinea and New Britain; then to crofs the line, and fail down among the fpice iflands to Java, as we were in want of many kinds of provifions, particularly fugar, falt, oil, tea, and tobacco: our fpirits alfo very low: and, as to bread, we had not had any for upwards of fix months, and our fails were nearly worn out.

Something has already been mentioned refpecting the language of the New-Zealanders, and of its affinity to that of the people of Otaheite; the following Vocabulary will more fully fhew this agreement, which is a very extraordinary cir-cumftance, and leads us to conclude that one place was originally peopled from the other, though they are at near two thoufand miles diftance, and nothing but the ocean intervenes, at leaft to our knowledge; and fuch a long navigation, we fhould hardly believe, could be practicable in their fmall canoes, the only veffels that they appear to have ever poffeffed; yet what fhould lead too diftinct people, having no communication with each other, to affix the fame founds to the fame things, would be hard to account for in any other manner. This opinion is farther corroborated, by comparing their cuftoms and manners, as alfo their inftruments of war and houfehold utenfils, which will be found to agree in many particulars. The migra-tion was probably from New-Zealand to Otaheite; as the inhabitants of the former place were totally unacquainted with the ufe of bows and arrows till we firft taught them; whereas the people of the latter ifland ufe them with great dexterity, having doubtlefs difcovered the ufe of them by fome accident after their feparation; and it cannot be fuppofed that the New-Zealanders would have loft fo beneficial an acquifi-tion, if they had ever been acquainted with it.

A VOCABULARY

~~~~~~

A VOCABULARY of the LANGUAGE of NEW ZEALAND.

Papa,	*Father.*
Hetamàéh,	*A boy, or son.*
He aowpohó,	*The head.*
He ai,	*The brow.*
He matta,	*The eyes.*
He toogge matta,	*The eye-brows.*
He gammo,	*The eye-lids.*
He eih,	*The nose.*
He peeapeea,	*The nostrils.*
He papaeh,	*The cheeks.*
He gaōwai,	*The mouth.*
He neeho,	*The teeth.*
He gooteh,	*The lips.*
Haiàeeò,	*The tongue.*
Egoorree,	*A dog.*
Teyka,	*Fish.*
Hewhài,	*A skate.*
Eraperape,	*The fish called Chimæra.*
Hepaooa,	*Ear-shells.*
Hekohooà,	*Small ear-shells.*
Heràiyanno,	*The small biting fly.*
Heaow,	*A leaf.*
Hèànoohe,	*Fern root.*
Tracaow,	*Wood.*
Po whattoo,	*A stone.*
Whakabeete,	*The large peaked hill.*
Hewai,	*Water.*

Hèàwhài,

Hěàwhài,	*A house.*
Patéeà,	*A hedge or fence.*
Ewhàò,	*A nail.*
Tochee,	*A hatchet, or adze.*
Eëi,	*Victuals.*
Eàowtè,	*Indian cloth.*
Hecacahoo,	*A garment.*
Opoonamoo,	*A green ear-ring.*
Potai,	*The feather ornament on their head.*
Heebeekee,	*A bunch of scarlet feathers which they stick in their hair.*
Emaho,	*Tataow.*
Kaowaowaow,	*A small flute.*
Hewaca,	*A canoe.*
Hewhaiwhai,	*A bile.*
Hoggee,	*To paddle.*
Patoopatoo,	*To throw stones, to threaten.*
Oweerree,	*To roll up.*
Orero,	*To speak, or a speech.*
Apoorotoo,	*Good.*
Ekeeno,	*Bad.*
Matto,	*Steep.*
Mai whattoo,	*Stronger, or very strong.*
Keeànooe,	*Too small.*
Keeàmaow,	*Larger.*
A, a,	*Yes.*
Kaowra,	*No.*
Na, na,	*What say you?*
Eeha, teneega?	*What's that? or what call you that?*
Eta eta,	*Look you; here, here.*
Ma dooge dooge,	*Let me see it, or let me look.*

NUMERATION

NUMERATION.

Katahè,	*One.*
Karooa,	*Two.*
Katarroo,	*Three.*
Kawha,	*Four.*
Kareema,	*Five.*
Kàònoo,	*Six.*
Kawheetoo,	*Seven.*
Kawarroo,	*Eight.*
Kàeeva,	*Nine.*
Kacahaowroo,	*Ten.*

Having given a plate, containing principally the figures of the New-Zealand houfehold and warlike Instruments, it may be proper here to give a defcription of them. [See pl. XXVI.]

Fig. 1. An Ornament for the Neck, made of three round pieces of Auris Marina, or ear-fhell, the infide of which is a beautiful coloured pearl.   Thefe pieces are notched on the edges, and ftrung on a piece of plaited tape, made of white flax, and coloured red.   It hangs loofely about the neck, and is two feet, eight inches and a' half long.

2. One of their common Paddles; when ufed it is held by one hand at the top of the handle, in which there is a hole, and by the other at the bottom, where it is carved very neatly, being five feet, nine inches and a half long.

3. A Fifh-hook, made of wood, and pointed with bone, which is tied on with twine; three inches and three quarters long.

4. A

Plate XXVI.

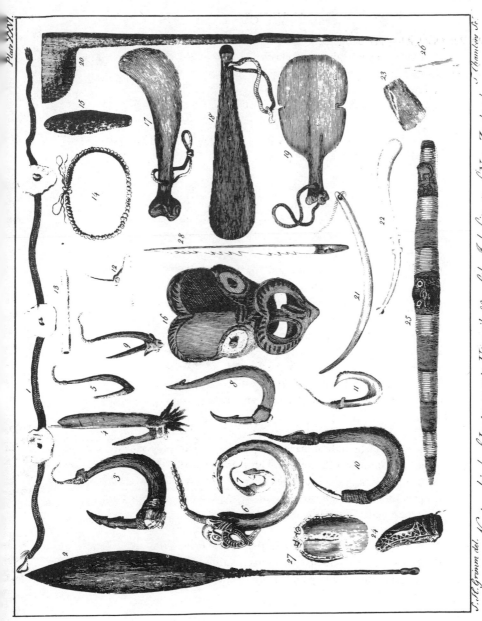

J. F. Grimm del.

Various kinds of Instruments Utensils &c. of the Inhabitants of New Zealand. J. Chambers F.

with some Ornaments &c. of the People of Terra del Fuego & New Holland.

4. A Fiſh-hook, made of two pieces of bone tied together ; the line is faſtened both at top and bottom : and, to the latter part, they tie ſome ſmall feathers. The length of this hook is 4 ⅜ inches.

5. A Fiſh-hook, made of wood, pointed with bone ; about two inches and a half long.

6. A large Fiſh-hook, made of wood, and pointed with bone, having the end, to which the line is faſtened, curiouſly carved ; eight inches and a half long.

7. A Fiſh-hook, made of human bone ; one inch and a quarter long.

8. A Fiſh-hook, made of wood, pointed with ſhell ; five inches ⅜ in length.

9. A Fiſh-hook, made of wood, and pointed with a ſubſtance that looked like one part of the beak of a ſmall bird ; two inches and a half long.

10. A Fiſh-hook, made of wood, and pointed with bone ; three inches and a half long.

11. A Fiſh-hook, made of bone ; one inch and a quarter long.

12. An Ornament made of bone, probably of ſome deceaſed relation, and worn in the ear ; one inch and three quarters long.

13. and 14. are treated of in the accounts of Terra del Fuego and New-Hol-land.

15. A piece of Wood, part of the head of a canoe, ſingularly carved ; nine inches and a quarter in length.

16. A favourite Ornament, which reſembles a human face, made of wood, co-loured red, and is much like ſome of the Roman maſks. The eyes are made

of the fine coloured ear-fhell mentioned No. 1, laid into the wood. This was fix inches long ; but they have different fizes. Some of the fmaller ones have handles carved very ingenioufly ; thefe they frequently held up when they approached the fhip : perhaps it may be the figure of fome idol which they worfhip.

17, 18, and 19, are Figures of Patta-pattoos, or War-bludgeons. They have holes in the handles of them, through which a ftring is paffed and tied round the wrift when they make ufe of them. Numbers 17 and 19, are made of wood ; the former is about fourteen inches long, and the latter twelve. Number 18 is about fourteen inches in length, made of a hard black ftone, a kind of bafaltes, and fimilar to the ftone of which the Otaheiteans pafte-beaters and hatchets are made.

20. Is a kind of Battle-axe, ufed either as a lance or as a patta-pattoo. The length of thefe is from five to fix feet. The middle part of them is very ingenioufly carved.

21. An Ivory Needle, made of the tooth of fome large marine animal, with which they faften on their cloaks. This is about fix inches ¾ in length ; but they have of various fizes ; and fome of them are made of the circular edge of the ear-fhell mentioned in No. 1.

22. An Inftrument made of the bone of fome large animal, probably of a grampus, which is ufed fometimes as a paddle, and at others as a patta-pattoo, and is about five feet long.

23. A Wedge or Chifel, made of the green ftone, or Poonammoo, as they call it, and fometimes of the Bafaltes. Thefe wedges they fometimes tie to a wooden handle, and then ufe them as hatchets and hoes. They are of various fizes, from one to eight inches in length.

24. A Whiftle, made of wood, having the out-fide curioufly carved. Befides the mouth-hole they have feveral for the fingers to play upon. Thefe, which are

worn

worn about the neck, are three inches and a half in length, and yield a fhrill
found.

25. A Trumpet, nineteen inches and a half in length, made of a hard brown
wood, which they fplit, and carefully hollow out each fide fo as to fit neatly
again, leaving an edge on each fide ; and joining them together, they are bound
tight with withes made of cane : it is broadeft in the middle, which is rather
flat, and gradually tapers to the ends that are open. In the middle of it there
is a large hole which reprefents the mouth of a figure fomewhat like a human
one, having hands and feet, the parts of which are carved round the inftrument : the head is not unlike the mafk, No. 16. Another fuch like mafk is
alfo carved near one end of the trumpet. They produce a harfh fhrill found.

26. Is fpoken of in the account of the people of Terra del Fuego.

27. A fingular kind of hand-fcoop, or water-bailer, made of one piece of wood :
the handle of it proceeds from the edge and hangs over the middle, and both
it and the edge are very ingenioufly carved. It is about eleven inches long,
eight inches wide, and near fix inches deep under the handle.

28. The head of a fpear, made of bone, about fix inches in length.

A JOURNAL

A

J O U R N A L

O F A

V O Y A G E to the S O U T H   S E A S,

In his Majesty's Ship The E N D E A V O U R.

P A R T   III.

O N the 31st, in the morning, we weighed anchor, having a fine breeze from the S. E. left the coast of New Zealand, and steered our course toward New Holland, taking our departure from a point of land near Blind Bay, which point we named Cape Farewell. We had fine weather and a fair wind till the 9th; then we saw one of the tropic birds, although we were in latitude 38° 34′, thermometer 73. We were becalmed nine days, from the 9th to the 17th, and then the wind blew from the S. S. W. and S. W. and we had a broken sea that caused the ship to pitch and roll very much at the same time; we shipped a sea fore and aft, which deluged the decks, and had like to have washed several of us overboard: we were then in latitude 38° 46′ and 22 degrees west of Cape Farewell, out of sight of land: so that the land of Van Diemen, if not

an

an ifland, muft have tended away abruptly tothe eaft, or we fhould have feen it before this time. We continued our courfe, but nothing worthy of note occurred till the 19th, in the morning, and then we difcovered the land of New Holland, extending a great way to the fouth, and to the eaftward. It is moderately high : part of it appeared to be flat, and covered with fand ; but, the weather being foggy, we had not a good view of it. We were obliged to fteer E. N. E. to clear it ; and faw three water fpouts, one of which continued very near a quarter of an hour. Latitude 37° 51'.

On the 20th, we failed along fhore with a fine brifk breeze, but we found no harbour. The land appeared rather level, with here and there a gentle afcent covered entirely with wood, fome of which appeared large. About noon we faw fome fmoke afcending out of a wood near the fea fide. Latitude 36° 51'.

On the 21ft, we had fine clear weather, and a brifk gale : the coaft appeared much the fame as it did the day before, excepting that it was rather lower. In the evening the land appeared very low and ftrait, ftretching away to the N.E. and was well covered with trees. We faw fome clouds of fmoke rifing from them a good way up the country, but we found no harbour. Latitude 35° 51'.

On the 22d, the coaft made a good view, being flat, level, and covered with verdure. The hills within land were remarkably flat : we difcovered five men upon them, through our glaffes, who were quite naked. It is probable they live upon the produce of the earth, as we did not fee any canoes, and the coaft feems to be unfavourable for fifhing. Latitude 35° 27'.

On the 25th, we were in latitude 34° 22'. The weather was very fine, but we were often becalmed. The land appeared ftill flat, remarkably level, and ftrait on the top. We faw feveral fires along the coaft lit up one after another, which might have been defigned as fignals to us.

On the 27th, in the morning, the wind being againft us, we ftood off and on fhore. At noon, being about one mile from land, fome of our men were fent on fhore in a boat, which foon returned, not being able to land for the furf,

which

which ran very high all along the coaſt. They eſpied three men, ſitting on the beach, who were naked, and of a very dark colour; but, on the boat's approaching nearer toward them, they fled into the woods. Our people alſo diſcovered ſeveral canoes drawn upon the beach, and a kind of houſe or wig-wam adjacent. We alſo, from the ſhip, ſaw five men walking, two of whom carried a canoe on their ſhoulders. The country looked very pleaſant and fertile; and the trees, quite free from underwood, appeared like plantations in a gentleman's park.

On the 28th, we got into a fine bay, and ſome of our people went on ſhore on one ſide of it, where we ſaw ſome houſes. On our approaching the ſhore, two men, with different kinds of weapons, came out and made toward us. Their countenance beſpoke diſpleaſure; they threatened us, and diſcovered hoſtile intentions, often crying to us, Warra warra wai. We made ſigns to them to be peaceable, and threw them ſome trinkets; but they kept aloof, and dared us to come on ſhore. We attempted to frighten them by firing off a gun loaded with ſmall ſhot; but attempted it in vain. One of them repaired to a houſe immediately, and brought out a ſhield, of an oval figure, painted white in the middle, with two holes in it to ſee through, and alſo a wooden ſword, and then they advanced boldly, [ſee pl. XXVII.] gathering up ſtones as they came along, which they threw at us. After we had landed, they threw two of their lances at us; one of which fell between my feet. Our people fired again, and wounded one of them; at which they took the alarm and were very frantic and furious, ſhouting for aſſiſtance, calling Hala, hala, mae; that is, (as we afterwards learned,) Come hither; while their wives and children ſet up a moſt horrid howl. We endeavoured to pacify them, but to no purpoſe, for they ſeemed implacable, and, at length, ran howling away, leaving their wives and children, who hid themſelves in one of the huts behind a piece of bark. After looking about us a little while, we left ſome nails upon the ſpot and embarked, taking with us their weapons; and then proceeded to the other ſide of the bay, where we had ſeen a number of people, as we came in, round a fire, ſome of whom were painted white, having a ſtreak round their thighs, two below their knees, one like a ſaſh over their ſhoulders, which ran diagonally downwards, and another acroſs their foreheads. Both men and women were quite naked, very lean and raw-boned; their complexion was dark, their hair black and frizzled, their heads unadorned, and the beards of the men

buſhy.

Plate *XXVII*

Two of the Natives of New-Holland, Advancing to Combat.

bufhy. Their canoes were made of one piece of bark, gathered at the two ends, and extended in the middle by two fticks. Their paddles were very fmall, two of which they ufed at one time ; and we found a large lump of yellow gum in their gigs which feemed to be for ftriking fifh. Some of their weapons had a kind of chifel fixed at their ends, but of what fubftance they were formed we could not learn.

The natives often reconnoitred us, but we could not prevail on them to come near us or to be focial; for, as foon as we advanced, they fled as nimbly as deer, excepting at one time, when they feemed determined to face us: then they came armed with fpears, having their breafts painted white ; but, as foon as they faw our boat go off from the fhip, they retreated. Conftrained by hunger, they often came into the bay to fifh ; but they kept in the fhallows, and as near as poffible to the fhore. In one of their houfes, at the top of the bay, we had laid fome nails, pieces of cloth, and various trinkets ; and though the natives had been there in our abfence, yet they had not taken any of them.

This bay is in latitude 34° 6′, and makes a good harbour, being only two or three points open to the eaftward; but the water is in general fhallow ; and it has feveral arms extending from it, which are alfo fhallow. On thefe fhallows we found a great number of rays, fome fhell-fifh, and a few fharks. The rays are of an enormous fize: one of them which we caught weighed two hundred and thirty-nine pounds, and another three hundred and twenty-fix. They tafted very much like the European rays, and the vifcera had an agreeable flavour, not unlike ftewed turtle. Thefe rays, and fhell-fifh, are the natives chief food.

The country is very level and fertile ; the foil, a kind of grey fand ; and the climate mild : and though it was the beginning of winter when we arrived, every thing feemed in perfection. There is a variety of flowering fhrubs ; a tree that yields gum ; and a fpecies of palm, [*Borafus flabellifer,*] the berries of which are of two forts ; one fmall, eaten by the hogs, and the other, as large as a cherry, has a ftone in it; it is of a pale crimfon colour, and has the tafte of a fweet acid. We alfo found a fpecies of Salvia Fortea.

We

We met with but one quadruped on the ifland, which was about the fize of a hare: we found alfo the fkin of a fnake, and faw a great number of birds of a beautiful plumage; among which were two forts of parroquets, and a beautiful loriquet: we fhot a few of them, which we made into a pie, and they ate very well. We alfo met with a black bird, very much like our crow, and fhot fome of them too, which alfo tafted agreeably. From the number of curious plants we met with on fhore, we called the bay Botany-Bay.

Having got on board a good ftock of hay for our fheep, on the 6th of May we weighed anchor, and left this bay. On this day, Forbes Sutherland, a native of the Orkneys, who had departed this life, was carried on fhore, and decently interred.

Having only moderate breezes from the N. and N.E. we made but little way till the 9th. In the evening of that day we faw two of the moft beautiful rainbows my eyes ever beheld: the colours were ftrong, clear, and lively; thofe of the inner one were fo bright as to reflect its fhadow on the water. They formed a complete femicircle; and the fpace between them was much darker than the reft of the fky.

In latitude 32° 51', on the 10th, the land appeared confiderably higher, and more broken, very fandy, and lefs fertile. We faw feveral clufters of iflands; among which, it is probable, there may be fome good harbours.

On the 11th, we paffed high broken land, having feveral diftinct peaks and hills, an extenfive flat along the fhore covered with pretty large trees, and a fandy beach. We faw alfo many fnakes, and three remarkable hills, which we called The Three Brothers. Latitude 32° 2'.

On the 14th, latitude 30° 22', the land appeared high, and well covered with wood; but, being three or four leagues from it, we could not diftinguifh many particulars upon it, though we faw clouds of fmoke arife from different diftant parts of the country. The wind was very variable after our leaving the laft bay, and we had fome calms. The wind hangs moftly between the N. and E. on this coaft, blows very gently, and then dies away to a ftark calm; but this day we had a frefh breeze from the S.W.

On

On the 15th, we were in the latitude of 28° 40′. The breeze continued brisk from the S. W. the land appeared very uneven ; and we saw a remarkable high peak, with three points at the top : behind it were three other hills, with round tops ; and the nearest land was well covered with wood. We saw six men, quite naked, walking upon a strait, white, sandy beach ; and, in the evening, having a low point of land a-head, we discovered several breakers, at a considerable distance from the shore. The wind freshening, we stood to the east ; and, soon after dark, brought to, continued sounding every half-hour, and found thirty fathoms water.

On the 16th, we were in latitude 27° 40′, and saw a vast tract of low land, with, here and there, a rising hill.

On the 17th, the land appeared higher, having many remarkable peaks ; one of which was like a glass-house : we also saw some smoke, and the appearance of a large river ; the water of which was of a pale green colour. Latitude 26° 28′.

On the 18th, in latitude 25° 36′, the land appeared to rise perpendicular, of an unequal height, and looked like a wall along the coast, without having any break ; which prevented us from seeing the back land ; and it was covered with great patches of white sand and stinted shrubs. The sea was full of a sort of orange-coloured powder, like that we saw on the coast of Brazil. On this day, we saw a water-snake.

On the 20th, in the forenoon, we were a-breast of a point which seemed to be the last of the land to the north, and tended away abruptly to the south. From this point there runs a very large shoal, on several parts of which the water broke. We sailed along-side of it, and had from seventeen to nine fathoms water. Before night came on, we got round it, and kept our course westward, as we had seen the looming of land in that quarter. The barren sandy land continued to this point, and was uninhabited. We saw a large turtle, some large grampusses that leaped out of the water, a great number of porpoises, many sharks which would not take bait, and several men-of-war birds. Latitude 24° 24′.

On

On the 21ft, in the forenoon, we difcovered land again, extending a great way, and forming a curve. It was very flat, level, and covered with trees, with a few hills within-land. We failed along it, to look for a harbour, to the N. W. There was no appearance of land to the S. W. fo that it is very probable there is a river in that part. We found no current, and our courfe was very fhallow, as we had but from feven to twenty fathoms water at a great diftance from land.

On the 22d, in the evening, we anchored in an open road or bay, round the north cape of the great bay. As we failed along, this day, the country appeared very barren and fandy, having only a few low fhrubs.*

On the 23d, the captain and fome others went on fhore, and faw a few of the natives, but could not get near them. We faw, too, about twenty of them from the fhip, who ftood gazing at us upon the beach ; alfo fmoke arifing out of the woods, which, perhaps, was only an artifice of theirs, to make us think they were numerous. We obferved nothing worthy of note on land, excepting a great variety of plants ; one of which bore a fruit like a fmall crab-apple, having a large ftone in it, the E awharra of Otaheite, and the dung of fome quadruped that fed on grafs. We hauled the feine, and tore it in pieces, but caught no fifh : though we faw great fhoals of them in this bay, they would not take the bait. We found a nautilus pompilius, and fome of a curious kind of hammer oyfters ; as alfo a number of porpoifes. We fhot a duck of a beautiful plumage, with a white beak, black body, and white and green on the wings. We likewife fhot another large bird, of the buftard kind, coloured black, white, and brown, which weighed feventeen pounds. The hills feen in this bay, which was called Buftard Bay, appeared very barren, having nothing upon them but a few diminutive fhrubs ; but we faw a large tract of low and flat land, that was covered with fmall wood, had feveral lagoons in it, and fome of the fame kind of plants which grow on the ifland of Otaheite and in the Eaft-Indies.

On

* This day the captain's clerk had his ears cut off, and his cloaths alfo cut off his back. The captain and officers offered, fome time after, at Batavia, a reward of fifteen guineas, to any one who fhould difcover the perfon or perfons who cut off his ears, and fifteen gallons of arrack, to any one that fhould difcover him or them who had cut off his cloaths.

On the 24th, in the morning, we weighed anchor, and left this bay. At noon, we were becalmed, and caught, with hook and line, feveral forts of beautiful-coloured fifhes. We faw fome very large pelicans, which were near five feet high, and the tail of fome quadruped, which we fuppofed might be a guanica. In lati-tude 23° 51' the land tended away from the fandy point in the great bay to the north-weft.

On the 25th, in the forenoon, we croffed the tropic of Capricorn. The land appeared very defolate, being little elfe than fand and rocks, parcelled out into fe-veral iflands and ragged points. We came to at night, in a fort of bay formed by the turning of the land, and found a confiderable tide flowing into it. There was the appearance of an opening in the land, which may poffibly be the mouth of a river.

On the 26th, we got in among a parcel of iflands, to get clear of which we propofed going by a paffage to the north-weft, which was next to the main ; but, finding our water fhoal very much, we fent fome men in a boat a-head of us, to found, and came into three and two and a half fathom water. They returned with an account that there was hardly water enough ; fo we tacked about and ftood out. The next morning, we had a fine breeze, and went through a paffage to the north-eaft, between two iflands : in this found, the tide fell thirteen feet. Our people, who went off in the boat, faw many of the natives upon one of the iflands, and they hallooed to them : they were of the fame fort as thofe we had feen before. On the land round about, we faw both high and low ridges, with fome peaks : part of it was well covered ; though there appeared fome large patches of white fand. Latitude 22° 52'.

On the 28th, refolving to keep the main clofe aboard, which continued tending away to the weft, we got into another clufter of iflands ; where we were much alarmed, having but three fathoms water, on a fudden, in a ripling tide : we put about, and hoifted out the boats, to feek for deeper water ; after which, as it was very gloomy and blew frefh, we kept an eafy fail to the weft, founding all the way ; and, at night, came to the entrance of a bay. This clufter of iflands is very much

variegated ;

variegated; fome of them are high, others low; fome exceedingly broken and mere barren rocks, others well cloathed. Part of the main land is very high, and has extenfive flats, covered with trees. Latitude 22° 8'.

On the 29th, in the morning, we paffed into the bay, which appears to be the entrance into fome river, by the ftrong tide that runs into the channel, which fell twelve feet in fix hours. The captain intended to ground the fhip here, in order to clean her bottom; but,

On the 31ft, we left this bay, not being able to find any frefh water, or any kind of provifions, not even fifh. The bay is open to the north; is very large and deep, and capable of containing a navy at anchor. There were many creeks, that feemed to end in a lagoon; but the captain could not determine whether the inlet, that led into the country, was a river. The country about the bay is but indifferently cloathed; the trees are fmall; and the foil on the hills is very ftony, and bare of grafs under the trees. That part of the fhore, which I faw, feemed to be a rock, compofed of broken ftones, cemented together with mud. On our firft view of this coaft, we conceived the moft pleafing hopes, but were unhappily difappointed. We faw only two of the Indians, but the marks of many more, and the footfteps of an animal that had a cloven hoof. We faw alfo many of the Yam-trees, the greater part of them having been ftripped of the bark; and feveral forts of ants, fome of which build their nefts of earth againft the fide of a tree, while others make them of leaves, glued together and hung upon the branches.

From a hill, at the entrance into the bay, we had thirty iflands in view. Through this labyrinth of iflands we paffed with fome difficulty, on account of the number of fhoals which we met with; one of which we fhould have been upon, had not the men in the boat given us timely notice. We were encouraged to attempt a paffage through them, from an expectation, we had formed, of finding one to the north fide of the land.

On the 2d of June, we were in the latitude of 20° 56', and ftill among iflands, through which we were obliged to fteer with great caution, keeping a boat out a-head, and coming to every night: we yet narrowly efcaped a bank, the foundings

were

were fo unequal. The land appeared very high, and much broken; had but an indifferent afpect, and feemed to be thinly inhabited.

On the 3d, in the morning, we had land on every quarter, excepting at fouth-eaft, and ftood to north-weft; where there appeared to be an opening, which carried us into a ftrait, in which we found deep water. This ftrait lies almoft north and fouth; is about feven leagues long, and one and a half broad. On the weft of it lies the main, and, on the eaft, a row of iflands which extend a confiderable way to the fouth. The land on both fides looked much better than that which we had feen before; being high, abounding in trees, and not fandy. We difcovered three perfons through our glaffes, and a canoe with out-riggers, like thofe of Otaheite. In the evening, we had almoft got out of the ftraits, the iflands failing, and the main tending more to the weft. Latitude 20° 27′.

On the 4th, we cleared the ftraits and iflands, and got into an open fea. The land upon the coaft was full of very high hills, whofe bowels are probably rich in ore; but their furface is poor indeed, being more barren, and fuller of ftones, than any land we had feen. We had clear and pleafant weather, and the land ftill tended away to the weft. Latitude 19° 48′.

On the 7th, we were between a parcel of iflands and the main. The main-land looked very barren and dreary: the hills upon it looked like a heap of rubbifh, on which nothing was to be feen, excepting a few low bufhes: but the iflands made a better appearance. We faw a few people in canoes, ftriking fifh, fome fmoke on the main, and fome palm-trees. Latitude 18° 48′.

On the 8th, the main land appeared ftill higher, and very barren. We difcovered feveral iflands that looked like fo many heaps of rubbifh, which had lain long enough to have a few weeds and bufhes grow on them. On one of them, which is not more than two miles in circumference, we faw a company of the natives, entirely naked, and of a dark complexion, ftanding quite ftill, and beholding the fhip with aftonifhment. At night we faw a fire, which yielded a very grateful odour, not unlike that produced by burning the wood of gum benjamin.

On

On the 10th, we continued our courfe to the north-weſt; and, about nine o'clock in the morning, we failed down a reef of coral-rocks. Our water ſhoaled very foon, from twenty-one to eight fathoms; which alarmed us very much: every countenance expreſſed furprize, and every heart felt fome trepidation. A-bout eleven, the ſhip ſtruck upon the rocks, and remained immoveable. We were, at this period, many thouſand leagues from our native land, (which we had left upwards of two years,) and on a barbarous coaſt, where, if the ſhip had been wrecked, and we had efcaped the perils of the fea, we ſhould have fallen into the rapacious hands of favages. Agitated and furprifed as we were, we attempted every apparent eligible method to efcape, if poſſible, from the brink of deſtruction. The fails were immediately handed, the boats launched, the yards and topmaſts ſtruck, and an anchor was carried to the fouthward: the ſhip ſtriking hard, an-other anchor was difpatched to the fouth-weſt. Night came on, which providentially was moon-light; and we weathered it out as patiently as poſſible, confider-ing the dreadful fufpenfe we were in.

On the 11th, early in the morning, we lightened the ſhip, by throwing over-board our ballaſt, fire-wood, fome of our ſtores, our water-caſks, all our water, and fix of our great guns; and fet the pumps at work, at which every man on board aſſiſted, the Captain, Mr. Banks, and all the officers, not excepted; relieving one another every quarter of an hour. About noon, the ſhip heaved much on one fide; upon which five anchors were carried out, and dropt at different parts; while all the hands on board plied the pumps inceſſantly, hoping to have heaved her off the rock, but hoping in vain. At four o'clock in the afternoon it was low water, and the ſhip, in feveral places, grounded on the rock. Between nine and ten, the tide rofe four feet, and the ſhip righted again; and, about ten, after fome farther attempts to clear her, ſhe providentially got off. This defirable event gave us fpirits; which, however, proved but the tranfient gleam of fun-ſhine, in a tem-peſtuous day; for they were foon depreſſed again, by obferving that the water in-creafed in the hold, faſter than we could throw it out; and we expected, every minute, that the ſhip would fink, or that we ſhould be obliged to run her again upon the rocks.

In

In the midſt of theſe gloomy proſpects and alarming apprehenſions, we found means to ſtop the leak, by a method ſuggeſted to us by an officer, who had, in a former voyage, made uſe of it with ſuccefs : we ſewed a great quantity of hair and oakum to a large piece of canvas, which we let down by two ropes, one on each ſide of the bow of the ſhip : in making way, ſhe ſucked this under, cloſe to her bottom ; and, when it reached the leak, it was forced in by the intruding water, and obſtructed its paſſage ſo much, that we kept it under with a ſingle pump. Providentially, too, at this inſtant, a breeze ſprang up, and we ſteered towards the land, the boats going before, in queſt of a harbour, which they alſo happily found, at about two or three leagues diſtance. On the 14th of June, we dropped anchor in the mouth of it ; but the entrance into it was ſo narrow, that we were obliged to place buoys all the way, to ſteer by. While we lay on the rock, it was calm ; and, from the time we left it, till this day, it blew gently ; but now it began to blow hard, which prevented us from getting into the bay till the 18th ; when we reached the deſired haven, though not without ſome danger, the ſhip having ſeveral times touched the ground.

When we threw the guns overboard, we fixed buoys to them, intending, if we eſcaped, to have heaved them up again ; but, on attempting it, we found it was impracticable.

Soon after we arrived in the bay, we laid the ſhip on a ſteep bank, on the ſide of a river ; ſet up tents on ſhore, unloaded her, carried all the cargo and proviſions into them, and there lodged and accommodated our ſick.

On the 22d, we examined the ſhip's bottom, and found a large hole, through the planks into the hold, which had a piece of coral-rock, half a yard ſquare, ſticking in it : the ſame rock, therefore, that endangered us, yielded us the principal means of our redemption ; for, had not this fragment intruded into the leak, in all probability the ſhip would have ſunk.

We loſt no time, but immediately ſet about repairing the ſhip's bottom, and in a few days made it ſound again. In the mean time, the boats were ſent out, in

ſearch

ſearch of another paſſage, which they found, and returned to the ſhip on the 3d of July.

On the 4th of July, the ſhip was carried to the other ſide of the river, and examined thoroughly ; but, being found in good condition, ſhe was ſoon placed in her former ſtation ; where ſhe was loaded, and properly fitted to proceed on the voyage.

During the time we ſtaid here, we picked up a great many natural curioſities from the reef we ſtruck upon, conſiſting of a variety of curious ſhells, moſt of which were entirely new to Mr. Banks and Dr. Solander. We met alſo with many new ſpecies of fiſh, Madrepores and other curious corals ; ſea-weed and other beautiful marine productions.

On ſhore we were not leſs ſucceſsful. Of vegetables, we found Glycine roſea, which yields a ſort of bean purſlain, that eats very well, boiled; Cicas circinalis, the kernels of which, roaſted, taſted like parched peaſe ; but it made ſome of our people ſick, who ate of it : of this fruit, they make a kind of ſago in the Eaſt-Indies : we cut down many of them for the cabbage, which is very good food. We found alſo a black purple fruit, with a kernel in it which had a flat ſweet taſte ; two ſorts of fruit like pears, having ſtony ſides, ſomewhat like the Guava, and of a very indifferent taſte ; a ſmall-leaved plant, that ſmelt like lemon and orange peel, and made an agreeable ſubſtitute for tea ; the E peea, Taro, E owhaee, and E peepee, of Otaheite : alſo wild Plantain, like the Meſia of Otaheite, which is very full of ſeed, and has hardly any pulp ; a ſort of fig-tree, that bears fruit on the main ſtem, which taſtes very inſipid ; the Etee and Eroa, of which the natives of Otaheite make the beſt lines; many gum-trees, and a great number of other plants, among which was a beautiful Nymphea, with blue and white petala.

Of birds, we found grey pigeons, with red beaks and reddiſh brown creſts, which ate very well ; two ſorts of ſmall doves; two ſorts of beautiful perroquets ; a very uncommon hawk, pied black and white; ſeveral other ſorts of hawks ; large black cocatoes, with ſcarlet and orange-coloured feathers on their tails, and ſome white ſpots between the beak and the ear, as well as one on each

wing ;

wing; the goat-fucker, or churn-owl; merops, or bee-eaters; large bats; a fmall
bird, with wattles of a deep orange red; a bird like a Tetrao, having wattles of a
fine ultramarine colour, and whofe beak and legs were black; an owl, having the
iris of its eyes gold colour, the pupil of them dark blue; a large black and white
gull, with a bright yellow beak, on the gibbous part of which was a fpot of fcarlet;
the corners of its mouth, and irides of the eyes, were of a bright fcarlet colour;
the legs and feet a greenifh yellow: a black-bird, of the oyfter-cracker genus, with
a bright red beak, except toward the point, where it was yellow; the iris of its
eyes fcarlet; the irides of them bright orange; the feet and legs of a pale-red
colour: a large olive-coloured bird of the loxia genus, having the iris of its eyes
of a gall-ftone colour, and the pupils of them black: a black and white fhag, the
iris of whofe eyes was of a fine dark-green colour, the pupils black; the fkin
which furrounded the eyes was of a verditer-green colour; the beak a pale grey;
on each fide of which was a bare yellow fpot; the feet were black: a large pigeon,
the iris of the eyes of which was of a blood colour, the pupils of them black; their
irides of a carmine colour; its legs and feet pale red. The two laft were taken in
a bay called Tafmano Bay. The black and white hawk before-mentioned, had
the iris of its eyes very broad, of a rich fcarlet colour, inclining to orange; the
beak was black, the cera dirty grey yellow; the feet were of a gold or deep buff
colour, like king's-yellow. Befides thefe, we faw many other curious birds.

Of quadrupeds, there are goats, wolves, a fmall red animal about the fize of a
fquirrel; a fpotted one of the viverra kind; and an animal of a kind nearly approaching the mus genus, about the fize of a grey-hound, that had a head like
a fawn's; lips and ears, which it throws back, like a hare's; on the upper jaw fix
large teeth; on the under one two only; with a fhort and fmall neck, near to
which are the fore-feet, which have five toes each, and five hooked claws; the
hinder legs are long, efpecially from the laft joint, which, from the callofity below it, feems as if it lies flat on the ground when the animal defcends any de-
clivity; and each foot had four long toes, two of them behind, placed a great way
back, the inner one of which has two claws; the two other toes were in the
middle, and refembled a hoof, but one of them was much larger than the other.
The tail, which is carried like a grey-hound's, was almoft as long as the body,

and

and tapered gradually to the end. The chief bulk of this animal is behind; the belly being largeſt, and the back riſing toward the poſteriors. The whole body is covered with ſhort aſh-coloured hair; and the fleſh of it taſted like a hare's, but has a more agreeable flavour.

Mr. Banks found, in the woods, an Opoſſum *, with two young ones ſucking at her breaſts.

There were many alligators on the coaſt, ſome of them very large, and we frequently ſaw them ſwimming round the ſhip.

We found alſo ſeveral ſorts of ſnakes, ants, and a ſmall culex, or fly, which is not bigger than a grain of ſand; the bite or ſting of which was venomous, and cauſed protuberances on the ſkin, which itched violently.

Of fiſh, we found many different ſorts, and a variety of beautiful ſhell-fiſh; among them three ſorts of oyſters; ſome were found in lagoons; ſome adhering to the mangrove; and others along the ſhore: large cavalhe, or ſcomber; large mullets, ſome flat-fiſh, a great number of ſmall ſcombri; and ſkate or ray-fiſh; one of which, that we caught, was curiouſly marked on the back with polygons finely coloured; and another of an orbicular figure, with a blue grey-coloured back, and white belly, which taſted like veal; ſome other parts like beef; and the entrails as agreeable as turtle. We caught alſo turtles of a bright green colour, ſome of which weighed near four hundred pounds †.

The natives, who were naked, though of a diminutive ſize, ran very ſwiftly, and were very merry and facetious. Their bones were ſo ſmall, that I could more than ſpan their ancles; and their arms too, above the elbow joint. The talleſt we ſaw meaſured but five feet nine inches; though their ſlimneſs made

* This creature has a membraneous bag near the ſtomach in which it conceals and carries its young when it is apprehenſive of danger.

† On opening a turtle that we caught we found part of a wooden lance in it, which had gone in by the breaſt before the calapee.

them

them appear taller, moſt of them were about five feet five inches; and were painted with red and white in various figures. The colour of their ſkin was like that of wood-ſoot. They had flattiſh noſes, moderate-ſized mouths, regular well-ſet large teeth, tinged with yellow. Moſt of them had cut off the hair from their heads ; but ſome of them wore their hair, which was curled and buſhy, and their beards frizzled. On their breaſts and hips were correſponding marks like ridges, or ſeams, raiſed above the reſt of the fleſh, which looked like the cicatrices of ill-healed wounds. Some of them were painted with red ſtreaks acroſs the body, and others ſtreaked over the face with white, which they called Car-banda. Some of them had a ſmall hair-rope about their loins, and one about an arm, made of human hair. They had alſo a bag that hung by their necks, which they carried ſhell-fiſh in. Their noſes had holes bored in them, through which they drew a piece of white bone about three or five inches long, and two round. [See pl. XXVI. fig. 13. and pl. XXVII.] One of them had his ears bored in like manner, and pieces of bone hung in them. Some of them had necklaces made of oval pieces of bright ſhells, which lay imbricated over one another, and linked together by two ſtrings. The women, who did not approach nearer to us than the oppoſite ſhore, had feathers ſtuck on the crown of their heads, faſtened, as we were informed, to a piece of gum.

They had lances and levers, very neatly made of a reddiſh wood ; and had two pieces of bone, joined together with pitch, that ſtood out at the end of them. To poliſh their lances they made uſe of the ficus riduola, which ſerved the purpoſe of a raſp. Their canoes were made out of the trunks of trees ; had an out-rigger ; and eight outriggers on which they laid their lances. Their paddles were long in the blade. To throw the water out of their canoes, they uſed a large ſhell called the Perſian-crown.

Their language was not harſh, as may be ſeen by the following vocabulary, and they articulated their words very diſtinctly, though, in ſpeaking, they made a great motion with their lips, and uttered their words vociferouſly, eſpecially when they meant to ſhew their diſſent or diſapprobation. When they were pleaſed, and would manifeſt approbation, they ſaid *Hee*, with a long flexion of the voice,

in

in a high and shrill tone. They often said Tut, tut, many times together, but we knew not what they meant by it, unless it was intended to express astonishment. At the end of this Tut, they sometimes added Urr, and often whistled when they were surprised.

XXXXXXXXXXXXXXXXXXXXXXXXXXXXXXXXXXXXXXXXXXXXXXXXXXXX

A VOCABULARY of the Language of the People of NEW HOLLAND.

Bamma,	*A man.*
Mootjel,	*A woman.*
Dunjo,	*A father.*
Tumurre, or jumurre,	*A son.*
Baityebai,	*Bones.*
Tulkoore,	*Hair.*
Garmbe,	*Blood.*
Wageegee,	*The head.*
Eiyamoac,	*The crown of the head.*
Morye, or moree,	*The hair of the head.*
Walloo,	*The temples.*
Peete,	*The forehead.*
Meül,	*The eyes.*
Garbar,	*The eye-brows.*
Poetya,	*The eye-lids.*
Melea,	*The ears.*
Bonjoo,	*The nose.*
Yembe,	*The lips.*
Mulère, or móle,	*The teeth.*
Unjar.	*The tongue.*
Jacal, or tacal,	*The chin.*
Waller, jeamball, or teamball,	*The beard.*
Dcomboo,	*The neck.*

Morco¹,

Morcol,	*The throat.*
Coyor,	*The breast.*
Coyoor,	*The nipples.*
Melmal,	*The pit of the stomach.*
Gippa,	*The belly.*
Toolpoor,	*The navel.*
Mocoo,	*The back.*
Eèimbar,	*The sides or ribs.*
Aco, or acol,	*The arms.*
Camor, or gamorga,	*The arm-pits.*
Mangal,	*The hands.*
Eboorbalga,	*The thumb.*
Egalbaiga,	*The three fingers next the thumb.*
Nakil, or eboornakil,	*The little finger.*
Coenjoo,	*The hips.*
Booca,	*The anus.*
Coman,	*The thighs.*
Atta,	*The ham.*
Pongo,	*The knees.*
Peegoorga,	*The legs.*
Chongarn,	*The ancle.*
Edamal,	*The feet.*
Kniororor,	*The heel.*
Chumal,	*The sole of the foot.*
Jambooingar, or tambooingar,	*The toes.*
Kolke,	*The nails.*
Pandal,	*A sore.*
Mòro,	*The scars on their bodies.*
Tennapuke, or jennapuke.	*The hole in their nostrils made for the bone ornament.*
Cotta,	*A dog.*
Kangooroo,	*The leaping quadruped.*
Taquol, or jaquol,	*An animal of the viverra kind.*

Waowa,

Waowa,	*The creft of a bird.*
Poetyo,	*A feather.*
Goromoco,	*A falcon.*
Wanda,	*A cockatoo.*
Perpore,	*The blue-headed loryquet.*
Baipai,	*The fpotted ftarling.*
Poteea,	*Fifh.*
Cooenda, or yolcumba,	*The fpotted fhark.*
Jckkerra,	*The ferrated bone of the fting ray.*
Putai,	*A turtle.*
Poenja,	*A male turtle.*
Mameingo,	*A female turtle.*
Maboo,	*The tail of a turtle.*
Mailetja,	*Echinus pentaphyloides, or flat fea-egg.*
Bingabinga,	*Echinus ovarius viridis, the greenifh prickly fea-egg.*
Kanawoongo,	*Haliotes, or ear-fhell.*
Gomego,	*Cyprea tygris, the tyger cowry.*
Metieul,	*The telefcope-fhell.*
Ebapee,	*The other mud-fhell, or lipped telefcope.*
Chicoai,	*The Perfian-crown fhell.*
Kurrow, or kurooee.	*Spondylus, the hinge oyfter.*
Moenje,	*Chama, or fmooth cockle.*
Tabugga, jabugga, or chapaua,	*A fly.*
Walboolbool,	*A butterfly.*
Wolbit,	*Plantains.*
Depoor,	*Ficus ridula.*
Badjoor,	*Cicas circinalis.*
Balanguir,	*Convolvulus Brafilienfis.*
Bandeer,	*Abrus pricatorius.*
Maracotn,	*Taro, or yam.*
Nampar,	*Bamboo.*
Maiye,	*A branch or ftalk.*
Dora,	*A leaf they chewed.*

Kere-

Keremande,	*A cocoa-nut-shell.*
Darnda,	*The redgum.*
Zoocoo,	*Wood.*
Maianang,	*Fire.*
Poorai,	*Water.*
Poapoa,	*Earth.*
Galan,	*The sun.*
Wulgar,	*The clouds.*
Kere,	*The sky.*
Walba,	*A stone.*
Toowal, or joowal,	*Sand.*
Yendoo, or jangoo,	*A basket.*
Goorga,	*A rope, or line.*
Paijall,	*A string made of a sinew.*
Charngala,	*A bag.*
Gulka,	*A lance.*
Melpairo, or melpier,	*The hand-board of the lance.*
Tapool,	*The bone ornament they wear through the septum nasi, or division of the nostrils.*
Geannar,	*A mother-of-pearl necklace.*
Carbanda, or carball,	*The white paint on their bodies.*
Maragau, or emaragu,	*A canoe.*
Malepair,	*The lever of the canoe.*
Garboora, or garburra,	*The out-rigger.*
Mairbarra,	*Smooth.*
Boota, bootina, yette, and yatta,	*To eat.*
Chuchala,	*To drink.*
Meerya,	*To roast or dress victuals.*
Tucai, or tucaiya,	*To sit down.*
Marra,	*To go.*
Mingoore,	*To dance.*
Mailelel,	*To swim.*
Pelenyo,	*To paddle.*
Aibuoje,	*To yawn.*

Poona,

Poona,	*To sleep or rest on.*
Wonananio,	*Asleep.*
Tocaya,	*Sit down.*
Kidde,	*Get along, or go before.*
Cowai,	*Let us go ; Come along.*
Hala, hala, máé,	*Come hither.*
Walgal, or walangal,	*Uncover ; take off ; shew.*
Walga,	*Strip, or uncover yourself.*
Gorra, gorra,	*Again, again.*
Chambara,	*Throw it away.*
Yeiye,	*Is it this ?*
Yarba,	*That's all.*
Cutjalla,	*Tie it on.*
Kono, kono,	*I cannot do it.*
Eya & ba,	*That, or this.*
Te,	*An article the same as A, or The.*
Chaloee,	*An expression of surprize !*
Yarea, & charo,	*Words uttered in a tone of pleasing surprize, on seeing the whiteness of some of our people's skin who had taken off their cloaths, in order to bathe.*
Yecalea,	*Expressed on seeing their spears that we had taken.*
Yerchee,	*Expressed on feeling the effects of a burning-glass.*

MENS NAMES.

Yappa Gadugoo,	Tapuolyer,	Dunggrea,
Yarconigo,	Balgomee,	Yaparico,
Garranattoo,	Goota,	Taijaputta.

Cabeeleelee, coyelaillo, halle-cutta, yerba, yerbe, yerga, are words they frequently made use of, but the meaning of them we could not find out.

As

As a mark of diffent, they faid Aipa, feveral times, and this was the only word, that we could diftinguifh, to accord with the Otaheitean language.

On our arrival, the natives fhewed themfelves, on the land oppofite to us, by degrees; and, after having thrown them fome fifh, they ventured to approach us in a canoe; landed by us; laid down their lances, and came forward to meet us, fhewing figns of amity as they came along; but they were fo much abafhed at firft, that they took but little notice of us, or of any thing about us, though they did not feem to be apprehenfive of danger. We made them fome prefents, which they accepted, but did not fhew much fondnefs for them. They became, at length, more free when only three of us were prefent, and made figns for us to take off fome of our garments, which we did accordingly. They viewed them with furprize; but they feemed to have had no idea of cloaths; nor did they exprefs a defire for any; and a fhirt, which we gave them, was found afterwards torn into rags.

The natives fhewed a great antipathy to our tame birds, and attempted to throw one of them over-board; and, a little before we left the land, they fet fire to the grafs round the fpot where we had pitched our tent; but, luckily for us, moft of our things were on-board, or they would, in all probability, have been confumed, as the fire burnt very fiercely, and had like to have deftroyed a litter of pigs, and fome other things. We fhot at one of them, who ran up the hill with a fire-brand, and wounded him. Several of them came to us afterwards, and made peace with us.

They feem to live moftly on fhell-fifh, the remains of which we frequently faw about their fires, which they procure by twirling a piece of wood in a hole, made in another piece, till it is lit up into a flame.

Some

Some of our people, in a pinnace, went in fearch of a paffage to go out of the bay, and landed on a coral reef, where they met with a great number of fhells; and, among the reft, the fpondylus, and a large fort of trochus, or top-fhell, with which they loaded the boat.

On the 4th of Auguft, in the morning, we weighed anchor, left the harbour, and fteered N. E. till we were near the Turtle Reefs; there we anchored again, and fent the boats on fhore, which returned with a turtle, a large fkate, and a great number of clams, a fort of cockle, fome of them very large.

On the 5th, it blew fo hard that we could not weigh anchor till afternoon, and then we ftood to the N. E. but, meeting with feveral fhoals, we were obliged to caft anchor again, as the wind blew frefh, and were detained till the 10th. On the morning of which we weighed anchor again, but the wind blowing hard from the S. S. E. we drove, and were obliged at length to let go two anchors, and rode by the firft with near two hundred fathoms of cable.

We had chiefly ftrong gales of wind after the fun's approach toward us from the tropic of Capricorn; and, on account of the many fhoals hereabout, we did not go directly out to fea, but kept near the fhore, and paffed by fome low iflands well covered with trees.

We alfo faw three high iflands, and failed betwixt them and the main: the latter appeared very low, barren, and fandy.

Toward evening we were on a fudden alarmed by the appearance of land all round us: the weather being hazy, and the wind blowing frefh, we hauled in our wind, and came to under a bluff point of the main.

On the 13th, in the morning, we weighed anchor, and ftood to the eaftward, clofe to one of the high iflands which we had paffed before, and fo on through a break of the reef, which was about half a mile wide. This reef, which the captain difcovered

covered from the top of the laſt-mentioned iſland, ran farther than the eye could reach, on the outermoſt ſide of all the reſt, like a wall, and the ſea broke very high upon it: We found no ſounding in the paſſage, latitude 14° 38′, and we ſtood to the N. E. in order to get out to ſea, intending to keep to the northward on the morrow.

On the 15th, about noon, we ſaw land again in latitude 13° S. alſo a continuation of the reef which ran along-ſide of it. In the evening, ſtanding right in for land, we were alarmed by ſuddenly diſcovering that reef extended to leeward of us, upon which we hauled in our wind, and crouded all the ſail we could, that we might be able to weather the fartheſt point of it. The wind was eaſterly this day, more moderate, and the ſwell of the ſea leſs.

On the 16th, at the dawn of day, we had a reef under our lee, at about a mile diſtance, which alarmed us much. When it was quite light, we ſaw breakers all round us excepting to windward, where we came in. The wind failing us about midnight, we tacked about, being afraid to ſtand any farther; and the wind's ſtill failing was the cauſe that we drove on the reef, which we now neared apace. In this dilemma, we firſt hoiſted out our ſmall boats (the long boat being ſtowed, and the pinnace repairing) to tow her off, and got a pair of ſweeps rigged out of the gun-room ports, to turn her head about. A ſlight puff of wind gave us ſome hopes of effecting it; but that failing, we approached ſo near the breakers, that there was but one heave of the ſwell between them and the ſhip. However, with our pulling, the alteration of the tide, and another ſlight puff of wind, we cleared her a little more from the reef, and ſtood to where we ſaw a break in the reef to leeward, there we hoped, at leaſt, to find ground to anchor upon; but, when we got to the entrance of it, we were driven off by a ripple of the tide that ſet out with great force; which, however, proved very providential, as we afterward found there were rocks in the paſſage, and that it was not a proper break. We then ſtood to windward, intending either to get out as we came in, or a little farther down to leeward, where the reef ſeemed detached; but, perceiving, ſoon after, the tops of ſome rocks in the paſſage, we declined attempting it. The wind again dying away, we were at a loſs what to do for the beſt; but, at laſt, determined on ſending ſome of our people in the boat to examine into the appearance

ance of another break still farther to leeward; and, a light breeze springing up from the east, we resolved to push in there, though the passage was but narrow, which we happily accomplished, being assisted by the tide; and we anchored between the reef and the shore, in fifteen fathoms water; though, at the very edge of these reefs, we had no sounding at one hundred and fifty-five fathoms. At our first entrance into this place we had very unequal soundings; sometimes finding no bottom; and one fathom farther finding it with twenty fathoms of line. This, we apprehended, was occasioned by the coral rocks which rise up almost perpendicular. Latitude 12° 36'.

On the 17th, in the morning, we sent some men in the boat to the reef for turtles and clams, but they returned without any of the former, and with but few clams, though they were of a large size.

The reefs were covered with a numberless variety of beautiful corallines of all colours and figures, having here and there interstices of very white sand. These made a pleasing appearance under water, which was smooth on the inside of the reef, while it broke all along the outside, and may be aptly compared to a grove of shrubs growing under water. Numbers of beautiful coloured fishes make their residence amongst these rocks, and may be caught by hand on the high part of the reef at low water. There are also crabs, molusca of various sorts, and a great variety of curious shell-fish, which adhere to the old dead coral that forms the reef.

On the 18th, we weighed anchor, and stood along shore on the inside of the reef, thinking that would be the safest and best way of finding the passage between New-Guinea and this land: we met with a great many islands, shoals, and reefs, and came to at night. We kept along shore till the 21st; and, at noon, in latitude 10° 36', we came to a great number of islands near the main land, which tended away to the S.W. We stood through between two of these islands, to the west, and found a very strong tide, which carried us along briskly, and gave us hopes that this was a passage between New Holland and New Guinea. At length we came to, and the pinnace was sent on shore to a spot where we saw some of the natives stand gazing at us; but when the boat's company landed, they immediately fled.

fled. The captain, and fome others, went up to the top of a hill, and, feeing a clear paffage, they hoifted a jack, and fired a volley, which was anfwered by the marines below, and the marines by three vollies from the fhip, and three cheers from the main fhrouds. The natives were armed with lances, and one of them had a bow in his hand. In other refpects they were much like the people we faw laft, being quite naked, and of a dark colour. This land was more rocky, and lefs fandy than we had lately feen, but ftill very barren; though the flats, indeed, were covered with many verdant trees. We alfo difcovered very high land at a great diftance to the N. E. which we took for the land of New Guinea.

We were obliged to keep a conftant look-out while we paffed between the reef and the land, as it was full of fhoals, reefs, fandy keys, and fmall iflands; and had we not come in again, we fhould not have found a paffage.

On the 23d, we had light breezes from the N. and S.W. with fome calms, and were certain of being in a ftrait, which feemed to be not very remote from the river Van Speult in Carpentaria; the land to the north being made up of a clufter of iflands. We found fhallow water all through this ftrait, which we named En-deavour Straits; and went over a bar that had only three fathoms and a half water. About noon, we faw a fmall ifland covered with birds-dung of a white colour; and fome of our people went off in a boat, and fhot a fcore of birds called Boobies.

On the 24th, in the morning, the cable broke in weighing up the anchor, which obliged us to drop another, and detained us all day fweeping for it with much trouble; but, the next morning, we got it up, and foon after were under way, and ftood on to the N. W. with a fine breeze from the eaft. About two o'clock, in the afternoon, we were much alarmed by finding ourfelves amongft a parcel of fmall fhoals. Thefe fhoals were difcovered by the water's appearing a little brownifh. They confifted of rocks upon which there were only two and three fathoms water; and, though there was a pretty large fwell, they did not break. There was one not half a cable's length from the fhip. We had not more than from fix to eleven fathoms water in this fea when we were out of fight of land. After examining around for the fafeft way to get clear of thefe fhoals, we weighed anchor and ftood out, firft foutherly, and then to the weft, till we deepened our water to eleven

fathoms;

fathoms; and then fuppofed that we paffed near fome part of that great fhoal, ftretching round part of the ifland of Hogeland, on the north of Carpentaria.

On the 26th, we fteered weft all day, with a fine breeze from the eaft, and deepened our water to twenty-five fathoms, in latitude 10° 10′.

On the 27th, fteering northward for the coaft of New Guinea, we were fur-prized again by the appearance of a fhoal all round us; on examination, however, we found it was only a fort of fpawn fwimming upon the water, fuch as we had often feen before, that gave it that appearance. We had, on this day, twenty-nine fathoms water and under. Latitude 9° 56′.

On the 28th, about noon, we got into very broken ground, the foundings being, on a fudden, from three fathoms to ten, and continued very irregular all the after-noon, with hard ground. This, however, did not prevent us from making all the fail we could, and without a boat ahead. About four o'clock in the afternoon, we faw low land. Toward the evening it blew very hard from the S. E. and we ftood E. N. E. and were in great danger of ftriking. As the water was fo fhoal, we ftood backwards and forwards all night; and, through the good providence of God, met with no accident. Latitude 8° 54′.

On the 29th, we ftood in for the land of New Guinea, which looked very flat, and was covered with trees, among which we faw a great many palms that over-topped the reft; but whether there were cocoa-nuts we could not get near enough, for the fhoals, to determine. We faw an opening which had the appearance of a river's mouth; and many fmokes on the land. In the afternoon we were abreaft of a point of land, which we fuppofed was that diftinguifhed in the maps by the name of Cape Valfch, or Falfe Cape : From this cape the land continued low, but did not tend to the S. E. as we expected. We could not keep near the fhore, the foundings being only from five to ten fathoms, at three or four leagues diftance from land. The water was very white and muddy, like that of a river, and had a fandy bottom. Latitude 8° 19′.

On

On the 30th, we coafted along about three or four leagues from the land, which was very flat. Our foundings were much the fame as the day before. This fand-bank extends about a league farther out to fea, as we judged from the dark-coloured water which we faw from the fhip. In the evening, the land feemed to end in a point, and tend away to the north. The fea was very full of fome ftuff like chaff, and we faw fome fmoke upon land. Latitude 8° 39′.

On the 31ft, in the night, a current carried us away fo far to weftward, that it was evening, the next day, before we made land again. We were now pretty certain that we had got round Cape Valfch by the fmoothnefs of the water, and thought the fand-bank would have broken off here, but it rather increafed, for we had only four fathoms water, and, at the fame time, could not fee the land.

After beating about for three days in queft of land, being prevented getting in with it by the wind fetting eaft, on the 3d, in the morning, we made the coaft again, and approached to within three or four leagues of the fhore : A party of our people went, in the pinnace, to examine the country while we ftood off and on. They foon returned with an account that a great number of the natives threatened them on the beach, who had pieces of bamboo, or canes, in their hands, out of which they puffed fome fmoke, and then threw fome darts at them about a fathom long, made of reeds, and pointed of Etoa wood, which were barbed, but very blunt. Our people fired upon them, but they did not appear to be inti-midated ; our men, therefore, thought proper to embark. They obferved that thefe people were not negroes, as has been reported, but are much like the natives of New Holland, having fhock hair, and being entirely naked. They alfo faw a plenty of cocoa-nuts growing on the trees, as well as lying in heaps on the ground ; and plantains, bread-fruit, and Peea. The country appeared very fertile, having a great number of different forts of trees, which formed very thick woods. The foil is very rich, and produces much larger plants than grow on the iflands. Latitude 6° 15′.

On the 5th, in the morning, which was moon-light, about one o'clock, we paffed two low iflands, which, we fuppofed, are the fouthermoft of the Arow
Ifles

Ifles that are fet down about this parallel. There is a fine frefh trade-wind, which generally blows eafterly in the day time, but comes about at night more foutherly, and blows much ftronger. We kept a W. S. W. courfe, being in latitude 7° 24' fouth, about twelve degrees from the ifland of Timor. Since the 3d inftant we have had from twelve to twenty fathoms water till this day, and then our foundings were much deeper.

The Arow Ifles belong to the Dutch Eaft-India company, who go there from Banda, and trade for fago, birds of paradife, and New-Guinea flaves.

On the 6th, in the forenoon, in latitude of 8° 15', we faw an ifland to the N.W. of us, of confiderable extent, being about fix or feven leagues of flat level land; and, by the latitude we were in, we fuppofed it was Timor land, which is laid down in the maps more to the weftward. We had a very frefh trade-wind from the S. E. and no foundings.

On the 7th, we had a frefh trade-wind from the eaft, with clear weather, latitude 9° 31', and faw abundance of very fmall flying-fifh, and fome porpoifes.

On the 9th, we had light breezes, or calms, all day. Mr. Banks went out in the fmall boat, and fhot between thirty and forty large boobies, which prey upon the flying-fifh. In the evening we faw land to the N. W. of us, and fuppofed it to be about twenty leagues diftant, which being very high, we thought, at firft, it had been clouds. Latitude 9° 46'.

On the 10th, we had light breezes or calms all day, and were ftill at a great diftance from land. We made an obfervation of the fun this day, and of the moon at night, to determine the longitude, and found ourfelves in 233° 33' weft from London; and our latitude, by obfervation, was 10° 1' fouth, by which we were certain that a current had driven us to the fouth, as we kept our courfe to the weft. We faw feveral fharks, dolphins, and barracootas, about the fhip, and caught a large fhark.

On

On the 12th, in the morning, we had light breezes from the weft, but, in the afternoon, it veered round to the fouth. We were on the eaft fide of Timor, and about one mile and a half from the fhore, which is very ftrait, and has a fandy beach ; the inner fide of which has a fkirting of Etoa trees. We faw the opening of a river which might make a fnug harbour. Both the high and low land is covered with wood, amongft which are many palms on the hills : we faw no houfe, or any human being, but a great many fmokes.

On the 15th, after having been troubled feveral days with light breezes from the S. W. we had the wind N. E. and E. and ftood fouthward to weather it. The land, this day, appeared very fcabby to the naked eye, but, viewed through our glaffes, we difcovered thefe to be clear places, many of which were fenced about, and had houfes upon them, the eaves of which reached to the ground. We faw alfo a great many palm-trees on the beach, as well as on the hills, fome parts of which were cultivated. We had a bold fhore, with hardly any beach. Toward evening the land near the fhore appeared much flatter and more level; behind which, at a great diftance, we difcovered many high hills. Latitude 10° 1′.

On the 16th, in the morning, we had a brifk trade-wind from the eaft, and a view of the ifland of Rotté, which lies off the fouth end of Timor, and paffed between it and Anamaboo, which lies to the S. W. of Timor. Both thefe iflands were much lower than Timor ; neither did they appear fo fertile. We faw no houfes, fmoke, or cultivated land upon them, but many palms of a kind we were not acquainted with. We had a fine brifk trade-wind this day, but no foundings; latitude, by obfervation, was 10° 24′, about four or five leagues from the fouthermoft part of Timor. In the night, between ten and eleven o'clock, before the moon was up, we faw a remarkable phænomenon, which appeared in the fouth quarter, extending one point weft, and two eaft, and was about twenty degrees high, like a glow of red rifing from fire, ftriped with white, which fhot up from the horizon in a perpendicular direction, alternately appearing and difappearing.

On

On the 17th in the morning, we faw a fmall ifland, which, by its appearance, promifed nothing, being brown, and almoft bare, excepting of palms, and a few other trees.   On our approaching nearer to it, we faw feveral forts of cattle, which induced us to fteer to leeward and fend the boat on fhore; in the mean time, ftanding off and on, feveral of the natives came to them on horfeback, who fpoke a little Portugueze, and told them there was a bay on the other fide of the next point where the fhip might anchor, and we might meet with a fupply of provifions. We purfued our courfe round the point, and anchored in a very large bay.   In the evening we faw a village, fituate on the fide of a hill, that had Dutch colours hoifted in it.   The next morning fome of us went on fhore, and waited on the Raja, or king, who received us very gracioufly, and promifed to fupply us with every thing, if the Dutchman pleafed: The Dutchman vouchfafed to confent, and made us a vifit on board, in company with the Raja and his attendants : they dined with us; were very ceremonious, and left us, after having made fpecious profef-fions of friendfhip.   The next day fome of our people returned the vifit, and dined with them.   After much fhuffling on their part, we made fhift to obtain a large number of fowls, eight bullocks, feveral goats, hogs, a great quantity of fyrup, and a few fruits.

They informed us that they had been without rain in the country for feven months, and that the herbage was almoft burnt up.

This ifland, which is divided into five diftricts, is about thirty miles long; is called Savoo, and lies fouth of India.   It contains near nine thoufand inhabitants, and for thefe nine years paft has been poffeffed by the Dutch, who have a refident here, and trade to India, Macaffar, and Timor ; and, from this ifland, furnifh Concordia with provifions.   It was formerly in the poffeffion of the Portuguefe, who left it about an hundred years fince.

As we were not permitted to examine the country, or its products, the Dutch-man not fuffering us to go any where without a ftrong guard, I amufed myfelf in picking up, from the natives of the ifland, what particulars I could learn in refpect to their language, from which I afterwards formed the following vocabulary.

A

A VOCABULARY of the LANGUAGE of the Natives of the Island of SAVOO.

Momonne,	*A man.*
Neekeeng-ïro,	*A grown man.*
Monama,	*An old man.*
Monecopai,	*A boy.*
Mobunne,	*A woman.*
Anawuneekee,	*A child.*
Càtoo,	*The head.*
Row catoo,	*The hair of the head.*
Bocòlo,	*The crown of the head.*
Otaïle,	*The temples.*
Tangarei,	*The forehead.*
Màdda,	*The eyes.*
Ròw na màdda,	*The eye-brows.*
Dungèena madda,	*The eye-lids.*
Roòpa-gàpoong,	*The eye-lashes.*
Wodeèloo,	*The ears.*
Sivànga,	*The nose.*
Roä fivànga,	*The nostrils.*
Cavarànga,	*The cheeks.*
Larà-voòboo,	*The mouth.*
Kooring-voòboo deeda,	*The upper lip.*
Kooring-voòboo vàva,	*The under lip.*
Sungeèdee,	*The gums.*
Ingootoo deeda,	*The upper teeth.*
Ingootoo vàva,	*The under teeth.*
Vaio,	*The tongue.*

Pàgavee,

Pàgavee,	*The chin.*
Row, na voobo,	*The muſtachios.*
Row, vee,	*The beard.*
Lacòco,	*The neck.*
Làdogòro,	*The throat.*
Sooſoo,	*The breaſts.*
Caboo ſooſoo,	*The nipples.*
Dùloo,	*The belly.*
Aſſoo,	*The navel.*
Kòlogoòno,	*The ſhoulders.*
Càmacoò,	*The arms.*
Làrabòrro,	*The arm-pits.*
Vosëoo,	*The elbows,*
Baibaö,	*The wriſt.*
Wùlaba,	*The hand.*
Daraba,	*The palm of the hand.*
Dunëäba,	*The back of the hand.*
Kiſooë aïaï,	*The thumb.*
Kiſoë Aïyooyoo,	*The forefinger.*
Kiſooë Aïtororro,	*The two next fingers.*
Kiſooë Eikee,	*The little finger.*
Koo-oo,	*The nails.*
Voorai,	*The backſide.*
Tooga,	*The thighs.*
Roòtoo,	*The knees.*
Làracrùkee,	*The hams.*
Baibo,	*The legs.*
Dooloomoònoo baibo,	*The calves of the legs.*
Pàcalaï,	*The ancles.*
Duneeäla,	*The feet.*
Woterdo,	*The heel.*
Dara yïlla,	*The ſole of the foot.*
Kiſoòei yìlla,	*The toes.*

Racăee,

Racäee,	*The skin.*
Killooë,	*The veins.*
Macoocooree,	*The flesh.*
Munje,	*Fat.*
Row,	*Hair.*
Cabao,	*A buffalo.*
Dejaro, or diaro,	*A horse.*
Vavee,	*A hog.*
Gnaca,	*A dog.*
Badoo gnaca,	*The barking of a dog.*
Kesàvoo,	*A goat.*
Doomba,	*A sheep.*
Keë,	*A ewe.*
Maiö,	*A cat.*
Roolai,	*The tail of a quadruped.*
Doleela,	*A bird.*
Pangootoo,	*The beak of a bird.*
Carrow,	*The tail of a bird.*
Row-mannoo,	*Feathers.*
Dulloo,	*An egg.*
Manoo,	*A cock or hen.*
Raree-manoo,	*The comb of a cock.*
Tutuo-manoo,	*Cock-crowing.*
Kidicoo-manoo,	*Clucking of a hen.*
Nudoo,	*A fish.*
Unjoo,	*A turtle.*
Toodoolai,	*A libellula, or dragon-fly.*
Samala,	*A muscheater.*
Sotee,	*Nautilus pompilius. The large chambered nautilus, or sailor-shell.*
Kerogga,	*Coralline.*
Adjoo,	*A tree, and wood.*
La,	*The trunk of a tree.*
Coree, or koree,	*The bark of a tree.*

Calai,

Calai,	*A branch.*
Row,	*A leaf.*
Vooe,	*Fruit.*
Dooe, or Dooa,	*The fyrup palm.*
Kililla,	*Areca.*
Ao,	*Chinam.*
Cananna,	*Piper betle.*
Nai,	*Tobacco.*
Vomoo,	*Plantains.*
Chevoos, ava,	*Oomarra, or fweet potatoes.*
Oobee,	*Ignames or yams.*
Cleeoo,	*Bamboo.*
Dubboo,	*Sugar Cane.*
Leebee,	*Avirrhoa bilimbc.*
Boa feeree,	*Palm-fruit.*
Wafilaggee,	*Tamarinds.*
Wudyarroo,	*Limes.*
Yirroo,	*Oranges.*
Nicu,	*Cocoa-nuts.*
Arre,	*Rice.*
Kivoonoo,	*Cocoa-nut rind.*
Cadjoo manoo,	*Cinnamon.*
Mangooroong-ootoo,	*Nutmegs.*
Wowdulloo,	*Cloves.*
Vopaio,	*Black-pepper.*
Cootoo-codo,	*Ginger.*
Lodo,	*The fun.*
Wurroo,	*The moon.*
Leeroo,	*The fky.*
Miramoo,	*The clouds.*
Capoa-reero,	*The horizon.*
Demoo,	*The Eaft.*
Va,	*The weft.*
Wodai,	*The north.*
Wullow,	*The fouth.*

Sabooai,

Sabooai,	Smoke.
Mireèngee,	Cold.
Kibàſoo,	Heat.
Aee,	Fire.
Ailei,	Water.
Aidàſſèe,	The ſea.
Nova,	The ſurf of the ſea.
Vorai, or raee,	The earth.
Càco,	The land.
Collolaide,	The hills.
Wawadoo,	A ſtone.
Laſilai,	Sand.
Buſſee,	Iron.
Bulido,	Lead.
Millapoòdee,	Silver,
Millalàrra,	Gold.
Umoo,	A houſe.
Bagoo,	A ſtool.
Cabeeſſa,	A baſket.
Dupee,	A mat.
Lèöravoo,	A looking-glaſs.
Baraco,	A box.
Retaca,	An axe.
Ingootoo-tumoo,	A comb.
Toodee,	A knife.
Toodee-yampoo,	A caſe-knife.
Yobe,	A ſword.
Kepocke,	A long ſpear.
Kepovarena,	A cannon.
Daire,	A drum.
Goola,	Palm ſyrup.
Booro,	Bread.
Dàgee,	Mutton.
Gàrra,	Salt.
Munje,	Oil.

Leepa,

Leepa,	*Cotton cheque.*
Seegee,	*The cotton cloth made on the island.*
Codo,	*A callico gown.*
Singoodoo,	*A palm bonnet.*
Oodoo,	*Beads.*
Gaddee,	*Large ivory rings.*
Tàtà,	*Tataow, or marks made in the skin.*
Màànadoo,	*A fish-hook.*
Cova,	*A boat.*
Joolee, or toolee.	*A large canoe.*
Capa,	*A ship.*
Dupoodeo,	*White.*
Cairara,	*Yellow.*
Damuddee,	*Blue.*
Mingaroo,	*Green.*
Sooree,	*Red.*
Bulla,	*Black.*
Sao-lodo,	*The morning.*
Deeda-lodo,	*The forenoon.*
Nutoo-lodo,	*Noon.*
Maceo-lodo,	*Afternoon.*
Munda-lodo,	*The evening.*
Mudda,	*Midnight.*
Pooai,	*More.*
Taro,	*There.*
O,	*Yes.*
Tiràmacoòsee,	*Farewell.*
Bolè,	*Stay, wait a little.*
Buffoo,	*Enough, I am satisfied.*
Sillaèo,	*To see.*
Roädeèloo,	*To hear.*
Taïyiggee,	*To feel.*
Kìffoo,	*To smell.*
Gnaä,	*To eat.*
Neenawei,	*To drink.*

Neeno-

Neeno-darao,	*To drink to one.*
Toonoo,	*To roaſt or bake.*
Varitai,	*To kindle or light.*
Jugge, or tugge,	*To kick.*
Tookoo,	*To Row.*
Voſſee,	*To paddle.*
Ta laco,	*To bend.*
Ta puceo,	*To break.*
Ta ſeeo,	*To tear.*
Ta te,	*To cut.*
Ta ſoonne,	*To hide.*
Ta tucke,	*To lay by.*
Ta ingaree,	*To ſhew or take out.*
Ta teetoo,	*To riſe.*
Ta tooe,	*To fall.*
Midyadee,	*To ſit down.*
Ta eaco,	*To walk.*
Ta rai,	*To run.*
Ta mudje,	*To talk.*
Painyee marunga,	*To blow the noſe.*
Painyee roo elloo,	*To ſpit.*
Ta bunge,	*To ſneeze.*
Ta maia,	*To cough.*
Ta marree,	*To laugh.*
Picoongaca,	*To whine.*
Ta tanjee,	*To cry.*
Ta budje,	*To ſleep.*
Maddee,	*To dye.*
Manu Diami,	*The Governor's name.*

NUMERATION.

NUMERATION.

Iſſe, or uſſe,	*One.*
Rooe,	*Two.*
Tulloo,	*Three.*
Uppa,	*Four.*
Lumee,	*Five.*
Unna,	*Six.*
Petoo,	*Seven.*
Aroo,	*Eight.*
Saio,	*Nine.*
Singooroo,	*Ten.*
Singooroo iſſe,	*Eleven.*
Singooroo rooe,	*Twelve, &c.*
Rooingooroo,	*Twenty.*
Rooingooroo iſſe,	*Twenty-one, &c.*
Tulloomooroo,	*Thirty.*
Tulloomooroo iſſe,	*Thirty-one, &c.*
Uppangooroo,	*Forty.*
Lumingooroo,	*Fifty.*
Unnangooroo,	*Sixty.*
Peetoongooroo,	*Seventy.*
Aroongooroo,	*Eighty.*
Saiongooroo,	*Ninety.*
Singaſſoo,	*One hundred.*
Looang aſſoo,	*Two hundred.*
Setuppah,	*One thouſand.*
Roo ſetuppah,	*Two thouſand.*
Selacuſſa,	*Ten thouſand.*
Serata,	*One hundred thouſand.*
Sereboo,	*A million.*

After

After a ſtay of two or three days, we left Savoo, and, on the 1ſt of October, in the morning, diſcovered Java and Prince's Iſlands. We directed our courſe through the Straits of Sundy; and, in the afternoon, paſſed a ſmall iſland, upon which we ſaw a very high hill, of a conical figure, and ſeveral ſmall ones. This is called the Iſle of Crocata: We ſaw alſo Pepper-Point. In the night, the weather was ſqually, and we had rain, with thunder and lightening. By our reckoning we found that Java Head is about 14° 22′ to the weſt of Timor. We had a briſk trade-wind from the S. E. and very near over-ſhot the Straits; but not finding land, we hauled to the eaſtward, and luckily got into the Straits to the leeward of Prince's Iſland. Our latitude, at noon, was 6° 9′.

On the 2d, we ſailed up as far as Angor Point, where we were becalmed, and waited for the current, which ſets to the ſouth till the monſoon ſhifts. We ſaw two Indiamen at anchor in Angor Bay. This was a pleaſing ſight; and, being impatient to hear news from England, the pinnace was hoiſted out, and ſome of our people went on board of them, who learned that the Swallow had arrived ſafe in the Engliſh channel; that freſh diſturbances had ariſen at home, in reſpect to the miniſters, and in America on account of taxes; that the flame of war was like to break out; that the Ruſſians, Poles, and Turks, were already embroiled in a war; and that the Ruſſians had made ſome vigorous attacks upon the Turks both by ſea and land. We ſent the boat on ſhore for ſome plantains and cocoa-nuts; and, in the evening, having a gentle breeze, we weighed anchor, and ſtood through between Angor Point and the oppoſite ſhore, and paſt Keita Iſland. The land of Sumatra ſeemed very near, and appeared to be exceeding high. We had alſo a more diſtinct view of Java, which was woody, and very high, particularly Bantam-hill, which is to be ſeen at a great diſtance.

On the 3d, we got up near to Bantam Point, or Point St. Nicholas, where we were becalmed, and dropped anchor. We ſaw a Chineſe veſſel paſs along the Straits, with Chineſe colours flying, which were white, and had a broad border, partly blue and partly black: in the middle of it ſeveral Chineſe characters, and a ſtar, which were painted of the latter colour. She had one maſt; an oblong ſquare ſail, a bamboo yard, and an awning, or houſe, in the middle.

In

In the afternoon, fome people came off to us, in a boat, from Angor-Point, to enquire who we were, and brought plantains, pumplenofes, oranges, turtles, parrots, domeftic poultry, fome fmall birds, and monkeys, which they offered to fale. They told us that the Prince-George, captain Riddle, was loft laft June off Batavia, and that the crew were carried by a Dutch fhip to Bengal.

In the evening we weighed anchor, but, having only a light breeze, we made no way.

On the 4th, we had a northerly wind, which was directly againft us, and the current ran very ftrong. Finding that we had loft ground, we anchored at night off Pulo Pifane; and, while we lay at anchor, fome of our people went on fhore in a boat, and bought fome cocoas, and Paddy, or rice in the hufk. On the evening of the next day, a light breeze fprang up from the Weft; but we were foon becalmed, and dropped anchor again. The weather was very fultry. Thermometer 86.

On the 7th, we weighed and dropped anchor feveral times, having light breezes and calms: however, the tide fhifting in our favour, we reached, that day, as far as Pulo Babi, which lies in the bay of Bantam, and paffed Pulo Panjang.

On the 8th, having light breezes, with calms, and the current running ftrong againft us, we made but very little way. This day we failed between the Milles Ifles, Pulo Tidong, and Pulo Pare. Thefe are moftly fmall and low iflands, covered with trees; and, by the lights which we faw on fhore, we concluded that fome of them were inhabited; and were not deceived in our conjectures; for, at night, fome of the natives came off to us, and brought fome turtles, pumpkins, and dried fifh.

On the 10th, we anchored in the road of Batavia, in which we found fixteen large fhips, three of which were Britifh; one of them an Indiaman that had loft its paffage to China, and the other two private merchantmen. A lieutenant, in the pinnace, was difpatched to the deputy-governor with a meffage, who told him, he

fhould

should be glad to see captain Cook, and that it would be proper to present his requests to the council in writing, who were to meet the next day. The pinnace returned to the ship, loaded with pine-apples, plantains, water-melons, and a bundle of London news-papers, which were very acceptable presents.

The Dutch commodore sent a messenger on-board of us, to enquire who we were; and by him we learned that the Falmouth man-of-war fell to pieces in this road about four months before we arrived.

Batavia, formerly called Jocatra, is situated in a very large open bay, in which is a great number of low islands; the principal of which, called the Milles Isles, lie off the bay. It is walled round, and has many canals cut through it, supplied by a river, which is divided into several streams, that run through the town. The main canal, which is large enough to admit small vessels, is carried a long way into the sea by means of a mole. The mountainous part of this country is at a great distance within land; and the plain flat land, which surrounds the city, is of considerable extent, very fertile, and watered with a great many rivulets; which renders the communication between different parts very easy. The roads which lead from the city are many, and as good as ours in England; they extend a long way into the country, and are so many avenues, planted with Tamarind, Cocoa, Pisang, Bread-fruit, Jacca, Duriam, and Allango, trees, which render them very pleasant. There is a great number of villas all along these roads, many of which have a magnificent appearance. In brief, the whole country looks like a garden, divided into different plantations by hedge-rows of trees and canals. But these canals, which are so convenient and enrich the views of the country, are supposed to be prejudicial to the health of the inhabitants: for, in the dry season, they stagnate, become putrid, and, being exhaled by the sun, the air is charged with noxious vapours: while the great number of trees prevents them from being dispersed by the winds, and occasions that kind of putrid fever, which is so common, rages so much, and is so fatal amongst them, insomuch that it carries off a patient in a few days; and indeed the climate is so unhealthy, that even the slaves, brought here from other parts of India, feel the effects of it. Fluxes too are also very common and dangerous at Batavia; and their intermittents, which the inhabitants think trivial, are very prejudicial

judicial to foreigners; but it muft be allowed, however, that they moftly prove fo for want of obferving a proper regimen.

The houfes in the city are moftly built of brick, and plaiftered over; many of them are very fpacious, and furnifhed very fumptuoufly, efpecially on the ground-floor; the bed-chambers, in general, having but little furniture in them. There are five gates to the city, with draw-bridges to each, which are fhut at night. The fuburbs, which furround the town, cover a large piece of ground, but are meanly built. The Campan China, which is largeft, is on the fouth fide.

The public buildings, in this city, are the caftle, a town-hall, and feveral churches. The caftle is fquare, furrounded by a ditch, and confifts of feveral fquare courts, in one of which is depofited a great number of warlike inftruments, efpecially of guns and balls.

The town-hall and the great church are handfome edifices. The church is of an octagon figure, having a dome and lanthorn of the fame form, and has a very fine organ. Ruyter's kirk, belonging to the Lutherans, is fmall, but a very neat building. The Portuguefe church is of an oblong fquare; and the priefts, belonging to it, preach in the Malay as well as the Portuguefe language.

The ftreets of Batavia are paved on both fides, are very regular and ftraight, and a canal runs through the middle of moft of them, both fides of which are planted with trees, which have a very agreeable effect; and, as all kinds of goods are conveyed by water, the ftreets are in good repair. The bazar, or market-place, is large and fquare, interfected by rows of ftails, and abounds with different fruits and garden herbage, alfo with poultry, pork, dried fifh, and a variety of other commodities. Near it is another fquare bazar, for fifh, fhell-fifh, and meat; but the chief market for vegetables is held at a place, called Tannabank, a little diftance from the town, on every Saturday morning, where they may be had very cheap.

This city is the feat of the Dutch governor-general and council of the Indies, and is, with feveral neighbouring fettlements of that nation, immediately under their direction; and to them all the other governments, belonging to their Eaft-

India

India company, are fubject. They meet, for the difpatch of bufinefs, feveral times in a week. There are alfo two fabanders, who, amongft other things, tranfact the bufinefs of foreigners with the council; a mayor of the city ; and a land and water fifchal for criminal affairs.

The Dutch, by their induftry, have done more here than any other power in Europe has done in India ; and, by means of their policy, have rendered it one of the moft flourifhing cities in this part of the world, where moft European, as well as Indian, commodities may be purchafed ; but it is not a good market for Indian goods ; for you meet with but few of them, and thofe few are very dear. This city is the chief rendezvous of the Dutch trade for the Eaft-Indies, and from this port the fhips for Europe take their departure. Here is a large houfe, appointed by the company, as a hotel for the accommodation of all European ftrangers, where they are obliged to refide, and pay two rix-dollars a day for a maintenance, while the Dutch may live for twenty-five rix-dollars a month. There is not, perhaps, any city in the world that contains a greater variety of people. One would imagine there were affembled, of different human beings, from every nation under heaven, who, for the moft part, retain their feveral peculiar dreffes, and are allowed to live after the manner of their refpective countries. Of whites, there are Dutch, who are mafters ; but the greater part of the company's fervants, and of the inhabitants, are Germans, Danes, Swedes, and Hungarians ; with a few Englifh, French, and Italians ; of thefe the foreign merchants are chiefly compofed ; and moft of them keep their chariots, and live in great luxury and elegance. A great number of flaves precede and follow their chariots ; and, when the women go abroad, the female flaves fit on the fteps of the chariot. The men are dreffed exceffively gay, having filk and velvet garments, richly laced and embroidered, with laced hats, and finely-dreffed wigs. Their waiftcoats have fleeves ; and, when they fit in a houfe, they always take off their coats. Amongft the middle clafs of people, a pair of drawers, which have two gold buttons and reach above their breeches, is reckoned a great piece of finery. The women drefs moftly in chintzes, made generally in the European, though fometimes in the Malay, fafhion : they are feldom feen walking in the ftreets, ufually riding in carriages. Both men and women have a fickly complexion, without any colour in their cheeks ; but palenefs, it feems, is reckoned one mark of beauty among the ladies. Befides chariots, which are open and richly

ornamented,

crnamented, they have fedans, with wooden lattices, carved and gilt, and fhort
fpokes, which make an aukward appearance to a ftranger: and, for their children,
they have a fort of oblong fquare box, with a lattice at the fides, and a roof fafh-
ioned like the eaves of a houfe; this has a fpoke at each end, and is carried by two
men on their fhoulders, and the child within fits all along on the bottom of it.

Their manner of living is pretty much the fame in all feafons of the year. They
rife as foon as it is light, and drink tea or coffee; then tranfact their bufinefs, either
within or without doors, till nine o'clock in the morning, at which time it is too hot
to be in the open air; and they negotiate bufinefs, or divert themfelves otherwife,
within doors, till about noon, and then dine. After dinner, they ftrip themfelves
of every thing, except a pair of drawers and a fhort cotton gown, and go to bed.
At four or five o'clock in the afternoon they rife again, drink tea, and, if they have
no bufinefs to tranfact, as there are no public places of diverfion, they take an airing
in their carriages; come home, fup, and go to bed again about eleven at night.
Thofe born here of European parents, who are not many and are of a mixed breed,
generally follow the Malay cuftoms.

The inhabitants are moftly Chinefe, and their number is very great both in town
and country. The China town, which is on the fouth fide of the city, is pretty large,
but meanly built, as the better fort of Chinefe live within the city. The greater number of fhopkeepers are Chinefe; they make all the arrack and fugar; nor can any
perfon hold an arrack-houfe without having it under the name of fome Chinefe.
They alfo cultivate all the variety of garden-ftuff with which Batavia is furnifhed;
and of them there are filver-fmiths, pewterers, carpenters, joiners, mafons, calkers,
barbers, hawkers, dealers, and chapmen. There is not any trade, however mean
and fervile, which they do not follow: and, though the Dutch have laid them under
many reftrictions, yet they find means to acquire a comfortable fubfiftence, and
often accumulate wealth. The Dutch have impofed a poll-tax on them of a duca-
toon, or fix fhillings and eight pence, a month.

The Chinefe in and about Batavia have a fallow complexion, black eyes, and tole-
rable good nofes, but they pluck their beards up by the roots, and make, upon the
whole, a very effeminate appearance.

They

They form two fects, and keep moftly to their own cuftoms. One of them wears all their own hair; and the other, which is by far the moft numerous, fhaves all the head except the crown. Thefe different modes arife from a peculiar religious tenet held amongft them. When a rich man has a child, and thinks he can maintain it, independent of any fervile employment, he fuffers the hair on its head to grow, which is wound up, tied upon the crown, and ornamented with a gold bodkin or two, and it muft never afterwards be fhaven; thefe are of high rank amongft them. The other children have their heads fhaven nine months after their birth, and on every ninth day afterwards, till they attain a certain age; and then they are at liberty either to wear it growing or have it fhaved: the lock of hair, left on the crown of fome of their heads, grows to a great length, reaching down to their pofteriors. Their drefs is excellently adapted to a hot climate, being generally white taffety, or callico; and confifts of a pair of trowfers, over which they wear a frock with wide fleeves, which buttons before: a purfe, wrought with filk, hangs beneath the upper garment; and a pair of Chinefe pampouches completes their drefs. The old men fometimes wear a fort of white boots, that reach up to their knees; and they always carry a fan in their hands, to fhade their heads from the fun. Their ufual falutation is, Adda bai ké, *how do you do, fir?* and they are very courteous in their addrefs and behaviour, efpecially to Britons, whofe generofity, I fuppofe, they have often experienced. The hawkers, amongft them, who outdo the Jews in low artifice, will afk twenty dollars for a thing, and take one; and have acquired, even among themfelves, the character of great cheats.

Before the rebellion in 1740, the Chinefe were intirely governed by two of their own nation, who were judges in all cafes, and fat in council. At prefent, they have a captain and two lieutenants, one of whom fits every forenoon, with a jury of twelve, in a hall they have for that purpofe, to hear and make up fuits and quarrels, which happen amongft them, if poffible, before they go before a Dutch court of judicature; and this the Chinefe muft do, if they defign to live in harmony with their community. To the faid hall they all repair, the three firft days of the month, to pay their head-money; at which time there is a Dutch enfign hoifted on a ftaff before the gate.

The

The Chinefe have four pagodas, or places of worfhip, in Batavia; but they do not feem to be a religious people, and are very carelefs and inattentive in the time of worfhip. I went into one of their pagodas, where I faw a company of them playing at cards in the principal part of it, that had an alcove, with feveral images in it, and lamps burning before them; fome little boxes full of afhes, on which they burnt paper before their idols; and, on the wall, a number of Chinefe charaćters; in other parts of the edifice there were lamps, images, and feveral fmall ftoves. I faw a ceremony performed in one of the ftreets, on the deceafe of a perfon, which, for its fingularity, may be worth relating. —— Having made a large fire, with flips of paper, they brought out, one after another, a great number of paper pageants, gilt and coloured, with feveral human figures compofed of the fame materials, and kept feeding the fire with them, till they were all confumed; then they threw a parcel of cups and bottles into the fire, that had fomething in them, but I could not learn what, went into the houfe, and the ceremony ended. Their mourning for the deceafed is a white turban.

There is, it feems, but one Chinefe woman in Batavia, and fhe is but feldom feen: It is deemed a crime to bring them from China; fuch of the Chinefe, who defign to continue here, and incline to marry, take to wife one of the Malay women.

The Malays of both fexes, who are moftly flaves, are very numerous: Every white man keeps a number of them; and they are the only fervants employed within-doors and without. Under this name are comprehended many forts of people, who come from Sumatra, Amboyna, Banda, and Ceram. Thofe that come from the coaft of Malabar, are diftinguifhed by their flimnefs and complexion, which is jet black. The Orang Bougees, or fuch as come from the ifland of Celebes, are remarkable for their fine black hair; and thofe from Timor are pretty black: Thefe, with all others from the eaftern ifles, are, in general, called Malays; and all fpeak the low Malay, though their languages are different in their refpećtive countries. Moft of them have flattifh nofes, and are, in general, fhort; the women, efpecially, are very fmall.

The

The dress of the male Malays, who are slaves, is very simple; consisting of a pair of short drawers, and a long shirt, or frock, above, made of striped or plain cotton, which buttons about the wrist with six small buttons; and those who can afford it have two or three gold buttons at the neck. They are accustomed to hold one hand on their heads, placed in a particular manner. The free-men are better clad, and affect, in some respects, the European dress and customs, having black sattin breeches, and waistcoats with sleeves, and carry their hats under their arms; but they wear neither shoes nor stockings.

The women-slaves wear a long piece of cotton check wrapped about their loins, which serves instead of petticoats; and, over that, a very short white callico jacket, which buttons at the wrist, and is close before. They have remarkable good hair, which they tie upon the tops of their heads, and stick two or three silver or gold bodkins into it; this, with a silver peenang box which hangs to a girdle, and a handkerchief, with searee, put over their shoulders, makes them appear very gaudy. The free-women, who are called Noonga Cabaia, wear a long chintz banjan, called a Cabai, which reaches down to their heels; and they have square-toed slippers, turned up at the points very high, with which they make shift to hobble along.

The Malays, and many of the white people, bathe in the river at least once in the day, and sometimes twice. The men are much addicted to gaming; and all of them chew the Penang and Searee, which blackens their teeth; but they have an expeditious method of cleaning them with betle: They also chew tobacco, cardamums, and gaimbre. They are reckoned to be an indolent revengeful people; and, when they think themselves injured, they repair to a gaming-house, and smoak opium till they are mad-drunk, and then sally out, with a creefs in their hand, to seek their enemy; attempting to kill every person that opposes them; and are often killed themselves, before they are apprehended: This is called an Amock, and is very common in Batavia. The criminal, if taken alive, is broke upon the wheel.

The Malays are Mahometans, and have several mosques about Batavia.

There

There is another fet of people called Portuguefe; whom the Malays call Orrang Cerami, or people of Ceram; but for what reafon I could not learn: They are very dark-coloured, but you may diftinguifh European features amongft them.

Other people, of which there are many to be feen at Batavia, are Banjans, or Gentoos; the Malays call them Orrang Codjo: Their heads are fhaven, and covered with a conical cap; the other parts of their drefs are a fhort petticoat, or wrapper, about their loins; and, over that, a banjan. The Javanefe, who refide here, are dreffed much in the fame manner, except the cap: they are all free, as the taking them for flaves is prohibited under a very fevere penalty. Here are alfo Armenians, Perfians, Moguls, people from many parts of India, as well as negroes from Madagafcar, Mofambique, and all the eaftern parts of Africa.

Batavia is plentifully furnifhed with all forts of provifions; but, in this city, as well as in others that are very populous, moft articles bear a high price. Here are fome bullocks, but many more buffaloes, which are fold on reafonable terms, and their flefh eats pretty well; alfo Cambeong, or goat-fheep; but they are lean, dry, and indifferent food: Hogs of the Chinefe and European breed; the former are very fat, eat very well, and are cheap; but the Europeans defpife them, and prefer the latter, which are very dear. They have alfo tame fowls in abundance, which are cheap. I have likewife feen wild-fowls. Their ducks are not fo good as ours, and are of another kind. Mufcovy ducks and geefe are bought reafonable; but turkeys and pigeons are dear. They have a plentiful market of fifh, which is the favourite food of the Malays, but no great variety: Claw-fifh, fhell-fifh, and particularly oyfters, though fmall, are pretty good food; but their turtle, of which they have a plenty, is remarkably bad, and is only eaten by the common people. I believe there is not any place can equal Batavia for the variety of provifions, which may be bought at ftalls, and are hawked about the ftreets, ready cooked, or cooking. They are furnifhed with flour from the Cape, and their bread is very good and cheap; but rice is more generally ufed, which grows in Java, and is very plentiful. Their common drink is arrack punch. The beft arrack is fold for fifteen-pence the gallon. By what I could learn, the principal ingredient in it is fugar; with the beft fort they mix Dooae, or palm-fyrup; but whether they ufe rice I cannot tell.

Claret

Claret and Rhenish are the moſt common wines drank at Batavia : Claret you may buy at eighteen-pence the bottle ; but beer ſells at twenty-pence. Sugar is another article which they have in great plenty ; the beſt ſells for about twopence-farthing the pound ; and ſugar-candy at threepence-halfpenny. They have a great quantity of coffee, which grows at Java : It is a company's trade, but may be bought, ſmuggled, for twopence-halfpenny the pound. They make as good butter as need be eaten ; and have a ſufficient quantity of it to ſerve moſt of the inhabitants with their coffee and tea : they have alſo ſome good butter from the Cape. Of garden-ſtuff, they have peaſe, French-beans, aſparagus, cos-lettuce, parſley, purſlain, onions, white radiſhes, potatoes, cabbages, ſpinage, cucumbers, celery, endive, and theſe all the year long : beſides theſe, which are exotics, they have ſeveral ſorts of Cajang, or beans, Oobe, or yams, ſweet potatoes, pumpkins, muſhrooms, Vuevues, which taſte like muſhrooms when roaſted, garlick, and a ſort of ſmall onions that taſte like ſhallots, Chabe, or red-bird pepper ; with a variety of other pot-herbs, too tedious to enumerate.

The beſt fruits they have at Batavia are the Mangaſteen, which is ſo wholeſome, that it may be eaten in a fever : the Ramboutan, about the ſize of a large plumb, growing in bunches, and covered with a thick huſk, of a bright red colour, full of ſoft prickles, which gives it a furzy appearance ; the inſide, which is about the ſize of a pigeon's egg, is tranſparent, and yields a very rich juice, which has an agreeable poignancy. Pine-apples, which are alſo very good and plentiful, may be bought for an halfpenny or a farthing each. The Nanca and Durian are much admired by the natives ; but they are very diſagreeable to foreigners, as they ſmell like onions and garlick, mixed with ſugar : the Nanca is rather long, divided into four equal parts within, has a ſtone in each, and is as large as a half-peck loaf : they grow on the trunk of a tree ; the outſide of the fruit is of a green colour, and the inſide of a yellow : they are covered with a bag, before they are ripe, which preſerves them from the vermin. The Durian is conſiderably leſs, quite round, and covered with ſpiny tubercles. They have bread-fruit, too ; but, being full of ſeed, it is never eaten. Alſo a plenty of mangoes, of ſeveral ſorts, which, in my opinion, eat beſt when they are green, with pepper and ſalt. Oranges are very ſcarce and very indifferent ; but they have plenty of limes, and ſome Namnams too, which eat very well fried. They alſo have a fruit, produced by a ſort of rattan, called Salae, which is

covered

covered over with fmall brown fcales, and taftes like cheefe, apples, and onions. Guavas, though deemed good of their kind, fmell fo difagreeably, that I could not endure them. Of Jamboo, they have many forts, fome large, fome fmall, fome round, and others long; white, pink, crimfon, and fcarlet. They have alfo a plenty of cocoa-nuts, of which they generally make their oil. Their other fruits are Pifang, or plantains, Manco, or water-melons, anona fquamofa, cuftard-apples, anona reticulata, grapes, pumplenofes, citrons, and acajou apples.

All the fhips, which are careened and hove-down here, go to a fmall ifland in the bay, called Unruft, about feven miles from Batavia; where there is proper tackle to heave them down, and a bafs, or overfeer, to manage all matters. The whole ifland is one dock-yard, inhabited entirely by carpenters, and others, who belong to the fhips that are there. * Near Unruft is another ifland, called the Kuypers, or Coopers, which is full of warehoufes, where fhips depofit their goods while they are heaving-down. About a mile from this, there is another ifland, called Palmirante, where there is an hofpital for fick feamen: and upon this ifland the fhips

---

* At this place our fhip was examined; and we found that many of her planks, and her keel, were much-damaged; one part of her not being above one-eighth of an inch thick, which was luckily before one of the timbers, or, in all probability, fhe would have funk long before we reached the bay of Batavia. While our fhip was repairing at Unruft, moft of the crew were at Cooper's-Ifland, where they were taken with a putrid dyfentery; three of whom, the fteward of the gun-room, one of the feamen, and a boy, died. The diforder alfo carried off Toobaiah, and the lad Taiyota, natives of Otaheite, whom we defigned to have brought to England. They had been feveral times up to Batavia, and expreffed great furprize at the many various objects to which they had been unaccuftomed: they were particularly ftruck with the fight of carriages drawn by horfes; and were very inquifitive in refpect of what they faw, that was new to them; having, before our arrival at Batavia, made great progrefs in the Englifh tongue, in which they were greatly affifted by Mr. Green, the aftronomer, who took much pains therein, particularly with Taiyota. When Taiyota was feized with the fatal diforder, as if certain of his approaching diffolution, he frequently faid to thofe of us who were his intimates, Tyau mate oee, " my friends, I am dying." He took any medicines that were offered him; but Toobaiah, who was ill at the fame time, and furvived him but a few days, refufed every thing of that kind, and gave himfelf up to grief; regretting, in the higheft degree, that he had left his own country; and, when he heard of Taiyota's death, he was quite inconfolable, crying out frequently, Taiyota! Taiyota! They were both buried in the ifland of Eadam. During our ftay at Batavia, moft of us were fickly; Mr. Monkhoufe, our furgeon, and the aftronomer's fervant, died; and fome others hardly efcaped with life.

companies

companies inter their dead. There are many other iflands in the bay, named Am-
fterdam, Rotterdam, and Eadam, where the company have rope-manufactories,
and fend their felons.

The ifland of Java abounds with monkies, cockatoos, parrots, and wild poultry :
there are alfo a great many horfes, which are fmall, but very fpirited.

The wefterly monfoon fets in about October or November, and fometimes later ;
and then the rainy feafon comes on : the eafterly fets in about April or May.

The general language fpoken at Batavia is low Malay ; and it is neceffary that
every perfon, who defigns to ftay long there, fhould learn it. This language is
very different from the high and proper Malay, which is fpoken on the continent of
India ; and may be compared to the Lingua-Franca, being a compound of feveral
other languages ; viz. of Malay, Portuguefe, and thofe of the eaftern ifles. A fhort
vocabulary of each is here annexed as a fpecimen ; as alfo vocabularies of the languages of other nations, in the neighbourhood of Batavia, which I collected from
natives of the different places, during my ftay in that city.

A VOCABULARY

A VOCABULARY of the MALAYAN LANGUAGE, as spoke at BATAVIA, usually called there the Low MALAY.

Alla, or Alla t'alla,	*God.*
Tooäng Alla,	*The Lord God.*
Soorga,	*Heaven.*
Nooraka,	*Hell.*
Saitang, Mamadee, or Booleefs,	*The devil.*
Orrang Saitang,	*A demon, or ghost.*
Appee,	*Fire.*
Aier,	*Water.*
Detanna, or Negree,	*The earth.*
Laot,	*The sea.*
Langee,	*The sky.*
Matt'aree,	*The sun.*
Boolang,	*The moon.*
Beentang,	*The stars.*
Trang,	*Light.*
Glap,	*Darkness.*
Panafs,	*Heat.*
Deengin,	*Cold.*
Angin,	*The wind.*
Waitan,	*The East.*
Coolon,	*The west.*
Keedol,	*The north.*
Lorr,	*The south.*
Tarang,	*The clouds.*
Oojang,	*Rain.*
Greemifs,	*A mizling rain.*
Amboon,	*The dew.*
Awang awang,	*A fog, or mist.*

Affup,

Assup,	Smoke.
Keelap,	Lightening.
Goontoor,	Thunder.
Oontor,	The rainbow.
Leendo,	An earthquake.
Orang,	Men, mankind, or people.
Lakee lakee,	A man.
Orang tooa,	An old man.
Parampooan,	A woman, or a young woman.
Anna paraowan,	A virgin.
Booda, or Anna lakee lakee,	A boy.
Anna parampooan,	A girl.
Annae or anna,	A child.
Cumbar,	Twins.
Bappa, or pappa,	A father.
Ma,	A mother.
Cakè,	A grandfather.
Naimai,	A grandmother.
Bappa teerree,	A step-father.
Mateeree,	A step-mother.
Anna lakee,	A son.
Anna parampooan,	A daughter.
Soodara lakee,	A brother.
Soodara parampooan,	A sister.
Lakee,	A husband.
Beene,	A wife.
Cawin,	A wedding.
Orang cawin,	The bridegroom.
Boodjang,	A widow.
Peeatoo,	An orphan.
Anna foondal,	A bastard.
Taman,	A friend.
Manchoree,	A thief.
Orang boota,	A blind man.

Orang

Orang Balanda,	*A Dutchman.*
Orang Engrefe,	*An Englishman.*
Orang Cerami,	*A Portuguese.*
Orang Codja, or Codjo.	*A Moor, Gentoo, Mogul, or Banyan.*
Orang China,	*A Chinese.*
Orang Maleiyo,	*A Malay.*
Orang Bugeefs,	*A native of the Celebes.*
Orang Papooa,	*A negroe, or caffre.*
Badang,	*The whole body.*
Capalla,	*The head.*
Atufcapalla,	*The crown of the head.*
Ramboo,	*The hair of the head.*
Mooca,	*The face.*
Taleenga,	*The temples.*
Matta,	*The eyes.*
Beedjee matta,	*The eye-balls.*
Rambco matta,	*The eye-brows.*
Atus matta,	*The eye-lids.*
Pooloo matta,	*The eye-lashes.*
Cooping,	*The ears.*
Edong,	*The nose.*
Enga,	*The noftrils.*
Peepee,	*The cheeks.*
Leeda,	*The mouth.*
Beebir, or moloo,	*The lips.*
Geegee,	*The teeth.*
Oojoo leeda,	*The tongue.*
Daga,	*The chin.*
Yenga, or coomifs,	*The beard.*
Lehair,	*The throat.*
Watta lehair,	*The neck.*
Dada,	*The breafts.*
Soofoo,	*The nipples.*
Purroo, or prott,	*The belly.*

Pooffar,

Pooffar,	*The navel.*
Balacang,	*The back.*
Peengang,	*The fides.*
Poonda,	*The fhoulders.*
Catea,	*The arm-pits.*
Tangan,	*The whole arm and hand.*
Seecoo,	*The elbow.*
Balacang tangan,	*The back of the hand.*
Pala tangan,	*The palm of the hand.*
Manjaree,	*The thumb.*
Yereeggee,	*The fingers.*
Taree,	*The forefinger.*
Taree tanga,	*The middle finger.*
Jeregee, or jereejee,	*The fourth finger.*
Anna, or jintee,	*The little finger.*
Pantar,	*The hips.*
Fanta,	*The haunches.*
Panco,	*The thighs.*
Lootoo,	*The knees.*
Palpalla,	*The hams.*
Cakee,	*The leg and foot.*
Toocakee,	*The calves of the legs.*
Sapatoo,	*The foot.*
Balcakee,	*The fole of the foot.*
Yereeggee cakee,	*The toes.*
Boolo,	*The hair.*
Coolit,	*The fkin.*
Gomoe,	*The fat.*
Daging,	*The flefh.*
Darra,	*Blood.*
Oorat,	*A vein.*
Toolang,	*The bones.*
Soom fom,	*The marrow.*
Otae,	*The brains.*

Oofoofs,

Oofoofs,	*The ſtomach.*
Atee,	*The heart.*
Oofo,	*The guts.*
Toole toole,	*The kidneys.*
Tullum boongan,	*The bladder.*
Soofoo,	*The milk.*
Aier matta,	*Tears.*
Beengata, or beenatang,	*A beaſt.*
Beenatang ootang,	*A wild beaſt.*
Tandoo,	*The horns.*
Coolit,	*The hide, ſkin, or leather.*
Booloo,	*The hair, or wool.*
Aicor,	*The tail.*
Moenje,	*An ape, or a monkey.*
Coocang,	*Lemur tardigradus.* [Vide Linnæus.]
Gaidja, or gadja,	*An elephant.*
Matcha,	*A tyger.*
Cootching,	*A cat.*
Tecoofs,	*A rat.*
Unjing, or anjing,	*A dog.*
Babee,	*A hog.*
Coodda,	*A horſe.*
Onta,	*An aſs.*
Sampee-lakee,	*A bull.*
Sampee-parampooan,	*A cow.*
Carbao,	*A buffalo.*
Cambeeng,	*A goat, or Guinea ſheep.*
Cambeeng-Balanda,	*An European ſheep.*
Keedang, or manjae.	*A deer, common in Java.*
Cantcheell,	*A hog-deer, no bigger than a rabbit.*
Choree choree,	*A bat.*
Boorong, or booloo,	*A bird.*
Mooloo booloo,	*The beak of a bird.*
Saiap,	*The wings.*

Aicor,	*The tail.*
Booloo boorong,	*A feather.*
Sarran boorong,	*A bird's neft.*
Tullor,	*An egg.*
Ulang,	*An eagle.*
Cocatooa, or kacatooa,	*A cockatoo.*
Papagai,	*A parrot.*
Noree, or looree,	*A lory.*
Baiyo,	*Gracula religiofa, the mino.*
Aiam,	*Poultry.*
Aiam lakee lakee,	*A cock.*
Jengir,	*A cock's comb.*
Aiam parampooan,	*A hen.*
Aiam balanda,	*A turkey.*
Gangfa,	*A goofe.*
Baibai,	*A duck.*
Maraae,	*A peacock.*
Boorong darra,	*A pigeon.*
Eacang,	*A fifh.*
Lomba lomba,	*A grampus.*
Punyoo,	*A turtle.*
Koora koora,	*A land-turtle, or tortoife.*
Chicao,	*A lizard.*
Kaico, or tocke.	*A lizard which haunts houfes, and has a particular fort of cry.*
Codda,	*A toad.*
Oolar,	*A fnake, or ferpent.*
Cullaculla.	*A cockroach.*
Tangcreek,	*A cricket.*
Keenjang,	*A butterfly.*
Lallar,	*A fly.*
Smootallang,	*A fmall black ant.*
Pootoo,	*A loufe.*
Oodang,	*Lobfters, cray-fifh, &c.*

Rooma,

Rooma,	*A house.*
Maja boondar,	*A round table.*
Maja panyang,	*A square table.*
Peesoo, or peesooe,	*A knife.*
Gor,	*A fork.*
Saindoo, or sandue.	*A spoon.*
Gandang,	*A drum.*
Panching,	*A fishhook.*
Jaring, or taring,	*A net, or sein.*
Barang,	*Cloaths.*
Cameeja,	*A shirt.*
Sapalloo,	*Shoes or slippers.*
Bantar,	*A pillow.*
Macanan,	*Victuals.*
Macan pagee,	*Breakfast.*
Macan teng aree,	*Dinner.*
Macan mallam,	*Supper.*
Rotee,	*Bread.*
Nassee,	*Boiled rice.*
Curree,	*A high-seasoned soup.*
Caldoo,	*Chicken broth.*
Montega,	*Butter.*
Caidjoo,	*Cheese.*
Garrum,	*Salt.*
Meenja, or meenyae,	*Oil.*
Chooca,	*Vinegar.*
Lada,	*Pepper.*
Atchar,	*Cayan-pepper.*
Goola paseer,	*Sugar.*
Goola batoo,	*Sugar-candy.*
Tambaco,	*Tobacco.*
Meeno, or meenum,	*Drink.*
Aier meeno,	*Water for drinking.*
Angor,	*Wine.*

Angor

Angor de maira.	*Red wine.*
Angor pootee,	*White wine.*
Angor affum,	*Rhenish wine.*
Angor dooae,	*Palm wine.*
Samfhoo,	*A particular fort of cold liquor.*
Aier callappa,	*Cocoa-nut milk.*
Pagee,	*The morning.*
Matáree teenge,	*The forenoon.*
Taingaree,	*Ncon.*
Matáree meeree.	*The afternoon.*
Matáree toroo,	*Sun-fet.*
Soree,	*The evening.*
Tainga mallam,	*Midnight.*
Calim aree dowloo,	*The day before yefterday.*
Calim aree dowloo mallam,	*The night before laft.*
Calim aree,	*Yefterday.*
Eniee aree,	*To-day.*
Baifoo, or baifue,	*To-morrow.*
Looffa,	*The day after to-morrow.*
Seang feang,	*In the day.*
Baifoo dattang,	*Another day, or another time.*
Poocol, or jam,	*An hour.*
Stainga poocol,	*Half an hour.*
Sa jamahat,	*A week.*

DAYS of the WEEK.

Aree jamahat,	*Friday.*
Aree faptoo,	*Saturday.*
Aree gnahat,	*Sunday.*
Aree ifneen,	*Monday.*
Aree falaffa,	*Tuefday.*
Aree rubo,	*Weanefday.*
..ee camefs,	*Thurfday.*

Sa boolan,	*A month.*
Sa taong,	*A year.*
Taong baroo,	*The new-year.*
Mooda,	*Young.*
Tooa,	*Old.*
Lapar,	*Hungry.*
Ramboo butal,	*Lank hair.*
Ramboo eekal,	*Curled hair.*
Ramboo beeneering,	*Frizzled hair.*
De dallam,	*Within.*
Delawar,	*Without.*
Kanna,	*The right.*
Keeree,	*The left.*
Penda, or pendue,	*Short.*
Panyang,	*Long.*
Tepiſs,	*Thin.*
Tabal,	*Thick.*
Laibar,	*Narrow.*
Coran laibar,	*Broad.*
Boondar,	*Round.*
Panyang,	*Square.*
Canja,	*Full.*
Puſſar,	*Big, or large.*
Ootang,	*In the country wild.*
Stainga,	*Half.*
Cucheel,	*A little.*
Tooga,	*A thing, or piece.*
Gooa,	*Me.*
Loo,	*You.*
Loo poonya,	*You, or yours.*
Gooa poonya,	*My, or mine.*
Deea,	*Him.*
Deea poonya,	*His or hers.*
Itooling,	*Them.*

Eenee,

Eenee,	*This.*
Eedoo or eetoo,	*That.*
De feennee,	*Here.*
De fanna,	*There.*
Seennee,	*This place, or here.*
Tarra de feetoor,	*That place, or there.*
Mana,	*Which.*
Appa,	*What.*
Adda,	*Yes.*
Ambeel,	*To fetch.*
Anoat,	*To take away.*
Panya,	*To roaft.*
Tootoo,	*To cover.*
Tarabang,	*To fly.*
Badeeree,	*To rife.*
Nampas,	*To puff or blow.*
Meeno,	*To fuck.*
Potong,	*To cut.*
Saindo,	*To fup.*
Gegit,	*To bite.*
Buffeela,	*To fit crofs-legged.*
Balek,	*To turn.*
Tootoo matta,	*To wink.*
Booang,	*To empty.*
Sallin,	*To fill.*
Floit,	*To whiftle.*
Munyanye,	*To fing.*
Tatawa,	*To laugh.*
Manangas,	*To cry.*
Loopa,	*To forget.*
Looda gillap,	*It is dark.*
Oojang attang,	*It rains.*

Sooda,

Sooda,	*It is done.*
Tallalo mahal,	*It is too much.*
Adda bai,	*They are good.*
Trada bai,	*They are not good.*
Adda,	*I have.*
Troda,	*I have not.*
Caffee gooa,	*Give me.*
Marro de feinne,	*Come hither.*
Pafang leeling,	*Light the candle.*
Goonte leeling,	*Snuff the candle.*
Boingoos,	*Blow your nose.*
Sapo camre,	*Sweep the chamber.*
Barapee,	*How much ?*
Barapee faloo rupea,	*How many for a rupee ?*
Barapee maon,	*What is the price of this ?*
Adda cowfs footra,	*Have you got any filk stockings ?*
Appa catta,	*What fays he ?*
Dee manna,	*Where is fuch a one ?*
Jallang dee fanne,	*Which is the way ?*
Salama tidor,	*Good night.*

A VOCABULARY

✖✖✖✖✖✖✖✖✖✖✖✖✖✖✖✖✖✖✖✖✖✖✖✖✖✖✖✖✖✖✖✖✖✖✖✖✖

A VOCABULARY of the LANGUAGE fpoken at ANJENGA, on the
  Coaft of MALABAR, called at BATAVIA the high or proper
  M A L A Y.

Veiloo,	*The fun.*
Saoo,	*The moon.*
Nacaiftrum,	*The ftars.*
Vanum,	*The fky.*
Vaigum,	*The clouds.*
Menal,	*Lightening.*
Eeree,	*Thunder.*
Tanee,	*Water.*
Maya,	*Rain.*
Tee,	*Fire.*
Cairo,	*Land.*
Manizen,	*A man.*
Oroopinnoo,	*A woman.*
Talla,	*The head.*
Otehe,	*The crown of the head.*
Talla moodee,	*The hair of the head.*
Mocom,	*The face.*
Naitee,	*The brow.*
Canna,	*The eyes.*
Cadoo,	*The ears.*
Moco,	*The nofe.*
Caowda,	*The cheeks.*
Waa,	*The mouth.*
Choondoo,	*The lips.*
Pailoo,	*The teeth.*
Nacoo,	*The tongue.*

Taree,

T'aree,	*The chin.*
Veeja,	*The beard.*
Carittoo,	*The neck.*
Ninyoo,	*The breaft.*
Mola,	*The nipples.*
Bagroo,	*The belly.*
Corelloo,	*The navel.*
Ooroopoo,	*The fhoulders.*
Cai,	*The whole arm.*
Mootooe,	*The elbow.*
Eai,	*The hand.*
Oolung-eai,	*The palm of the hand.*
Poorang-eai,	*The back of the hand.*
Veraloo,	*The fingers.*
Chande,	*The hips.*
Torra,	*The thighs.*
Mootoo,	*The knees.*
Caloo,	*The legs and feet.*
Raloo-veraloo,	*The toes.*
Oolung caloo,	*The fole of the foot.*
Nacong,	*The nails.*
Majaroo,	*The hair.*
Caluttoo,	*Morning.*
Ooteha,	*Noon.*
Eraoo,	*Evening.*
Erittoo,	*Night.*
Enalla,	*Day.*
Teenoo,	*To eat.*
Koree,	*To drink.*
Nada,	*To walk.*
Odóo,	*To run.*
Nokoo,	*To fee.*
Caloo,	*To hear.*

Mana,

Mana,	*To smell.*
Chulloo,	*To speak.*

NUMERATION.

Onoo,	*One.*
Randoo,	*Two.*
Mono,	*Three.*
Nalieu,	*Four.*
Unjoo,	*Five.*
Aroo,	*Six.*
Yalloo,	*Seven.*
Yuttoo,	*Eight.*
Weinbuthoo,	*Nine.*
Patoo,	*Ten.*
Patoo nonoo,	*Eleven, &c.*
Eeroowadoo,	*Twenty.*
Moopada,	*Thirty.*
Nailpada,	*Forty.*
Unpada,	*Fifty.*
Aroopada,	*Sixty.*
Irrewothe,	*Seventy.*
Unbuthoo,	*Eighty.*
Tonorra,	*Ninety.*
Norra,	*One hundred.*

A VOCA-

A Vocabulary of the Language of the Natives of the Island of Sumatra, in the East-Indies.

Jet,	*The sun.*
Gù or geuex,	*The moon.*
Tchee,	*The stars.*
Thee,	*The sky.*
Hoïn,	*The clouds.*
Hò,	*Rain.*
Gowshù,	*The rainbow.*
Haï,	*The sea.*
Whang,	*Wind.*
Lang,	*People.*
Tapò,	*A man.*
Tsawà,	*A woman.*
Taow,	*The head.*
Tamung,	*The hair of the head.*
Beeïn,	*The face.*
Bwaclieu,	*The eyes.*
Vacvaï,	*The eye-brows.*
Vactoojin,	*The eye-lids.*
Pee,	*The nose.*
Tsooë,	*The mouth.*
Tsooë toon,	*The lips.*
Tsooë kee,	*The teeth.*
Tsooë eta,	*The chin.*
Tchee,	*The tongue.*
Amcooë,	*The neck.*
Semgua,	*The breast.*
Deeïn,	*The nipples.*
Pacto,	*The belly.*

Patsa,

Patſa,	*The navel.*
Padja,	*The back.*
Pakow peeng,	*The ſides.*
Quintaow,	*The ſhoulders.*
Tchoo,	*The arms.*
Cöai,	*The arm-pits.*
Tche aowtee,	*The elbow.*
Tchoo pooä,	*The band.*
Tchoo tang ſeeäm,	*The palm of the band.*
Tſung taow,	*The fingers.*
Cajang,	*The hips.*
Cada tooë,	*The thighs.*
Cadaow,	*The knees.*
Cäooto,	*The legs.*
Catſat,	*The ancles.*
Ca,	*The foot.*
Cojang taow,	*The toes.*
Catchù atù,	*The ſole of the foot.*

NUMERATION.

Chit.	*One.*
Nung,	*Two.*
Sa,	*Three.*
See,	*Four.*
Ingo,	*Five.*
La,	*Six.*
Chee,	*Seven.*
Poë,	*Eight.*
Ca,	*Nine.*
Tſap,	*Ten.*
Tſapet,	*Eleven.*
Tſapgee,	*Twelve.*
Tſee tſap,	*Twenty.*
Tſee et,	*Twenty-one.*

Tſa

Tſa tſap,	*Thirty.*
Chippa,	*One hundred.*
Chet cheang,	*One thouſand.*
Chet bang,	*Ten thouſand.*
Chet ſabang,	*One hundred thouſand.*
Chet pawang,	*A million.*

NUMERATION of the Natives of CERAM, an Iſland in the EAST-INDIES.

O eenta,	*One.*
O looa,	*Two.*
O toloo,	*Three.*
O patoo,	*Four.*
O leema,	*Five.*
O loma,	*Six.*
O peeto,	*Seven.*
O aloo,	*Eight.*
O teeo,	*Nine.*
O pooloo,	*Ten.*

A VOCABULARY

A VOCABULARY of the LANGUAGE ſpoken by the People of the Iſland of MADAGASCAR.

Delanna,	*The earth.*
Greemiſs,	*A mizzling rain.*
Cumbar,	*Twins.*
Loha or dooha,	*The head.*
Voolaon dooha,	*The hair of the head.*
Handing,	*The face.*
Maſſoo,	*The eyes.*
Vooloo maſſoo,	*The eye-brows.*
Soofi,	*The ears.*
Oroong,	*The noſe.*
Bava,	*The cheeks.*
Mooloor,	*The mouth.*
Neefee,	*The teeth.*
Leula,	*The tongue.*
Vaow,	*The chin.*
Vooſſoon,	*The neck.*
Dada,	*The breaſt.*
Nooroo,	*The nipples.*
Reeboo,	*The belly.*
Foit,	*The navel.*
Voohoo,	*The back.*
Vooha,	*The ſides.*
Soorooka,	*The ſhoulders.*
Tangan,	*The whole arm and hand.*
Hailik,	*The arm-pits.*
Keehow,	*The elbows.*

Voohan

Voohan tangan,	*The back of the hand.*
Falla tangan,	*The palm of the hand.*
Ranjang tangan,	*The fingers.*
Foonee,	*The hips.*
Fai,	*The thighs.*
Lohalka,	*The knees.*
Randjao,	*The legs.*
Boobeechee,	*The calves of the leg.*
Ungoor,	*The foot.*
Ambanee ungoor,	*The sole of the foot.*
Ranjang ungoor,	*The toes.*
Matcha,	*A tiger.*
Onta,	*A camel.*
Onta,	*An afs.*
Oolar or boolar,	*A fnake.*
Smootallang,	*An ant.*
Cumbang fapatoo,	*Scarlet hibifcus.*
Manga mattang,	*Grecn mangas.*
Manga bapang,	*Ripe mangas.*
Cobong,	*A garden.*
Bafar,	*A market.*
Cointchee,	*A key.*
Cointchee fapatoo,	*Buckles.*
Leyang or loyang,	*Brafs.*
Sootra,	*Silk.*
Tampalooda,	*A fpitting-pot.*
Gaingong,	*A reed mufical inftrument.*
Cajin,	*A Malay garment.*
Baidjoo,	*An upper white fhort jacket.*
Tomeat,	*A cane.*
Corro corro,	*A java proe.*
Maddat appiam,	*Opium.*
Ratchang,	*Poifon.*
Curjeedoo,	*A cure.*

Orrang

Orrang buggeefs,	*A Macaſſar man.*
Orrang meenta,	*A beggar.*
Cabeezee,	*An eunuch.*
Orrang geela,	*A lunatic.*
Bodda,	*A fool.*
Orrang oodal or oofta,	*A liar.*
Boodjang,	*A batchelor.*
Doocoon,	*A doctor.*
Ɛmai,	*A title of reſpect.*
Noonya,	*Miſtreſs.*
Noona,	*Miſs.*
Cawin,	*A wedding.*
Pacattan,	*A language.*
Soondal,	*A lie.*
Carmarran dooloo mallam,	*The night before laſt.*
Baifoo dattang,	*The day after to-morrow.*
Poocool or jam,	*An hour.*

DAYS of the WEEK.

Aree Jamahat,	*Friday.*
Aree Saptoo,	*Saturday.*
Aree Gnahat,	*Sunday.*
Aree Seenen,	*Monday.*
Aree Salaſſa,	*Tueſday.*
Aree Rubo,	*Wedneſday.*
Aree Cameſs,	*Thurſday.*
Tongbarroo,	*The new year.*
Mabooe,	*Drunk.*
Lammoo,	*Moon-eyed.*
Matapoota, or mataboota,	*Blind, or blindneſs.*
Toolee,	*Deaf.*
Gagoo,	*Dumb.*
Bainco,	*Lame.*

Tangallang,

Tangallang,	*Drowned.*
Jahat,	*Cruel.*
Suffue,	*Narrow, or ſtrait.*
Longar,	*Broad or wide.*
Craſs,	*Loud, ſwift, or ſtrong.*
Maira mooda,	*Light-red.*
Maira looa,	*Dark-red.*
Paffeer,	*Pleaſed or glad.*
Talalloo,	*A ſuperfluity, as* Talalloo bagoos, *too fine.*
Morra,	*Cheap.*
Malengkit bagitta,	*Adheſive, or gluey.*
Paffang,	*A pair.*
Dooadooa,	*Both.*
Laian,	*Another.*
Seedeecoot,	*Few, little.*
Sarre,	*Every.*
Nantee dowloo,	*Perhaps.*
Dowloo,	*Before.*
Baroo ſang,	*Juſt now.*
Sampee,	*Until, or till.*
Begeenne, or begeetoo,	*So, like that or this; in this or that manner.*
Belair malay,	*To ſail.*
Goffoe peefoo,	*To ſharpen a knife.*
Pangeel,	*To call, or name.*
Teembool,	*To grow.*
Batcha,	*To read.*
Potong,	*To cut.*
Curja or beeking,	*To make.*
Tarro,	*To lay, to ſet, to put or place a thing.*
Boonte,	*To be with child.*
Sambayam,	*To pray.*
Bole,	*To be able.*

Gaigar,

Gaigar,	*To hurry or haften.*
Peecool, or bawa,	*To carry.*
Paffang,	*To light.*
Yattoo,	*To tumble.*
Tadda tadda,	*To tack.*
Jangan,	*Don't, or get along.*
Lalloo de feetoo,	*Get away from thence.*
Sappatow,	*Who knows?*
Sapeetoo,	*Who is there?*
Appa maon,	*What do you want?*
Soocoo fooca,	*Do you chufe?*
Maon,	*Will you?*
De manna boole dappa,	*Where can I get fuch a thing?*
Maon appa tradda ambeel,	*Why did they not fetch it?*
Curjappa,	*What do you make of it?*
Cappang belair,	*When do you go to fea?*

NUMERATION.

Iffee or effa,	*One.*
Rooe,	*Two.*
Tulloo or tailoo,	*Three.*
Efax or efar,	*Four.*
Leman or lime,	*Five.*
One or aine,	*Six.*
Heitoo or petoo,	*Seven.*
Balloo,	*Eight.*
Seeva,	*Nine.*
Fooroo or fooloo,	*Ten.*

NUMERATION

NUMERATION of the Negroes on the River GAMBIA in AFRICA.

Killing,	*One.*
Foola,	*Two.*
Saba,	*Three.*
Nane,	*Four.*
Looloo,	*Five.*
Owrou,	*Six.*
Oronglo,	*Seven.*
Sae,	*Eight.*
Conunte,	*Nine.*
Tang,	*Ten.*
Tang killing,	*Eleven, &c.*
Emva,	*Twenty.*
Emva killing,	*Twenty-one, &c.*
Emva ning tang,	*Thirty.*

They

✖✖✖✖✖✖✖✖✖✖✖✖✖✖✖✖✖✖✖✖✖✖✖✖✖✖✖✖✖✖✖✖✖✖✖✖✖✖✖

They keep their accounts at Batavia in ſtivers and dollars; forty-eight ſtivers make one rix-dollar. The current coin that paſſes here is made up of doits, dublekes, ſchillings, Surat and Bengal rupees; ducatoons, and half ducatoons, old and new; Spaniſh dollars, German crowns, and ducats. Theſe all paſs for their full value.

	s.	d.
10 doits, 1 dubleke	0	2½
3 dublekes, 1 ſchilling	0	7½
4 ſchillings, 1 Surat rupee	2	6
10 dublekes, 8 doits, 1 Bengal rupee	2	3
2 rupees, 8 dublekes, 1 duckatoon	6	8
4 rupees, 4 dublekes, 8 doits, 1 ducat	11	0

As for the Malays and Chineſe, they count with ſawangs, ſatalees, ſoocoos, rupees, and reals.

8 doits, 1 awang, or ſawang.
2 awang, 4 doits, or 2 ſawang, 1 arroo, 1 alee, or ſatalee.
5 awang, or 2 ſatalee, 4 ſawang, 1 arroo, 1 ſocoo, or ſaſacoo.
3 ſocoo, 1 rupee; 4 ſoocoo, 4 awangs, 1 real.

WEIGHTS.

100 catee, or 125 lb. 1 peecol.
27 peecol ———— 1 coyang.

One of our midſhipmen ran away from us here, and it was ſuſpected that he was the perſon who cut off Orton's ears.

On the 26th of December, we weighed anchor, and ſailed from the bay of Batavia; and, on the 5th of January, 1771, we arrived and anchored at Prince's Iſland,

Ifland, on the eaft fide, (the water of which was very deep clofe to the fhore) and ftaid there till the 16th.   Here we were plentifully fupplied with turtle, and fine fifh of different forts ; cocoa-nuts, plantains, mangoes, limes and lemons : alfo with deer about the fize of a calf ; and a fort of fmaller deer about as large as a rabbit, which ate much like them : a great quantity of poultry, with which the ifland abounds ; young Indian corn, Tagaree, fugar, and fome ducks.   Their turtles were very lean, and far inferior to thofe we caught on the coaft of New Holland, which I fuppofed might be owing to their having been kept long in crawles.   We had alfo very fine water-melons, and bread-fruit, which would have been better had it not been fo young.

This fide of the ifland is pretty high, and covered with wood, excepting plantations of rice, upon which we faw feveral houfes.   The other fide is plain flat ground, and abounds with plantations of pifang, calappa, and other fruits.   The people who are upon it have been there between three and four years, and came from the main land of Java; and it is moft likely difpoffeffed the former inhabitants.   They are all Mahometans.   It was the month of Ramezan when we were there, and in this month they never eat in the day-time.   They have a Radja, or king, who, indeed, is but a poor one.   They wear a piece of cotton check about their waifts, which reaches to their knees, and another piece over their fhoulders. Their hair is very mean, and unlike that of the Malays, which is very fine *.

* Here ends S. Parkinfon's journal.

CONTINUATION

C O N T I N U A T I O N

O F A

J O U R N A L

O F A

V O Y A G E to the S O U T H S E A S,

In his Majefty's Ship The E N D E A V O U R.

P A R T IV.

O N the 16th of January, we took our departure from this ifland; and, a few days after, the diforder with which feveral of our company had been attacked, and died at Batavia and Cooper's Ifland, began to rage among us with great violence, and, in a few days, carried off Mr. Charles Green, the aftronomer; Mr. Sydney Parkinfon, Mr. David Spoving, clerk to Mr. Banks, and many of the common men. Mr. Green, being early feized with a delirium, unfortunately left fome of his minutes fo loofe and incorrect, that it is feared it will be difficult to render them intelligible.

On

On our arrival at the Cape, we were in great diſtreſs, not having more than ſix men capable of duty; but, providentially for us, the Pocock Eaſt-Indiaman was there, homeward bound, and captain Riddle generouſly ſent his boat to us with a ſupply of fruits, and other vegetables, as the wind blew hard, and we could not ſend our boat on ſhore.

The next day, the Captain, Mr. Banks, Dr. Solander, and ſeveral others of our principal people, went on ſhore; were kindly received by the governor; and met with a different treatment from that at Rio de Janeiro. He gave them a grant to hire a houſe for the ſick, who were all landed the next day; and, from the wholeſomeneſs of the climate, and a proper diet, moſt of them ſoon recovered. We ſtaid there about a month; a great part of which time Dr. Solander was very ill. Mr. Banks ſpared neither time nor expence in collecting of plants, inſects, ſkins of wild beaſts, and other curious animals; and employed a number of people to aſſiſt him, ſome of whom he ſent up a long way into the country for plants. Lieutenant Gore, with only one attendant, a ſlave belonging to Mr. Brand, a burgher at the Cape town, made an excurſion, out of curioſity, to the top of the table-hill, where they ſaw ſeveral tigers and wolves, and brought ſome curious plants, in flower, which he preſented to Mr. Banks, to whom they were very acceptable.

After the ſick had recovered, and we had taken in all neceſſary ſupplies, and had engaged ſome Portugueze to ſupply the loſs of our ſailors, we left the Cape, and proceeded on our voyage homeward. Three days after we left the Cape, Mr. Robert Molineux, the maſter of our ſhip, died.

After a paſſage of eighteen days, during which time nothing remarkable happened, we arrived at St. Helena, where we found his majeſty's ſhip, the Portland, commanded by captain Elliot, with twelve Eaſt-Indiamen under her convoy. In going into the road we ran foul of one of the Indiamen; but, with the aſſiſtance of ſome boats, we happily got clear of her, without much damage, except to our upper-works. The Portland being under ſailing orders, and we under captain Elliot's command, as ſenior officer, we were aſſiſted, by his people, in procuring

wood

wood and water; and he furnished us with some European provisions. We stayed there but four days, and then the whole fleet, consisting of fourteen sail, weighed anchor, and steered homeward.

Twelve days after we left St. Helena, our first lieutenant, Mr. Zachariah Hicks, died. About a month after we fell in with a schooner from Rhode-island, who was whaling off the western islands. We sent a boat on board for news; and were informed, to our great joy, that all was peaceable in England when she left it. Through our heavy sailing in the night, we lost sight of the fleet; and, in a few days, saw another whaling schooner, who confirmed the account which we had received from the former, and told us, that two days before they had chased a large whale into a harbour of St. Michael's Island, and that, while they were pursuing it, they were fired upon by the Portuguese, and obliged to retreat, leaving the whale a prize to them, who, doubtless, made sure of it. We bought, of the master of the schooner, some fine salt cod, with some fresh fish; also some New-England rum. This vessel, it seemed, had been out twenty-one days, and was in want of beef, and seemed distressed.

About sixteen days after we left the schooner, we got into soundings; and, in a few more days, beat into the Chops of the Channel; and the wind, which had been before at N. E. coming about to the S. W., we proceeded directly to the Downs, where we arrived on the 12th of July, 1771, after having been absent from England within a few days of three years. We immediately sent our sick on shore; and, after staying three days, received orders to proceed round to Woolwich, where we anchored on the 20th of the same month.

It may not be amiss to inform the curious in natural subjects, that Mr. Banks and Dr. Solander have discovered, in the course of this adventure, many thousand species of plants heretofore unknown: among the rest, one that produceth a kind of white silk flax, which, as it grows under the same parallel of latitude with England, it is presumed, will also thrive here, if properly cultivated. They have also brought over with them a quantity of seed, which, if it succeeds on this island, may, in all probability, be of much national advantage to Great-Britain.

They

They have alfo defcribed a great variety of birds and beafts, heretofore unknown, or but indifferently treated of; and above three hundred new fpecies of fifh, and have brought home with them many of the feveral kinds; with about one hundred fpecies of new fhells; and a great number of curious infects, fome of them of a new genus; and corals; alfo of other marine animals, particularly of the Molufca tribe.

Copious defcriptions of all thefe curiofities, with elegant engravings annexed, are now preparing to be publifhed to the world by the above-mentioned gentlemen.

THE END.

ERRATA.

Page 2, after line 16, insert, *A large eel was caught by one of our people, which was of a purple nutmeg colour, clouded with irregular spots of a darker colour, and was also full of small white dots.*

Page 4, line 17, for *island,* read, *place.*

—— 5, —— 20, dele, *when the air was not so dry.*

—— 7, —— 10, dele, *to the rest.*

———————— 25, after *forehead,* insert, *and is tied behind with the tendons of some animal.*

———————— 29, for, *We saw also an ornament made of shells,* read, *We saw one of these ornaments.*

—— 8, —— 4, for, *the,* read, *these.*

———————— 12, for, *hill,* read, *hills.*

———————— 28, for, *it,* read, *the fire.*

—— 16, —— 22, after, *figure,* insert, *Notwithstanding these flies are so great an inconvenience, the natives, from a religious notion, will not kill any of them.*

—— 17, —— 10, after, *paste,* insert, *or pudding.*

———————— 11, for, *Makey,* read, *Mahey.*

Ibid.   ibid. for, *and a substance called Meya,* read, *and Meya, a species of wild plantain.*

Page 20, line 6, for, *Tobiah,* read, *Toobaiah.*

———————— 31, dele, *but.*

———————— 33, for, *ate,* read, *eat.*

—— 21, —— 2, after, *island,* insert, *which the Otaheiteans hold sacred, as well as the flies, and therefore will not kill any of them.*

—— 22, —— 24, for, *was,* read, *they called.*

———————— 29, for, *VIII.* read, *VII.*

—— 23, —— 23, for, *joined at the bottom,* read, *the legs joined at the bottom, cross-ways.*

—— 24, —— 7, for, *purawei,* read, *parawei.**   [* An inner garment or shirt.]

———————— 15, for, *fig. 13,* read, *fig. 27.*

———————— 25, for, *or bunches of hair curiously plaited. They also wear teepootas,* read, *They also wear tamoous, or bunches of human hair curiously plaited.*

———————— 30, for, *taowree,* read, *taowdee.*

———————— 31, for, *whaow,* read, *waow.*

—— 25, —— 2, for, *the men,* read, *the two men.*

—— 26, —— 5, dele, *2.*

———————— 7, after, *ears,* insert, [*ibid. fig. 1 and 2.*]

—— 35, —— 13, for, *to a valley,* read, *up the great valley that leads.*

———————— 14, after, *Orowhaina,* insert, *a high peaked hill, so called.*

—— 38, —— 8, after, *monoe,* insert, *or cocoa-oil.*

—— 40, —— 15, for *small blue parrot,* read, *blue parroquet.*

—— 41, —— 24, for, *E neearohettee,* read, *E neearoheettee.*

—— 42, —— 3, for, *Eatooas,* read, *Ethooa, or god.*

—— 43, —— 6, after, *Venes,* insert, *or blue parroquet.*

—— 44, —— 1, for, *Etoa-casuarina.   Equisetifolia.* read, *Etoa.   Casuarina-equisetifolia.*

—— 57, for, *75,* the number of the page, read, *57.*

—— 63, after, *Potohe, Firstly,* insert, *Ea, Yes ; Aowra, No.*

—— 77, line 11, after, *ditto,* insert, *about three inches in length.*

—— 87, —— 28, for, *truncheon,* read, *bludgeon.* [*See pl.* XXVI. *fig.* 18.]

———————— 30, after, *XV.* insert, *and* XIX.

—— 93, —— 26, after, *paddles,* insert, *by the like number of men, who look the same way they row, striking their paddles into the water, with the points downward, at the same time bending their bodies forward, and as it were driving the waves behind them.*

—— 102, —— 5, dele, *which.*

—— 114, at the bottom insert the following notes. *Baracootas, a fish remarkably smooth, about seven or eight feet long.*
Flying-gurnards, a flying-fish of a remarkably fine gold colour.
Drum-fish, so called from the noise they make.
Chimera, a fish of a silver colour.

—— 115, —— 9, after, *wattles,* insert, *a bird about the size of a blackbird, remarkable for its fine singing, with two beautiful white curled feathers (by some called Wattles) under the throat.*

—— 124, —— 19, for, *month,* read, *months.*

Page

ERRATA.

Directions to the Binder for placing the Cuts.

Plate of SYDNEY PARKINSON to face the title.